◧ Contents

Climbing the Steps to Field Hockey Success

Field hockey is an extraordinary team game played by millions of male and female adults and youth in more than 118 countries and by member associations worldwide. Whether you are a novice or an experienced field hockey player, you will appreciate the game more as you improve your skills and your understanding of strategy.

The popularity of field hockey comes from the immense challenge the game demands for successful play. In field hockey, players must be able to defend as well as attack. They must be able to handle the ball, and they have to handle it under the pressures of time, limited space, physical exhaustion, and dogged challenges from opponents. Every time the hockey ball moves, the situation changes and the decision-making abilities of players are tested. The individual's ability to execute decisions that are essential to team play must be developed. *Field Hockey: Steps to Success* is written with that objective in mind.

As in the first edition of *Field Hockey: Steps to Success*, a thorough understanding of the three roles of attack and defense enables the field hockey enthusiast to communicate tactics while having a reason to select and execute proper skills. The second edition of *Field Hockey: Steps to Success* provides a progressive, 11-step plan for developing field hockey skills as well as a more comprehensive method of incorporating individual (role 1), group (roles 1 and 2), and team (roles 1, 2, and 3) tactics for all levels of players and coaches.

Follow the same sequence each step of the way:

1. Read the explanation of each skill, why the skill is important, and how to execute the skill.

2. Study the illustrations, which show exactly how to position your body to execute each skill successfully.

3. Read the instructions for each drill. Practice the drill and record the score.

4. Have a qualified observer—a teacher, coach, or trained partner—evaluate your skill technique once you've completed each set of drills. The observer can use the success checks with each drill to evaluate your execution of the skill.

5. At the end of each step, review your performance and total up your scores from the drills. Once you've achieved the indicated level of success with one step, move on to the next step.

This updated and expanded version is organized into 11 clearly defined steps that enable you to advance at your own pace. Each step provides an easy and logical transition to the next step. You cannot leap to the top of the staircase! You get to the top by climbing one step at a time. The first few steps provide a foundation of basic skills and concepts. As you progress through the book, you will learn how to use those skills to execute tactics and to work with teammates. Numerous illustrations further clarify the proper execution of field hockey skills and tactics, including those used by the goalkeeper. Drills are sprinkled throughout each step so that you can practice and improve fundamental skills and tactical concepts before engaging in more pressure-packed, simulated game situations. At the completion of all 11 steps, you will be a more knowledgeable and skilled field hockey player.

Second Edition

Field Hockey

STEPS TO SUCCESS

Human Kinetics

Library of Congress Cataloging-in-Publication Data

Anders, Elizabeth, 1951-
  Field hockey : steps to success / Elizabeth Anders with Sue Myers. --
2nd ed.
      p. cm. -- (Steps to success sports series.)
  ISBN-13: 978-0-7360-6837-6 (soft cover)
  ISBN-10: 0-7360-6837-6 (soft cover)
  1. Field hockey. I. Myers, Sue. II. Title.
  GV1017.H7A573 2008
  796.355--dc22

                              2008017200

ISBN-10: 0-7360-6837-6
ISBN-13: 978-0-7360-6837-6

The Web addresses cited in this text were current as of June 2008, unless otherwise noted.

Acquisitions Editor: Tom Heine; **Developmental Editor:** Cynthia McEntire; **Assistant Editor:** Scott Hawkins; **Copyeditor:** Erich Shuler; **Proofreader:** Kathy Bennett; **Graphic Designer:** Nancy Rasmus; **Graphic Artist:** Tara Welsch; **Cover Designer:** Keith Blomberg; **Photographer (cover):** Juan Mabromata/AFP/Getty Images; **Art Manager:** Kelly Hendren; **Associate Art Manager:** Alan L. Wilborn; **Line Drawings:** Paul To, Tim Offenstein; **Field Diagrams:** Joe Bellis, Alan L. Wilborn; **Printer:** Versa Press

Human Kinetics books are available at special discounts for bulk purchase. Special editions or book excerpts can also be created to specification. For details, contact the Special Sales Manager at Human Kinetics.

Printed in the United States of America   10 9 8 7 6 5 4 3 2

The paper in this book is certified under a sustainable forestry program.

Human Kinetics
Web site: www.HumanKinetics.com

United States: Human Kinetics
P.O. Box 5076
Champaign, IL 61825-5076
800-747-4457
e-mail: humank@hkusa.com

Canada: Human Kinetics
475 Devonshire Road, Unit 100
Windsor, ON N8Y 2L5
800-465-7301 (in Canada only)
e-mail: info@hkcanada.com

Europe: Human Kinetics
107 Bradford Road
Stanningley
Leeds LS28 6AT, United Kingdom
+44 (0)113 255 5665
e-mail: hk@hkeurope.com

Australia: Human Kinetics
57A Price Avenue
Lower Mitcham, South Australia 5062
08 8372 0999
e-mail: info@hkaustralia.com

New Zealand: Human Kinetics
Division of Sports Distributors NZ Ltd.
P.O. Box 300 226 Albany
North Shore City, Auckland
0064 9 448 1207
e-mail: info@humankinetics.co.nz

◧ Acknowledgments

Winning a championship in sports, especially in a team sport such as field hockey, requires a collective effort. Through my fortunate career as an athlete and coach, I have learned that teamwork is necessary for achievement and victory. Similarly, a team effort is required to write and publish a book.

Respectfully, I would like to acknowledge several people who have helped with this second edition. A huge thank you goes to Sue Myers and to Dr. Andrea Hoffman, who agreed to assist me again after the first edition of *Field Hockey: Steps to Success*. Special appreciation goes to my assistant coaches Char, Carla, Marcia, Sue, Yogi, Carol, Dawn, Robin, Amanda, Katie, Marina, and Gwen, who know that it takes a team to succeed, and to Melissa Baile, a friend and former athletic administrator, who knew how to make an opportunity happen. Thank you to the staff of Human Kinetics, particularly to Jana Hunter, for her patience and support! Ongoing thanks to all of my coaching colleagues who have worked with me, and to many others who are too numerous to mention by name. My mentors, who helped to shape my career—Libby Williams, Eleanor Snell, and Marge Watson—remain in my heart, along with the athletes who have played for me and for the programs we represented. My players make the word "team" so very special. They have all heard me say, "I am so proud of you as people and as players for the tradition and standard we have been able to create and share." I remain indebted to the extraordinary group of players I have had the privilege to coach at Old Dominion University. Last, but certainly not least, thanks to my parents, Alice and Stan Anders Jr., and my brother, Stanley Anders III, and his wife, Chris, and family for their continuous love and support.

The Sport of Field Hockey

Field hockey remains a historically popular team sport for men and women, and for youth and adults on nearly every continent. Known internationally as hockey, field hockey incorporates fitness, psychological skills, techniques, and tactics. While playing the sport, a field hockey player will encounter numerous mental and emotional challenges in addition to the physical demands. Although physical size is unrelated to success in field hockey, the successful player needs to quickly and skillfully execute fundamental techniques and use her intelligence and physical prowess, including proper body balance, core muscular strength, anaerobic endurance, flexibility, exceptional hand-eye coordination and ball-to-foot relationship, and agile, speedy movement. It is common for an international player who plays on a watered, swift, artificial surface to run more than 5 miles at a sprint during a 70-minute match while encountering individual and team problem-solving situations that require coordinated, technical skills. Field hockey players are among the best conditioned of all athletes.

Some form of field hockey has been played since ancient times. The sport was brought to Europe through the influence of the Roman Empire. Later the British Empire exposed hockey to their colonies in Asia, Africa, Australia, and America. Today the Federation of International Hockey (FIH) serves as the guardian of the sport. It is responsible for the sport's development and promotion with worldwide national and continental organizations. The FIH oversees five continental associations: Europe, Asia, Africa, Pan-America, and Oceania. The Unites States is a member of the Pan-American continental organization. As the governing body of world field hockey, the FIH has more than 118 member nations, which translates into millions of participants, both male and female, of all ages.

Although the number of male players is increasing, in the United States, men's field hockey takes a backseat to the women's game in terms of the total number of participants and overall opportunities in the scholastic and collegiate scene. Participation by both genders continues to significantly expand.

Field hockey is a speedy, technical team sport that gives enjoyment to many levels of players. The game can be modified to satisfy local conditions or age groups. Throughout this book, the conventional game of outdoor field hockey is described.

The Federation of International Hockey (FIH), the international governing body, has established 14 principal rules for field hockey. The rules cover every game situation, from the organization and conduct of the game through the game procedures. The FIH rules are standard throughout the world and pertain to all competition. Variances in some rules may occur in youth and school organizations and, in the United States, in college-sponsored programs. In this part of the book, we provide a condensed discourse of the rules governing hockey play. For the complete rules, contact the FIH. See the resources section on page xviii for their contact information.

PLAYER CLOTHING AND EQUIPMENT

Field players on the same team must wear uniform clothing. Players may not wear anything that is dangerous to other players. They are permitted to wear protective gloves that do not significantly increase the natural size of the hands.

Recommended equipment for field players include shin and ankle guards and mouth protection. For medical reasons only, players are permitted to wear a facemask that fits flush with the face; a soft, protective head covering; or eye protection in the form of goggles with soft, covered frames and plastic lenses.

Over her upper-body protective equipment, a goalkeeper must wear a shirt that is a different color than the shirts of both teams. Goalkeepers must wear protective equipment comprised of at least headgear, leg guards, and kickers. Clothing and goalkeeping equipment that significantly increase the size of the body or area of protection are not permitted. A fully protected goalkeeper may use body, upper arm, elbow, forearm, hand, and thigh protectors, as well as leg guards and kickers.

The Field Hockey Stick

The field hockey stick (figure 1) has a traditional shape, with a handle and a curved head that is flat on its left side. The stick must conform to the specifications set by the Hockey Rules Board. The hockey stick must be smooth and must not have any uneven or sharp parts. The minimum stick weight is 12 ounces (340.2 grams) while the total weight of the stick may not exceed 28 ounces or 737 grams. The stick and its optional additions may be made of, or may contain, any material other than metal or metallic components, provided that the material is not hazardous. Any curvature along the length of the stick (the rake or bow) must have a continuous, smooth profile along the whole length, it must occur along the face side or the back of the stick (but not both), and it must be limited to a depth of 1 inch (25 mm).

Including any additional coverings (such as grip tape), a field hockey stick must be able to pass through a ring (interior diameter of 2 inches, or 51 mm) from the head of the stick to the top of the handle. The playing surface of the stick is the flat

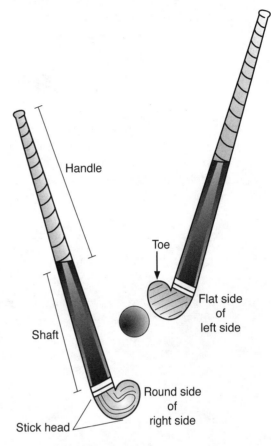

Figure 1 Field hockey stick.

side, sometimes referred to as the *left face* of the stick. It is permissible to use the edge of the stick to strike the ball, but players are not permitted to use the *right face,* or the rounded side, of the stick. Players must always use the flat side of the stick and stick edges to play the ball.

The Field Hockey Ball

The hockey ball is spherical, hard, and typically white. The hockey ball is similar in size to an American baseball, with a circumference of 8 13/16 inches to 9 1/4 inches (224 mm to 235 mm). The spherical ball is made of hard, natural or artificial materials with a hollow or solid interior. The weight may be between 5 1/2 ounces and 5 3/4 ounces (156 grams to 163 grams). The outer, hard surface of the ball can be smooth, or it can be dimpled like a golf ball. A seamless ball is preferred for an artificial playing surface. For international games in which the artificial surface is watered before the start of the match and during the halftime intermission, the best-performing ball has a plastic cover that does not absorb moisture, and it is well balanced to withstand friction and bounce. For international games, a white ball is used, but at other levels the team captains may agree on any color hockey ball as long as it contrasts with the field color.

THE FIELD

The field hockey field (figure 2) is the same length as an American football field but it is wider. The field of play is rectangular, 100 yards (91.40 m) long and 60 yards (55 m) wide. Before each game, the umpire checks for proper field lines, markings, and goal conditions. The width of all lines and shooting circles is 3 inches (75 mm). Players are not permitted to add marks or lines to the field of play. The perimeter lines of the hockey field are in the field of play and they are marked by the backlines, the goal lines (part of the backline between the goalposts), and the sidelines. The ball

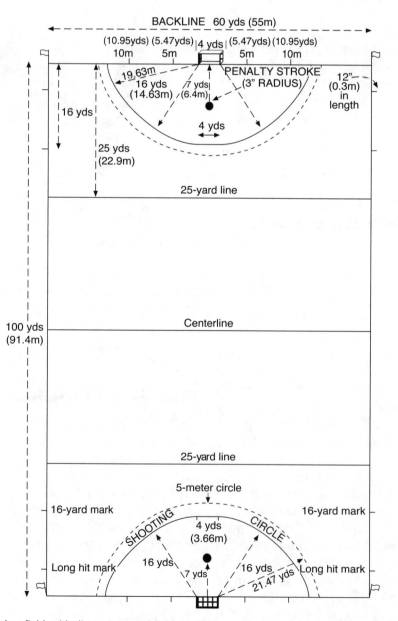

Figure 2 Field hockey field, with dimensions and field markings.

must travel wholly over a line to be considered out of play. The centerline is 50 yards (46 m) from the backlines. Two lines known as the 25-yard lines are marked across the field 25 yards (23 m) from each of the backlines. At each of the four corners of the field, a 4- to 5-foot (1.20 and 1.50 m) flag post is placed off, but near, the outer edge of the field corners.

A 16-yard mark is placed outside the field of play on each sideline. It is parallel to the backline, 16 yards (15 m) from the backline's inside border. The 16-yard mark must be 12 inches (30.5 cm) in length.

Other short lines include the penalty-corner hit marks. These marks are outside the field of play, on the backlines, at 5.47- and 10.95-yard intervals (5 and 10 m) as measured from the outer edge of both sides of the goalposts. Also on the outer edge of the sidelines are long-corner hit marks that are outside the field of play, 5.47 yards (5 m) from the corner of the field where the backline and sideline meet.

The penalty spot is a 6-inch (150 mm) diameter spot that is placed 7 yards (6.4 m) in from the center of the inner edge of the goal line. This spot marks where the ball is placed when a player takes a penalty stroke.

Shooting Circle

The shooting circle (figure 3) is a semicircle drawn from the backlines, 16 yards (14.63 m) from each outer edge of the goalposts. The shooting circle extends 16 yards into the field of play and includes a 4-yard (3.66 m) straight line that runs parallel to the goal line. The line that marks the shooting circle is 3 inches (7.5 cm) wide and is part of the space enclosed by the semicircle.

A ball that is wholly on the shooting circle or partly on the inside of the circle is considered inside the circle. A 5-meter circle is marked with broken lines, 5 meters from the outer edge of each circle. Each broken line starts with a solid section at the top center of the circle line, and each solid section is 300 mm long with 3-meter-long gaps between the solid sections.

Goals

A field hockey goal is rectangular. It is made up of two goalposts; a horizontal crossbar; a net that covers the sides, back, and top of the goal cage; a backboard; and two sideboards.

Goalposts are positioned perpendicular to the ground, 4 yards (3.66 m) apart, and they are connected by a horizontal crossbar that is 7 feet (2.14 m) from the ground. The goalposts may not extend beyond the crossbar nor may the crossbar extend beyond the goalposts. The 2-inch-wide posts and crossbar are painted white and are not more than 3 inches deep.

The 1 1/2-inch-diameter mesh net is attached to the back of the posts and crossbar at 6-inch notches and are secured solidly behind the goal and on the outside of the backboard and sideboards. Nets have a maximum mesh size

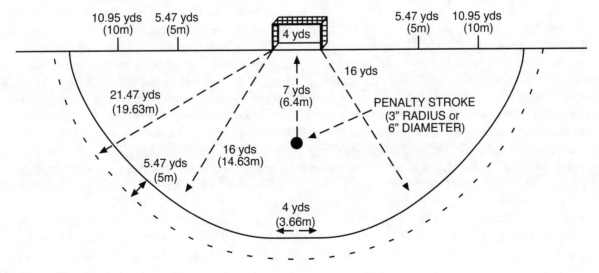

Figure 3 Shooting circle.

of 1 3/4 inches (45 mm) and are secured so as to prevent the ball from passing between the net and the goalposts, crossbar, sideboards, or backboards. The nets hang loosely outside the back- and sideboards in order to prevent the ball from rebounding.

Inside, all goals have a dark-colored backboard, 18 inches (46 cm) off the ground and 4 yards long.

The two sideboards are also 18 inches tall but must not be less than 4 feet long. They also are painted a dark color on the inside of the goal.

The goal cage is positioned at each end of the field, on the center of the goal line, so that the front base of each goalpost touches the back outer edge of the goal line or backline, with the center of the goal set 30 yards (27.5 m) from the sideline.

GAME PLAY

A field hockey game is played between two teams of 11 players each. A team may choose to play with a fully-protected goalkeeper who has goalkeeping privileges, to use 11 field players (no one has goalkeeping privileges), or to use a designated field player who has goalkeeping privileges only within her defensive shooting circle. A goalkeeper may wear full head and body protective equipment (leg guards, kickers, and headgear). A designated field player who has goalkeeping privileges within her defensive circle may wear only protective headgear. The goalkeeper or designated field player must wear a different color shirt. During a game, a team may remove the goalkeeper by making a substitution.

One player from each team is appointed as captain. The team captain wears a distinctive arm band or similarly distinguishing article on the upper arm or shoulder. The captain is responsible for the behavior of the players on her team and for ensuring that substitutions on her team are performed correctly. A replacement captain must be appointed if a captain is suspended.

Two umpires administer the rules and ensure fast and fair play. They take positions along the sidelines, venturing onto the field only when necessary. Each umpire maintains sole responsibility for calls in one half of the field for the entire game, including determining when the ball goes out of play anywhere along the full length of his or her nearer sideline and backline. Umpires call penalty corners, penalty strokes, and goals in their half of the field, and they call free hits in their circles. They also keep track of game time, call the end of each half, and ensure the completion of a penalty corner if a half is extended. (One or two timekeepers may help monitor game time from the scorer's table.) Umpires keep a written record of goals scored and of warnings and suspensions issued. The umpire blows a whistle to

- start and end each half of the game,
- signal fouls, enforce penalties, or suspend the game for any other reason,
- start and end a penalty stroke,
- signal a goal and then to restart the game after a goal is scored or after play is suspended,
- indicate that the ball is entirely out of bounds when it is not obvious to the players,
- restart the game after an unsuccessful penalty stroke attempt, and
- stop the game for the substitution of a goalkeeper in full protective gear and then to restart the game after the substitution.

Prior to the game, the team captains and umpires participate in a coin toss. The coin toss determines which team will start the game. The winner of the coin toss may choose the end of the field that her team will attack in the first half of play or she may choose to have possession of the ball at the start of the game. If the winner of the coin toss chooses to begin with ball possession, then the captain of the other team chooses which end of the field her team will attack in the first half. In the second half, direction of play is reversed. The team that didn't start with possession of the ball in the first half begins with ball possession in the second half.

The game starts with a center pass, or free hit, in any direction from the center of the field. The pass that starts the game may not lift the ball off the ground, and the opposing team must be at least 5 meters (about 5 1/2 yards) from the ball. All players, other than the player making the center pass, must be in their own halves of the field until the ball is in play. A center pass also restarts the game after halftime and after a goal is scored. After a goal is scored, the center pass is taken by the team that was scored on. As with all free hits, the ball must move at least 1 meter (about 1 yard), and the player making the initial pass may not touch the ball again until someone else has touched it.

Each team defends a goal. The aim of hockey is to move the hockey ball up the field, and once the ball is in the shooting circle, players hit, push, or lift the ball into the opposing goal cage using only a hockey stick. An attacker scores by using the flat side and edge of the field hockey stick to hit, push, or lift the ball from inside the shooting circle (an area 16-yards deep, or 14.63 m, from the goalposts) into the goal. For a goal to be counted, the ball must pass completely over the opponent's goal line (figure 4). The ball may not travel outside the circle before passing completely over the goal line and under the crossbar. The ball may be played by a defender or it may touch a defender's body before or after it is touched in the circle by an attacker. Each goal counts as one point. After a goal is scored, play resumes with a free hit in the center of the field by the team that was scored on.

Much like an ice hockey goalie, the field hockey goalkeeper's principal task is to protect the team's goal by using her body, feet, stick, or hands to block or redirect the ball. When a goalkeeper is outside the shooting circle, she is considered a field player; therefore, she may play the ball only with the flat side of the field hockey stick.

Once the game begins, play is continuous. The clock is stopped only after a goal or after a penalty stroke, or at the umpire's discretion, such as when a player is injured. The game clock keeps moving during the continuous, unlimited substitutions. Substitutions must take place within 5 meters (about 5 1/2 yards) of the centerline on the team-bench side of the field.

Player substitution in field hockey is similar to substitution in ice hockey. The player being replaced has unlimited reentry, and the number of players substituted during the course of a game is unlimited. The player being substituted must

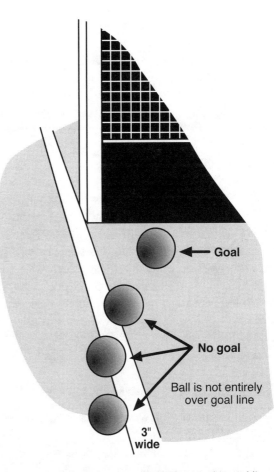

Figure 4 A shot must pass completely over the goal line and under the crossbar to count as a goal.

run completely off the side of the field, within 5 meters (about 5 1/2 yards) from the centerline, before the substitute may enter the field. Goalkeepers are permitted to leave and enter the field near the goal they are defending. The game clock continues keeping time during the rolling substitution unless the umpire has suspended play in order to attend to an injured player or to issue a card reprimand. Also, time is stopped during the substitution of a goalkeeper who is wearing full protective gear. If a player is injured, the umpire stops the game temporarily so that the injured player may leave the field to be treated. An injured or bleeding player must leave the field unless medical reasons prevent it. The player may not return until wounds have been covered and blood-stained clothing has been replaced.

A team cannot substitute players from the time a penalty corner is awarded until after the penalty corner is completed, unless the defending goalkeeper is injured or suspended. An eligible player may not be put into the game in place of a suspended player. His or her team must continue the game without the suspended player.

A regulation game has two 35-minute playing periods with a five-minute halftime intermission. Specific leagues or competitions may modify the time of the playing periods and halftime in order to accommodate different player levels. For example, college leagues may increase halftime length to 10 minutes in order to give the ground crew enough time to rewater the playing surface. High-school junior varsity games often are played with 25- or 30-minute halves. The team that scores the most goals wins the game. If the regulation period ends in a tie score, the match is a draw. Specific tournaments or leagues set their own rules regarding ways to resolve a tie game, perhaps by playing longer, by having a penalty-stroke competition, or by simply declaring the game a draw.

Ball Out of Bounds

The ball is out of play when it passes completely over the sideline or backline. A player on the team that did not touch or play the ball immediately before it went out of play restarts play.

When the ball travels over the sideline, play is resumed using the procedures for a free hit. By placing the ball on the sideline where the ball crossed the line, a player is ready to restart the play. When the ball goes outside the field of play, a player from the team that did not hit the ball out of bounds may take a free hit or free push from the sideline where the ball went out of play. The ball must be stationary and may not be raised. The player playing the ball may be on or off the playing field. Players from the opposing team must be at least 5 meters (about 5 1/2 yards) from the ball.

Sixteen-yard hits are similar to soccer's goal kicks. Defense hits, also called 15-meter hits, are taken by the defense when the attacking team plays the ball over the backline. The hit is taken from a spot exactly opposite from where the ball crossed the backline and not more than 16 yards (14.63 m) from the backline. Again free-hit rules apply.

If the defending team unintentionally plays the ball over the backline, then the attacking team takes a free hit from a spot on the sideline 5.47 yards (5 m) from the corner flag. This is called a long corner.

A penalty corner is awarded to the attack team if the defense intentionally hits or pushes the ball over the backline, unless the ball is deflected by the goalkeeper. For a goal to count during a penalty corner, the player must use a direct shot with a backswing, and the ball must hit the backboard or sideboard. A penalty corner is completed when a goal is scored; an attacker commits a foul; the ball travels more than 5 meters (about 5 1/2 yards) outside the circle; the ball travels outside the circle for a second time; the ball travels over the backline and another penalty corner is not awarded; a defender commits a foul and another penalty corner is not awarded; a penalty stroke is awarded; or a bully is awarded.

Bully

When play is stopped (due to an injury, for example), a bully is taken to resume play. The bully is taken close to where the ball was located when play was stopped, but not within 16 yards (14.63 m) of the backline. For the bully, the ball is placed between one player from each team. The players face each other, with the goal they are defending to their right. The two players start with their sticks on the ground to the right of the ball and then tap the flat faces of their sticks together once just above the ball. After the tap, each player tries to gain possession of the ball. All other players must be at least 5 meters (about 5 1/2 yards) from the ball. A bully is used to resume play whenever play is stopped but when no penalty is given.

PLAYER CONDUCT

Field hockey players are expected to act sensibly and with good sportsmanship at all times.

- A player must hold her stick and not use it in a dangerous manner, such as by lifting it over the heads of other players. The stick is considered dangerous when it is higher than a player's shoulders in crowded or occupied space (other players within 5 meters, about 5 1/2 yards).

- A player may not play the ball wildly or in a way that is dangerous or is likely to lead to dangerous play. A ball is considered dangerous when it is higher than the knee in crowded or occupied space (other players within 5 meters, about 5 1/2 yards).

- A player must not hit, touch, handle, or interfere with other players' bodies, sticks, or clothing.

- A player must not intimidate or impede another player.

- A player may not play the ball with the back of the stick.

- Hitting the ball hard on the forehand with the edge of the stick is prohibited, except in a controlled action, such as during a tackle, when raising the ball in a controlled manner over an opponent's stick or over a lying goalkeeper, or when using a long pushing motion along the ground. A player may hit the ball with the edge of the stick on the backhand as long as the player doesn't play the ball wildly, creating a dangerous situation.

- A player must not use any part of the stick to play a ball that is above shoulder height, although defenders are allowed to use the stick to stop or deflect a shot on goal at any height. A defender, however, may not hit a ball above the shoulders. A penalty stroke is awarded if a defender hits the ball above the shoulders to prevent a goal. If a ball is traveling toward the goal and a defender attempts to stop or deflect the ball, but if the ball would miss the goal if it were not deflected, then any use of the stick above the shoulder will be penalized by a penalty corner and not a penalty stroke. If dangerous play results after a legal stop or deflection, a penalty corner is awarded.

- A player may raise the ball off the ground as long the ball is not played dangerously and as long as it is not raised during a free hit.

- A player must not approach within 5 meters (about 5 1/2 yards) of an opponent who is receiving a descending raised ball until the ball is on the ground and has been received and controlled.

- A field player must not stop, kick, propel, pick up, throw, or carry the ball with any part of her body. It is a foul when a field player voluntarily uses her hand, foot, or body to stop or play the ball.

- When an opponent is attempting to play the ball, a player must not obstruct that opponent by backing into her, by physically interfering with her stick or body, or by shielding the ball from a lawful tackle with the stick or any part of the body. A third-party obstruction is called when a player runs in front or blocks an opponent in order to stop her from fairly playing or attempting to play the ball.

- A player must not tackle unless in a position to play the ball without body contact.

- An attacking player is not permitted to run behind the goal or into the goal being defended by the opponent.

- Unless the stick no longer meets specifications, a player may not change her stick between the award and completion of a penalty corner or penalty stroke.

- A player must not throw any object or piece of equipment onto the field, at the ball, or at another player, umpire, or person.

- A player may not delay the game by wasting time.

Goalkeepers also must conform to proper conduct on the field.

- A goalkeeper who wears full protective equipment may not take part in the game outside the 25-yard (23-meter) line area she is defending, except when taking a penalty stroke.

- A goalkeeper who wears only protective headgear may not play beyond the 25-yard line area she is defending unless the headgear is removed. The protective headgear must be worn, however, when the goalkeeper is defending a penalty corner or penalty stroke.

- When the ball is inside the shooting circle, the goalkeeper has special privileges to safely use her stick, protective equipment, or any part of her body to push the ball away, deflect the ball in any direction (including over the backline), or stop the ball. She may use her leg guards or kickers to propel the ball. In addition, the goalie, with the stick above her shoulder, can stop or deflect the ball, unless deemed dangerous by the umpire.

- The goalkeeper is not permitted to lie on the ball. This is an obstruction foul.
- When the ball is outside the circle she is defending, the goalkeeper is permitted to play the ball with her stick only.

PENALTY ENFORCEMENT AND PROCEDURES

For any offense, the offending player may be cautioned through a spoken warning, warned with a green card, temporarily suspended from the game with a yellow card, or permanently suspended from the game with a red card.

Umpires carry three different-colored and different-shaped cards, which they use to warn players of bad behavior or misconduct, rough and dangerous play, delay-of-game tactics, attitudinal and verbal misbehavior, and dead-ball fouls. The triangular-shaped green card acts as a warning or caution. A square yellow card is used to temporarily suspend a player from the game; his or her team must continue play with one less player. The minimum time duration of a suspension is five minutes. A round red card means that the player is ejected from the game. The player is sent off the field and its surrounding area for the rest of the game. His or her team may not substitute another player for the ejected player.

The advantage rule allows the game to flow even after a foul has occurred if enforcing the penalty would provide an unfair advantage to the team that committed the foul. A good umpire applies the advantage rule often and wisely by anticipating what will happen in the next few seconds.

Hockey players who break the rules are penalized with the umpire awarding a free hit, a penalty corner, or a penalty stroke to the other team.

Free Hit

A free hit is awarded when an attacker commits a foul or when a defensive player commits an unintentional foul outside his or her circle. A free hit is given when a defender commits a foul within 5 meters (about 5 1/2 yards) of the circle.

A free hit is taken from the area, or close to the area, where the foul occurred, except when an attacker commits a foul between the 16-yard line and the backline. In this case, the defending team takes the free hit near the spot of the foul or from a spot up to 16 yards from the backline. In the latter case, the spot must be exactly in line with the foul. If the offending team commits another foul before the free hit is taken, the umpire may move the free hit spot 10.95 more yards (10 m) toward the offending team's goal but not into the shooting circle.

All players of both teams, except the player taking the free hit, must be at least 5 meters (about 5 1/2 yards) from the ball. The opposing team must be 5 meters (about 5 1/2 yards) or more from the ball for all free hits between the 25-yard lines. The ball must be stationary, and the player taking the free hit may push or hit the ball but may not raise the ball into the air. The ball must move at least 1 meter (about 1 1/2 yards). After playing the ball, the striker may not play the ball again or approach within the playing distance of it until another player has played the ball.

Penalty Corner

A penalty corner is awarded against the defending team for deliberate fouls within the 25-yard area or for accidental fouls within the shooting circle. A penalty corner is also given when the ball becomes lodged in a defending player's clothing or equipment within the circle that the player is defending or when the defending team intentionally plays the ball over the backline. Exception: The goalkeeper can deflect the ball over the backline with her stick, protective equipment, or any part of her body.

The setup procedure for the penalty corner requires that not more than five defenders, including the goalkeeper if there is one, start with their sticks, hands, and feet behind the backline.

The remaining defenders position themselves beyond the centerline. The attack player serving the ball must have at least one foot behind the backline. The remaining attackers are on the field with their sticks, hands, and feet outside the shooting circle. The attacker executes the penalty corner by hitting or pushing the ball from a spot on the backline, but within the circle, 10.95 yards (10 meters) from the goalpost on either side the attacking team chooses. No player from either team can be within 5 meters (about 5 1/2 yards) of the ball, nor may they cross the backline or the centerline, nor may they enter the shooting circle until the attacker starting the penalty corner plays the ball.

To score from the penalty corner, the ball must travel outside the circle on the ground and be played into the circle before the shot is taken. If the first shot is a hit, as opposed to a push, flick, or scoop, the ball must cross the goal line at a height of not more than 18 inches (the height of the backboard) for a goal to be scored, unless it touches the stick of another player or a defender's body while traveling toward the goal. Slap hitting is considered a hit. On second and subsequent hits, flicks, deflections, and scoops at goal, the shot may be of any height but must not be dangerous. A shot is considered dangerous if a player is struck by a ball above knee height while within 5 meters (about 5 1/2 yards) of the shot at goal. The player serving the penalty corner from the backline may not score a goal directly from the push or hit, even if the ball is deflected into the goal by a defender.

If the ball travels more than 5 meters (about 5 1/2 yards) from outside the circle (beyond the 5-meter circle) or if the ball travels outside the circle for a second time, then the penalty corner rules no longer apply. For any violation of the rules by the attacking team, a free hit is awarded to the defending team. If the defending team violates the penalty corner rules, the attacking team either retakes the penalty corner or it may be awarded a penalty stroke if the defending team persistently fouls after a previous warning or penalty has been given. A game half cannot end on an awarded penalty corner. The penalty corner is played out until the defending team clears the ball 5 meters (about 5 1/2 yards) beyond the shooting circle or until the attacking team fouls.

Penalty Stroke

A penalty stroke is awarded to the attacking team when a defender commits either a deliberate foul within the shooting circle or an unintentional foul in the circle that prevents the probable scoring of a goal. Persistent early breaking over the backline at penalty corners will also merit a penalty stroke.

The game clock is stopped for a penalty stroke. The setup procedure for the penalty stroke places all players—other than one defending player (the goalkeeper or a designated field player) and the attacker who is taking the stroke—on the field beyond the nearer 25-yard (23-meter) line. The stroke is taken from a spot 7 yards (6.40 m) in front of the center of the goal line. The attack player taking the stroke must stand behind the ball and within playing distance of the ball before beginning the stroke. The defender must stand with both feet on the goal line and may not leave the goal line or move either foot until the ball has been played. If the player defending the stroke is a goalkeeper, she must wear protective headgear. A field player defending a stroke may wear a protective facemask and may use only her stick to stop the penalty stroke shot. The controlling umpire blows the whistle when both the attack player and the defender are in position. At the sound of the umpire's whistle, the attacker may take one or more forward steps in the approach to start the stroke. Without faking, using a backswing, or dragging the ball, the attacker is allowed to push or flick the ball at any height at the goal. The attacker may play the ball only once and may not subsequently approach either the ball or the defender.

A free hit is awarded to the defense if the attacker commits a foul during the penalty stroke. If the defender commits a foul to prevent a goal from being scored, such as by leaving the goal line or by moving either foot before the ball has been played, then the penalty stroke is retaken. With a first foul of this nature, the defender is warned with a green card, and any subsequent foul will result in a yellow card suspension. If the same defender commits any other foul during the penalty stroke that prevents a goal being scored, a goal is awarded.

For a foul by a defending player when a goal is not scored, the penalty stroke is retaken. For a foul by an attacking player when a goal is scored, the penalty stroke is retaken. If a goal was not scored or if the attacker taking the stroke committed a foul, a 16-yard free hit is given to the defending team at the top of the circle, 16 yards from the center of the backline.

PLAYER ROLES

Every player, except the specialized goalkeeper, must be proficient in both attacking and defending. The modern game of hockey places greater emphasis on the complete field hockey player than it used to. Although players can move anywhere on the field, each has exact responsibilities within the team's system of play or formation, whether the team plays with 10 field players and a goalkeeper or with 11 field players.

As in the first edition of *Field Hockey: Steps to Success*, attack roles and defense roles are defined to help field hockey players and coaches on all levels understand and improve their hockey skills and strategies within the team's formation. Through the execution of role responsibilities, hockey techniques and tactics are appropriately applied to develop a group of individuals who think and play together. For players to make good decisions, they must know what, why, when, and where to apply a game technique. This knowledge will lead players to develop decision-making skills and technical execution. Players will then exhibit quality performance, which is satisfying and fun!

Assigning roles to players according to who possesses the ball and where the ball is located on the field provides players with pertinent information in a given situation. The concept of role assignments is based on the location of the ball on the field and on the space on the field.

Attack play is the creation of space and the use of space by attack players, both by the player who has the ball and by the players who don't have it. Hockey defense is the organization of players to block and control space. Players participate in three roles both when their team possesses the ball (attack) and when the other team possesses the ball (defense).

Each of the three attack roles and three defense roles has specific responsibilities. When these responsibilities are understood and executed, all players on the field, regardless of game position within a formation, will be able to both attack and defend. It is important to note that a hockey player will possess the ball only 3 to 5 minutes on average and will be without the ball for 62 minutes or more in a 70-minute match. Therefore, the key to creating a steady flow of passing options is the intelligent movement of players who do not have the ball. Players must meet the responsibilities of the attack and defense roles and be able to move smoothly and effectively into any given role.

When field hockey players learn to retreat to defend and to advance to attack, they are ready for the game positions discussed in steps 7, 8, 9, and 10. Game positions define the overlapping and constantly interchanging roles of attack and defense. All players take on their attack roles when their team is in possession of the ball, and all players perform their defense roles when the opponent has the ball.

Attack Roles

Attack roles are based on moving the ball from one player to another in order to advance the ball toward the opposing goal. It takes two players to complete a pass and at least three players to provide continuity. Hockey is a passing game, and when a team has a sense of positional play along with the technical competence of passing, receiving, and controlling the ball, then the ball can move effectively from player to player.

Attack role 1 (AR1) is the player with the ball. Her primary role is to maintain ball possession for the team and to complete the pass. It is her responsibility to pass the ball in order to penetrate, secure an advantage, or merely maintain ball possession. If the pass is not immediately possible, AR1 uses ball control and dribbling to move to a new position from which to pass.

Attack role 2 (AR2) is the helper. She supports her leader, who is in possession of the ball. AR2 moves to a position less than 15 yards, or one pass, away from AR1 in order to be available for a direct pass.

Attack role 3 (AR3) is the assistant helper. She provides support for AR2 and moves more than 30 yards from the ball and 15 or more yards from AR2. AR3 positions herself two passes away from the ball and moves to create space for her AR2 teammates.

Defense Roles

Team defense roles require field hockey players to organize collectively in order to win back ball possession. Together, defenders position themselves to block space and to control the amount of space the opponent can use so that the ball can be successfully tackled or intercepted.

Defense role 1 (DR1) is the player closest to the ball. She has the responsibility of stopping the forward penetration of the ball carrier by putting herself directly in front of AR1. DR1's objective is to force AR1 to make a predictable pass. In general DR1 stays about 5 yards from AR1, although the distance can range from 3 yards up to 7 yards, according to their proximity to the goal, DR1's speed and ability, and the direction in which DR1 wants to force AR1.

Defense role 2 (DR2) is the player who is one pass away from the ball. She helps DR1 by closing off, and thereby controlling, the space between the ball and AR2 players. By stepping up to mark and intercept passes to the nearest opponent, DR2 prepares to help DR1 stop the ball carrier.

Defense role 3 (DR3) is the assistant helper for DR2. She is the farthest from the ball, two or more passes away. DR3's responsibility is to establish a help position for DR2, to provide balance, and to cover the penetrating space and the opponents in this space.

WARM-UP AND COOL-DOWN

Before every practice or game, perform a series of warm-up activities in order to prepare your body for effective performance. Warm-up exercises are designed to stimulate blood flow and to raise muscle temperature, thereby helping prevent muscle and joint injuries during the actual practice session or game. Warm-up exercises will also improve your muscular contraction, response time, and flexibility, and they will help reduce next-day soreness.

The length of the warm-up period will vary for each player, but 15 to 20 minutes is generally sufficient time to elevate your muscle temperature. A good indication that muscle temperature is elevated is that you start to perspire. It is important to elevate your heart rate (which increases blood flow to muscles) from its resting rate before performing flexibility exercises. Choose one or more exercises, such as dribbling with a ball or passing with a teammate while jogging, to increase the blood flow to the muscles and to raise the overall body temperature. Next, perform a series of stretching exercises that work the major muscle groups used in field hockey.

Field hockey players need flexibility to reach out and stop the ball or to tackle at a full stretch. Increased muscular flexibility will improve the range of motion around joints, which improves the performance of hockey skills. Stretching exercises promote circulation and are beneficial in many ways. Through stretching exercises, muscle tension is reduced and coordination is enhanced. A limited range of motion can restrict performance and can lead to injuries such as muscle strains. Static stretching that avoids bouncing and jerking movements will increase flexibility. Gradually extend the muscle or group of muscles to the point where you feel mild tension. Then relax and hold that position for 30 seconds. Stretch each muscle group twice, and be sure to include the hamstrings, quadriceps, lower back and hips, groin, calves and Achilles tendons, and shoulders and arms.

Your objective is to improve your range of motion in a safe, injury-free style, not to compete by outstretching your teammates. After performing static stretches, you are ready for the final phase of the warm-up. Ballistic activity and sprint running comprise the last step in preparing the body for success during the hockey practice or game. Ballistic exercises consist of dynamic stretching and sport-specific movements that are quick and forceful. Along with sprinting, ballistics improve initial-movement explosiveness and the speed of hockey skills. Because field hockey demands intense explosive and reactive movement in order to perform the skills of hitting, dribbling, and tackling, it is important to do ballistic exercises and accelerated sprints, which help develop and maintain muscular strength in the following muscle groups: abdominals, legs and hips, shoulders and chest, arms, and hands. Step 11 provides warm-up and conditioning activities that you can follow. Field hockey conditioning and fitness training should always consist of sport-specific movements. Refer to step 11 to plan your warm-up and training routine.

The warm-up is complete, and your body is now prepared for the hockey practice or game. At the end of each practice session or after a game, do a cool-down or warm-down. A cool-down consists of exercises that allow your body functions and heart rate to return to their resting levels. Perform jogging, walking, and stretching exercises for each of the major muscle groups. Stretching after a game or strenuous practice session will help prevent muscle soreness. Stretch each major muscle group for 30 seconds and repeat once if necessary.

In summary, since field hockey requires endurance and strength, a player must warm up in order to prevent or delay fatigue. Fatigue will affect a player's performance by reducing her skill and by impairing her ability to make good decisions. Hence a hockey player should understand that successful performance requires physical preparation and technical precision. Whenever possible, include a ball and stick in your warm-up exercises in order to incorporate skill training. Inadequate warm-ups and cool-downs will limit your ability to improve your skills. Take care of your body.

RESOURCES

The following organizations are under the jurisdiction of the FIH (Federation of International Hockey), and they administer field hockey competition in the United States and around the world. The USA Field Hockey Association directs field hockey competition. The National Collegiate Athletic Association (NCAA), the National Field Hockey Coaches Association (NFHCA), the National Association for Intercollegiate Athletes (NAIA), and the National Junior College Athletic Association (NJCAA) administer collegiate competition for both men and women.

International Organizations

Federation of International Hockey (FIH)
Residence du Parc
Rue du Valentin 61
1004 Lausanne
Switzerland
Phone: 41-21-641-0606
Fax: 41-21-641-0607
www.worldhockey.org

Pan American Hockey Federation
46 Barton Street
Ottawa, Ontario K1S 4R7
Canada
Phone: 1-819-956-8023
Fax: 1-819-956-8019
www.panamhockey.org

International Olympic Committee (IOC)
Chateau de Vidy
C.P. 356
1007 Lausanne
Switzerland
Phone: 41-21-621-6111
Fax: 41-21-621-6216
www.olympic.org

National Organizations

United States Olympic Committee (USOC)
National Headquarters
1 Olympic Plaza
Colorado Springs, CO 80909-5760
Phone: 719-632-5551
www.usoc.org

U.S. Field Hockey Association
1 Olympic Plaza
Colorado Springs, CO 80909-5774
Phone: 719-866-4567
Fax: 719-632-0979
www.usfieldhockey.com

National Field Hockey Coaches Association (NFHCA)
11921 Meadow Ridge Terrace
Glen Allen, VA 23059
Phone: 804-364-8700
Fax: 804-364-5467
www.nfhca.org

Amateur Athletic Union (AAU)
National Headquarters
P.O. Box 22409
Lake Buena Vista, FL 32830
Phone: 407-934-7200
Fax: 407-934-7242
www.aausports.org

Youth Sports Network (YSN)
4712 Admiralty Way #530
Marina de Rey, CA 90292
Phone: 310-822-0261
www.ysn.com

Scholastic Organizations

National Association of Intercollegiate Athletics (NAIA)
23500 W. 105th St.
P.O. Box 1325
Olathe, KS 66061
Phone: 913-791-0044
Fax: 913-791-9555
www.naia.org

National Collegiate Athletic Association (NCAA)
700 West Washington Street
P.O. Box 6222
Indianapolis, IN 46206-6222
Phone: 317-917-6222
Fax: 317-917-6888
www.ncaa.org

National Federation of State High School Association (NFHS)
P.O. Box 690
Indianapolis, IN 46206
Phone: 317-972-6900
Fax: 317-822-5700
www.nfhs.org

◲ Key to Diagrams

	Player
	Ball
∿∿➤	Dribble
– – ➤	Pass
➡	Player movement
AR1	Attack role 1 (player with the ball)
AR2	Attack role 2
AR3	Attack role 3
DR1	Defense role 1 (defender closest to attacker with the ball)
DR2	Defense role 2
DR3	Defense role 3
GK	Goalkeeper
F	Forward
RW	Right wing
CF	Center forward
LW	Left wing
RM	Right midfielder
RCM	Right center midfielder
CM	Center midfielder
LM	Left midfielder
LCM	Left center midfielder
RB	Right back
RIB	Right inside back
RC	Right cover
CB	Center back
LB	Left back
LIB	Left inside back
LC	Left cover
S	Sweeper
P	Post player

Balance and Footwork

The ability to play near your potential is the mark of a successful field hockey player and, ultimately, of a successful hockey team. Players who can properly and quickly execute fundamental hockey skills exemplify the beauty of team play. Because field hockey is a team game, a player must perform individual skills well before she can play well within a team. Receiving, hitting, pushing, ball control, and one-on-one defense are the five fundamental hockey skills to learn in order to effectively play attack and defense. No matter your present level of play, correct balance and footwork are the foundation for all hockey skills and team success.

Success in field hockey is often associated with speed, but balance and quick feet, or agility, are the most important physical attributes to possess. Little can be done to improve your innate sprint speed, but balance and foot agility can be improved significantly through practice. Proper body balance is controlled by the head, feet, and hands with the stick. When these extremities are in balance, your body is ready to move quickly and skillfully. It is essential to have control of the body, feet, and stick before attempting to perform skills rapidly. Rushing your execution of hockey techniques will only promote mistakes and bad habits, which reflect a lack of emotional balance as well as a lack of balance. Quickness is specific to the hockey skill being performed. The successful hockey player must seek a point of balance in

her relationship to the ball with every offensive and defensive technique.

Like the golfer who attempts to perfect her body posture before swinging the club, the field hockey player must also prepare the body for performing skills. Unlike the golfer who has plenty of time to position her feet, head, and hands before striking the ball, a hockey player is usually moving or running when performing a skill. Whether you are passing, receiving, dribbling, or tackling, the body must be momentarily in control before any skill can be performed successfully. Of course, the speed at which you can perform a skill correctly will be a primary factor in your progress. The hockey athlete must first try to perform a skill correctly and then to practice it to the point that its performance becomes a habit. Once you have reached this level, then you can try to perform the skill more quickly.

Balance is closely related to footwork, which is basic to all fundamental hockey skills. Effective footwork allows you to start, stop, and change direction with quickness and balance. Footwork also prepares the body to perform skills. Good footwork is important to all the attack roles and defense roles. As an attack player with or without the ball, you have an advantage over your defender in knowing what moves you are going to make and when you will make them. Attack footwork is used to shoot the ball, to fake your opponent off balance, to dribble around the reach of an opponent's stick, to cut to receive a pass, to avoid colliding with the opponent, and to maneuver in congested space in order to get to the goalkeeper's rebound.

Good footwork is particularly important when playing defense. Much of your defensive success will depend on your ability to move quickly in any direction and thereby to react instantly to the moves of your opponent and to the speed of the ball. With hard work, you can improve your footwork to the point where you can force your opponent to react to you. Good footwork can enable you to disrupt the attack plan of your opponent by forcing errors in ball handling and by forcing bad passing decisions that could result in an interception for your team.

By thoroughly understanding the basic mechanics of body balance and footwork, you can improve your agility and stick-handling skills.

BALANCED ATTACK STANCE

Hockey players must seek a point of balance in relationship to the ball. A well-balanced position (figure 1.1), essential in learning to play attack role 1 (attack player with the ball), will prepare you to dribble quickly in any direction; stop under control while keeping the ball close to your stick (with the stick head on the ground); pass or shoot the ball in any direction; and receive the ball from any direction.

Relax your body behind the ball. Keep your head forward, leading with the upper body (shoulders) as you bend forward toward the ball. Stagger your feet shoulder-width apart with your weight centered on the balls of your feet. Knees are flexed, and hips are lowered in a semi-crouched position, ready to move. Keep your arms away from your body. Both hands remain apart on the stick in a shake-hands position. Keep the head of the stick on the ground. If you have the ball, keep your stick very close to it.

Misstep

Your stick head is not comfortably touching the turf.

Correction

Bend your knees, and keep your hands and arms away from your body. Staggered feet must be 12 inches (30.5 cm) apart, the width of your shoulders, with your weight distributed equally on both feet.

Figure 1.1　Balanced Attack Stance

1. Shoulders and feet face the ball
2. Hands are in a separated shake-hands grip
3. Feet are shoulder-width apart on the power points of feet, with your knees flexed
4. If you are in possession of ball, stand with your feet at least 24 inches (61 cm) from the ball
5. Keep the ball on the stick or on the flat side facing the ball, if you do not have possession of the ball
6. Head is steady over the knees
7. Use short, quick steps
8. Head is up to see the field
9. Maintain a ready, balanced position in order to cut, dribble, pass, or shoot

Misstep

Your balance is off.

Correction

If you lose your balance forward, flex your knees in order to get low, rather than bending at the waist, so that you are ready to move backward as quickly as you can move forward. If you lose your balance backward, be sure to keep your heels off the ground and to stagger your feet shoulder-width apart. Knees must remain bent so that you can lean your head forward and maintain balance. If you easily lose balance to either side, spread your feet shoulder-width apart and flex the knees so that you are balanced and ready to move in any direction.

STICK HANDLING

Both left-handed and right-handed players use the shake-hands grip (figure 1.2a), or receiving grip, as the basic hockey stick grip and as the starting point for other grips. For the shake-hands grip, place the hockey stick on the ground with the stick's toe and forehand edge pointing up. Place both palms on top of the stick handle with fingers touching the ground on either side of the stick. Pick up the stick with both hands in a shake-hands position.

Misstep

The whites of your finger tips show.

Correction

Avoid the baseball-style grip. Relax your grip by establishing a slight trigger finger position with both index fingers.

The reverse shake-hands grip is used to play the ball's left side. The reverse grip is the same as the shake-hands grip except that the toe of the stick points down (figure 1.2b). Place the top of the handle in your left palm and grip it firmly. Pay extra attention to your left hand's position because your left hand's fingers will turn the flat side of the stick to the ball to dribble, receive,

a   b

Figure 1.2 Hands on the stick: *(a)* shake-hands grip; *(b)* reverse shake-hands grip.

pass, and tackle. Place your right hand, which should be somewhat more relaxed than the left, a comfortable distance (5 1/2 to 7 inches, or 14 to 18 cm) down the handle. Adjust this distance based on the skill you are performing and your distance to the ball. Each hand's forefinger and thumb form a V, which should be centered on a line from the toe up the middle of the handle. Keep your arms and stick away from your body.

Misstep

The flat (left) side of the stick faces the sky.

Correction

Each hand's forefinger and thumb should form a V, which should be centered on a line from the toe up to the middle of the handle.

Misstep

Loss of stick-handling speed when going to a reverse shake-hands grip.

Correction

The hands are too far apart on the stick. Separate the hands only 5 1/2 to 7 inches (14 to 18 cm), and relax the right hand grip. Remember to use the shake-hands grip with V alignment, and turn the stick with the left hand.

CONTROL BOX

For each player, there is a correct distance separating the ball and the feet. This distance will vary a little according to a player's height, body build, and point of balance. The ball is controlled in an imaginary control box area consisting of the space in front of the feet, a space that is about the width of the feet. The control box concept will help you realize your proper point of balance in relationship to the ball. Maintaining the head of the stick and the ball within the control box promotes proper body posture and balance. This in turn will enhance every hockey attack technique you attempt, such as dribbling, passing, and receiving.

To determine your control box, grip a hockey ball in your left hand and your hockey stick with your right hand. Squat down and place the ball out in front of your feet as far as you can reach without losing balance (figure 1.3a). Place the ball on the ground and stand up, keeping the feet the same distance from the stationary ball. Position your head, feet, hands, and stick in a balanced attack stance, an alert yet relaxed semi-crouched position, coiled for quick movement (figure 1.3b). Address the ball with the stick next to the ball's right side. Keep the ball within bounds of the width of the feet in order to keep from losing control of the ball.

Misstep

You frequently lose control of the ball.

Correction

The hands are too close together. Separate your hands 5 1/2 to 7 inches (14 to 18 cm) and bend your knees in order to establish your control box.

Misstep

Balance is disrupted, and you experience a loss of speed with the ball.

Correction

Your center of gravity is too low and the ball is too far from feet. Move your feet and head closer to the ball so that your head leads the upper body toward the ball.

Train your body to be a master of correct posture with precise ball-to-feet judgment so that your stick can complete the connection for proper skill execution. Establishing an imaginary control box is an integral component of executing hockey skills successfully.

Figure 1.3   Control Box

a   b

PREPARATION

1. Ball is in your left hand and the stick is in your right hand
2. Squat down
3. Reach forward and place ball in front of your feet, centered
4. Measure the distance from ball to your toes
5. Visualize your control box

EXECUTION

1. Use a shake-hands grip
2. Stick faces the right side of ball to move the ball left; it faces the left side to move the ball right
3. Strike the lower half of the ball with the stick
4. Maintain a measured distance of the ball from your feet
5. Be in a balanced attack stance
6. Keep your head over your wrist and focus on the ball

Misstep

Stick contact is made on the top half of the ball, resulting in a loss of ball control outside the control box. You have to overreach in order to get to the ball and you have a difficult time controlling it.

Correction

The ball is too far from the feet, so the player cannot reach the lower half of the ball. Move feet closer to the ball and bend your knees for good balance.

Misstep

Eyes strain to find the ball, and you frequently advance the ball with your feet.

Correction

Move the ball away from the feet and into your control box where you can see it.

Balance and Footwork Drill 1.
Mini-Bands for Lateral Balance

Place a mini-band around your ankles, and hold your hockey stick in both hands in a receiving grip. Set up an area 7 yards (6.4 m) long by placing cones at the start and end of 7 yards. As you drill, have a teammate observe and evaluate your work.

Stand at the first cone with your right side facing the second 7-yard cone. Move laterally to your right for 7 yards (6.4 m), keeping your head steady and your shoulders, hips, knees, and ankles in alignment. Maintain balance on the power points of your feet (the balls of your feet), equally distributing your body weight on both feet. As you push to the right, keep the mini-band taut in a shoulder-width stretch. As you move laterally to the right, the left foot is the trail, or recovery, foot. Quickly bring the trail foot back under the left shoulder and hip in order to maintain balance. Return to the start cone with the left side of your body leading the lateral footwork movement. Repeat the 7-yard (6.4 m) distance back and forth five times.

Your teammate should watch for balance errors such as bearing your body weight on the heels of your feet or moving your head or feet outside the width of your shoulders. Stick-handling errors include using an incorrect grip, holding the stick head more than 2 inches (5 cm) above the ground, and holding the stick so that the flat side is not facing forward.

Award yourself 2 points for each completed, back and forth, 7-yard (6.4 m) distance without a balance or stick-handling error.

To Increase Difficulty

- Position the cones 10 yards (9 m) apart.
- Increase the number of repetitions.
- Quicken the pace.
- Add a hockey ball and keep it in control.

To Decrease Difficulty

- Decrease the distance between cones.
- Reduce the number of repetitions.

Success Check

- Maintain balance and body control, with your feet shoulder-width apart.
- Use the power points of the feet during movement.
- Keep the head and shoulders aligned above the hips.
- Use the shake-hands grip with the flat side facing forward near the ground.
- Keep your head and eyes up, and look out at the field.

Score Your Success

Five repetitions without error = 10 points

Four repetitions without error = 8 points

Three repetitions without error = 6 points

Two repetitions without error = 4 points

One repetition without error = 2 points

Your score ___

Balance and Footwork Drill 2.
Breakaway for Quick First Step

Choose a partner for this drill. You both will work on quick, explosive first-step runs over a 16-yard (14.5 m) distance. Each of you attaches a Velcro breakaway belt around the waist. Attach the Velcro end of your belt to your partner's belt. Hold your hockey stick in your right hand halfway down the stick. Stand in a balanced ready or athletic position (feet shoulder-width apart on your power points) approximately 2 or 3 feet (0.6 to 0.9 m) in front of your partner, who is facing the same direction you are. Your objective is to break away from your partner, who will react to your first-step movement and will attempt to stay with you, preventing the separation of the breakaway belts. Use balanced short-run steps while exploding over the 16-yard (14.5 m) distance. Switch positions with your partner. Each player performs five repetitions in the front position as the quick starter. Complete two sets of five breakaway runs. On every start and while running, maintain balance on the power points of your feet (the balls of the feet). Be careful not to lose body control, or strike the heels of the feet during the footwork movement, or hold the stick incorrectly, or watch your feet instead of the field ahead. The front player scores 1 point for each successful breakaway from the react player, who is in the rear position.

To Increase Difficulty

- Decrease the distance to 10 yards (14.5 m).
- Increase the number of repetitions.
- Dribble a hockey ball.
- Change lateral direction, or fake, before sprinting.

To Decrease Difficulty

- Increase the distance to 25 yards (23 m).
- Reduce the number of repetitions.
- Do not hold a field hockey stick.

Success Check

- Maintain balance and body control with feet shoulder-width apart.
- Use the power points of the feet during movement.
- Keep the head and shoulders aligned above the hips.
- Use the shake-hands grip with the right hand halfway down the stick.
- Keep your head and eyes up, and look out at the field.

Score Your Success

Ten breakaways without error = 10 points

Eight or nine breakaways without error = 8 points

Six or seven breakaways without error = 6 points

Four or five breakaways without error = 4 points

Two or three breakaways without error = 2 points

Your score ___

Balance and Footwork Drill 3.
10-Yard (9 m) Weave Run

Mark a 10-yard distance, and set three cones in a straight line, equally spaced (approximately 24 inches, or 61 cm, apart). Mark a start line 3 yards (2.8 m) in front of the first cone and mark an end line 3 yards beyond the last cone. From the start line, run as fast as possible and weave around the cones to the end line. Run both feet over the end line and turn to weave back to the start line. Hold your hockey stick in your right hand halfway down the stick. Use short running steps, touching the ground with the power points of your feet. Do three sets of 20-second runs. Each completed run to the end line, with a return to the start line without an error, equals 2 points. Total the number of points for each set. Errors include knocking cones off line (demonstrated loss of body control), running on the heels, watching the feet instead of the field.

To Increase Difficulty

- Decrease the distance to 5 yards (4.5 m).
- Decrease the distance between the cones.
- Increase the amount of time.
- Run backward.
- Dribble a hockey ball.

To Decrease Difficulty

- Increase the distance between the cones.
- Reduce the amount of time.
- Do not hold a field hockey stick.

Success Check

- Maintain your balance and body control, with your feet shoulder-width apart.
- Use the power points of the feet during movement.
- Keep the head and shoulders aligned above the hips.
- Use the shake-hands grip, with the right hand halfway down the stick.
- Keep head and eyes up, and look out at the field.

ATTACK FOOTWORK

Movement with and without the ball is important for all three attack roles. An effective attack player uses her slight advantage over the defender (knowing what move is coming and when) and moves swiftly while remaining in balance. Once you have developed the skills, footwork and fakes will allow you to maintain balance as you attempt to get past your opponent. Moving continuously with and without the ball also demands superior fitness. Successful hockey players develop their physical conditioning as they master the skills necessary for excelling in the three attack roles.

When you are near the ball, both hands must remain on your stick in a shake-hands grip. When you are 30 yards (27.5 m) or more from the ball, you can grip your stick with only the right hand (figure 1.4) so that you can freely pump your arms and thereby run faster. But both hands must immediately grip the stick in preparation to play the ball as you approach it.

You should master three basic attack-footwork movements—breakdown steps, change of pace, and change of direction—so that you can perform the attack roles.

Breakdown Steps

Breakdown steps (figure 1.5) are used in both attack and defensive footwork, and it is the most fundamental skill for balance and foot movement. The attack hockey player uses breakdown steps to prepare the moving body for receiving and passing skills. When sprinting, you must quickly bring your body under control and into your basic attack stance.

To execute breakdown steps, shorten your running strides into quick, choppy steps without crossing your feet. Feet are staggered, with one foot up and one back as you keep your weight evenly distributed on the balls of the feet. Lower your hips by bending the knees. As the shorter strides slow your momentum, push off the power point of your back foot and step with the lead foot in order to briefly move into your attack stance. The head must be up in order to see the field and the ball, with both hands on the stick prepared to play the ball.

Figure 1.4 Stick grip when running.

Figure 1.5 Breakdown Steps

a

b

c

PREPARATION

1. Hold the stick with a shake-hands grip
2. Burst into a short run
3. Head leads a relaxed upper body

EXECUTION

1. Square your shoulders and toes to the ball
2. Shorten your strides to choppy steps and keep your feet shoulder-width apart
3. Flex your knees in a semi-crouched position, with your weight on the power points of your feet
4. Stick and arms are away from your body
5. Stick head moves down to touch the ground
6. Focus on the ball

FOLLOW-THROUGH

1. Maintain balance on the power points of your feet
2. Head is up to see the field
3. Be ready to play the ball

Misstep

You overrun the ball, and your stick is too close to your feet.

Correction

Begin shortening your strides sooner in order to get your body and feet in balance before the ball arrives.

Misstep

Your stick is too far from the ground, and you are not in balance.

Correction

Keep your heels off the ground and bend your knees in order to prepare the stick to play the ball.

Change of Pace

The change-of-pace footwork varies running speed so that you can fool a defender and break away from her. Without changing your basic running form and balance, change from a fast running speed to a slower pace and then quickly back to a fast run. The most frequently used change-of-pace footwork in field hockey is the *stutter step*, also called the *hesitation step* (figure 1.6).

As you run, keep your head up so that you can see the field and the ball. Take your first step with your back foot, crossing it in front of your lead foot. Run on the power points of your feet with your toes pointing in the direction you are going. Lean your upper body slightly forward and pump your arms in opposition to your legs, keeping your elbows flexed. Your stick grip will vary from a right-hand-only grip for open field runs to a shake-hands grip for preparing to play the ball. Completely extend your support leg. Lift your knee and thigh up and parallel to the ground as you bring the leg forward.

To execute the stutter step, move lightly on the balls of your feet, using short, choppy steps. Lead the upper body with your head and maintain body balance, slightly crouched, with every joint flexed and relaxed. Both hands remain on your stick as you pump your feet in place. Push off the rear foot to accelerate forward. The left foot pushes from the ground in order for you to go to your right; to go to your left, push off the power points of your right foot.

Figure 1.6   Stutter, or Hesitation, Step

a   b   c

PREPARATION

1. Hold your stick with a shake-hands grip
2. Burst into a short run
3. Head leads a relaxed upper body

EXECUTION

1. Square your shoulders and toes to the ball
2. Shorten your strides
3. Keep your feet shoulder-width apart
4. Flex your knees in a semi-crouched position and pump your feet
5. Burst into another short run

FOLLOW-THROUGH

1. Maintain balance on the power points of your feet
2. Head is up to see the field
3. Be ready to play the ball

Misstep

Change of speed does not evade your defender.

Correction

Pump your feet in place in order to get your defender to stop his feet, then lower your hips and push off into a burst of speed.

When attacking, you will be a step faster than a defender when you use change-of-pace footwork, which will enable you to win the space or get to the ball first. The stutter step, or hesitation step, will allow you to fool your opponent into slowing down or stopping, giving you an immediate advantage to change direction or to accelerate and break away from the defender. The deception of the change of pace comes from illusion and from quickness when changing speed. To slow your speed, shorten your stride or decrease your stride frequency. Use less force to push off your back foot and to avoid leaning your head and shoulders back as you slow your pace. To increase your speed, increase your stride frequency or lengthen your stride. To accelerate quickly to a faster speed, push forcefully off the back foot.

Misstep

Change from slow to fast is not quick.

Correction

Push forcefully off your back foot to quickly accelerate.

Misstep

The change from a fast speed to a slow speed is not deceptive.

Correction

Lean your head and upper body forward in order to prevent defenders from quickly spotting the change of pace.

Change of Direction

Change-of-direction footwork is especially important for getting open to receive a pass or for putting your defender off balance. An effective change of direction, such as the *stop and turn* (figure 1.7), depends on sharp cutting from one direction to another. The change of direction can be a simple attack move if you concentrate on a two-count move: right-left cadence or left-right cadence. To execute a basic change-of-direction move, begin with a three-quarter-length step with one foot, rather than with a full step. On your first step, flex your knee as you plant your foot firmly to stop your momentum, turn on the ball of your foot, and push off in the direction you want to go. Shift your weight and take a long step with your other foot, pointing your toes in the new direction. Keep your head up in order to see the field, and keep both hands on your stick if you are near the ball.

Figure 1.7   Stop and Turn

a

b

c

PREPARATION

1. Head is up to see the field and ball
2. Use a shake-hands grip
3. Burst into a short run

EXECUTION

1. Hop before you stop
2. Back foot lands first; lead foot lands second
3. Feet should be staggered shoulder-width apart with your knees flexed
4. Turn on the balls of your feet
5. Push off in a new direction and shift your weight
6. Make a long second step

FOLLOW-THROUGH

1. Maintain your balance
2. Eyes are focused on the ball
3. Stick head is low, ready to receive
4. Head is up to see the field

Misstep

You are not deceptive because you have a tendency to slow your speed too much on your approach to change direction.

Correction

Stay in your normal running form and concentrate on a two-count directional move such as right-left, left-right, or stop-turn.

Misstep

You run too great a distance, making your stops slow.

Correction

Use quick, brief breakdown steps or a short hop in order to stop.

The stop and turn allows you to change direction in order to create space between you and the opponent. The increased space will give you more time to successfully receive a pass from a teammate or, if you have the ball, to successfully dribble into the free space behind you. Before any turn or pivot can be made, you must learn to make a good stop after a short burst of speed. The quick burst of speed is used to fake your opponent into thinking that you are going to run by her.

It is important to lower your hips in a low, balanced position, with the knees bent and the head up to see the field. The head should remain above the midpoint of the feet. Stop your run by shortening your strides into a staggered hop and then lean in the opposite direction. Your rear foot is flexed at the knee in order to lower your body to a sitting position. The rear foot becomes the pivot foot, which turns the body. The other foot follows. After completing the turn, you should be facing the direction from which you want to receive the ball, with your feet shoulder-width apart, the body in good balance on the balls of your feet, and the ball away from the reach of the defender.

Misstep

Turns are rounded rather than sharp.

Correction

Use a three-quarter-length first step and flex your knee so that you can pivot sharply. Shift your weight and push off in the direction you want to go. The second step is a long, explosive step.

Misstep

The turn is slow and labored.

Correction

Feet are too wide. Keep your feet shoulder-width apart so that you can execute a long, second step with the back foot while pushing with the lead foot.

Attack Footwork Drill 1. *Fake and Accelerate*

In the center of a 12-yard (11 m) area, set two cones 2 yards (1.8 m) apart as the designated start area. Place one tennis ball 5 yards (4.5 m) from each side of both cones. Face a partner within the start area, keeping a minimum of 3 yards (2.8 m) between you and your partner. Begin as the attack player. Attempt a fake and then accelerate to pick up either tennis ball before your partner (the defender) tags you. Your partner cannot tag you while you are positioned in the start area. When both of your feet have left the start area, this is considered an attack try. Stay balanced while faking by maintaining a shoulder-width stance on the power points of your feet. Do five attempts and then exchange roles with your partner. Each player completes two sets of five attempts. Award yourself 1 point for each successful ball pick-up without being tagged.

To Increase Difficulty

- Increase the size of the playing area.
- Increase the number of attempts.
- Use a hockey stick and hockey balls.
- The attack player must get both balls during one attempt.

To Decrease Difficulty

- Decrease the size of the playing area.
- Reduce the number of attempts.

Success Check

- Maintain balance and body control with your feet shoulder-width apart.
- Use the power points of your feet to push in a direction.
- Shoulders and hips face forward in the direction of the ball.

Score Your Success

10 points = 10 points

8 or 9 points = 8 points

6 or 7 points = 6 points

4 or 5 points = 4 points

0 to 3 points = 2 points

Your score ___

Attack Footwork Drill 2.
Change of Direction With Agility Rings

Place four agility rings on the ground in a lateral row with 24 inches (61 cm) separating each ring. Grip your hockey stick with the right hand only. Start with your left foot in the first ring. For a change-of-direction movement from left to right, push off your left foot and land on your right foot inside the third ring. Immediately bring your left foot into the third ring. Establish balance and then push off the left foot and land your right foot inside the fourth agility ring. Remain on the power points of your feet at all times. Change direction back to the left. Push off the right foot (positioned in the fourth ring) and land on your left foot inside the second ring. Rapidly bring your right foot inside the second ring for balance and push off the right foot in order to land the left foot in the first agility ring. You have completed one repetition. Complete two sets of five repetitions. Have a partner watch and evaluate your technique. Change-of-direction errors include landing on the agility ring as the result of losing your balance, landing on your heels, or arms flailing out and away from your body. Avoid jumping up, and keep your feet under your hips and shoulders when executing a change of direction. Award yourself 1 point for each repetition completed without an error.

To Increase Difficulty

- Increase the distance between agility rings.
- Increase the number of repetitions.
- Increase the pace.
- Hold the hockey stick with a receiving grip.

To Decrease Difficulty

- Decrease the distance between agility rings.
- Reduce the number of repetitions.

Success Check

- Maintain balance and body control with your feet shoulder-width apart.
- Use the power points of the feet to push in a direction and to land on the ground.
- Shoulders and hips face forward.
- Keep your head steady.

Score Your Success

Zero errors = 10 points

One error = 8 points

Two errors = 6 points

Three errors = 4 points

Four errors = 2 points

Five errors or more = 1 point

Your score ____

Attack Footwork Drill 3. *Change-of-Direction Races*

Select a partner or organize into groups of equal numbers. Set three cones in a straight line, 2 feet apart. If you are organized into more than one group, set cones for each group. Place two tennis balls 7 yards (6.4 m) beyond the third cone. There should be 5 yards (4.5 m) between the tennis balls. Start 2 yards (1.8 m) behind the line of the first cone on the left side. Your partner starts behind the line of the first cone on the right side. With your feet shoulder-width apart, rise up on the power points of your feet. On a signal from the coach (clap hands or whistle), race against your partner to the second cone and turn back to the start (first)

cone. Immediately turn and run to the third cone and then turn back to the second cone. Turn and run to touch the tennis ball with your left hand. The first player who touches the tennis ball that is positioned 7 yards (6.4 m) out from third cone wins 1 point. Walk back to the start, switch sides with your partner, and repeat the race. Complete a total of 10 races. Be sure not to strike your heels on the ground; make wide, slow turns because your feet are outside your shoulders; or use the right hand instead of the left to touch the tennis ball. (Gripping a hockey stick with the left hand only gives you maximum reach to the ball.)

To Increase Difficulty

- Increase the distance of the race area.
- Increase the number of races.
- Pick up the tennis ball.
- Use hockey sticks and hockey balls.
- Racers start from different positions such as from the knees, from a push-up position, from a seated or lying position, from a one-legged squat position, or from a backward-facing position.

To Decrease Difficulty

- Decrease the distance of the race area.
- Reduce the number of races.
- Touch a volleyball, not a tennis ball.

Success Check

- Maintain balance and body control with your feet shoulder-width apart.
- Use the power points of your feet to push in a direction.
- Shoulders and hips face forward in the direction of the ball.

Score Your Success

10 points = 10 points

8 or 9 points = 8 points

6 or 7 points = 6 points

4 or 5 points = 4 points

0 to 3 points = 2 points

Your score ___

Attack Footwork Drill 4.
Agility Change-of-Direction Game

Select a teammate to compete against. Use four cones to mark a 10-by-10-yard (9 by 9 m) square playing area. On each side of the playing square, center two cones 1 yard (0.9 m) apart so that you have four 1-yard gates. Begin as the attack player who starts outside the square. Your teammate, the defender, will attempt to tag you. The defender starts in the middle of the square. Both of you can go in and outside the square through the gates only. During a 30-second period, if you are tagged, you are out of the game. If you can avoid being tagged during the 30-second period by demonstrating successful agility and change-of-direction footwork, you award yourself 1 point. Perform five 30-second periods and switch roles with your teammate. Complete two sets of five 30-second tag periods as the attack player. Avoid making wide turns around the square or through the gates as you will be running a farther distance than necessary. Use fakes and efficient footwork on the power points of the feet to change direction.

To Increase Difficulty

- Increase the distance between the gates.
- Increase the time period.
- Reduce the size of the square.
- The attack player uses a hockey stick and ball.
- Add more defenders and attackers.

To Decrease Difficulty

- Increase the size of the playing square.
- Reduce the time period.

Success Check

- Maintain balance and body control with your feet shoulder-width apart.
- Use the power points of your feet to push in the direction you want to go.
- Keep your head up and your eyes on the field.

Score Your Success

After 10 playing periods, the player or team with the most points wins.

Tagged zero times = 10 points

Tagged one time = 9 points

Tagged two times = 8 points

Tagged three times = 7 points

Tagged four times = 6 points

Tagged five times or more = 2 points

Your score ___

Attack Footwork Drill 5. *Chicken Tag Game*

Select a teammate to compete against. Use four cones to mark a 7-by-7-yard (6.5 by 6.5 m) square. The game objective is to be aggressive and to become the player who can successfully tag your "chicken" opponent. Stand behind the opposite end line from your opponent. Start the game by moving from behind your end line into the square. You are now in the chicken role and can be tagged by your opponent if he or she enters the square to pursue you. If you avoid being tagged and safely chicken back behind your own end line, you can become the tag player by re-entering the square. Now your opponent is the chicken and can become the tag player only by safely returning behind his or her own end line and re-entering the square. Tagging can happen only inside the square, and only the player who has the tag role may tag. The tag player wins a point for successfully tagging the chicken player. If a player steps out of bounds over a side-line, a point is awarded to the player who stayed in play. Play 10 games, alternating starting roles at the beginning of each game. The player who scores the most tags out of 10 games is the winner.

To Increase Difficulty

- Increase the size of the playing area.
- Increase the number of games.

- Add more players. The winner is the last player remaining.

To Decrease Difficulty

- Decrease the size of the playing area.
- Play fewer games.

Success Check

- Maintain balance and body control with your feet shoulder-width apart.
- Use the power points of your feet to push in the direction you want to go.
- Use a fake to unbalance the opponent.

Score Your Success

After 10 games, the player or team with the most points wins.

Nine or ten tags = 10 points

Seven or eight tags = 8 points

Five or six tags = 6 points

Three or four tags = 4 points

One or two tags = 2 points

Your score ___

Attack Footwork Drill 6. *Capture-the-Ball Team Game*

Divide into two teams of three players or more. Use four cones to mark a 20-by-20-yard (18.3 by 18.3 m) square area. Place 11 tennis balls in the center of the square, equidistant from each other. The game's objective is to use change-of-direction skills and agility in order to capture more tennis balls than your opponent. Each team starts behind a goal line. When the coach gives a signal, both teams enter the square. Once you enter the square to capture a tennis ball, an opponent can tag you. If you are tagged, you are out of the game and

your team plays with fewer players. Players can tag you at any time inside the square. If you are tagged while running with a ball, you must return the ball to the center of the square before leaving the game. To capture a ball, you must run it back and place it on the ground behind your goal line without your opponent tagging you. An opponent cannot tag you when you are behind your goal line. When all 11 balls have been captured, tally the score to determine which team won. Play the best out of five games.

To Increase Difficulty

- Decrease the size of the playing area.
- Use fewer balls.
- Use hockey sticks and balls.
- Add more players.
- Tagged players can stay in the game but must first return to the goal line.
- Play the best out of seven games.

To Decrease Difficulty

- Increase the size of the playing square.
- Play fewer games.
- Reduce the number of players per team.

Success Check

- Maintain balance and body control with your feet shoulder-width apart.
- Use the power points of your feet to push in the direction you want to go.
- Keep your head up and your eyes on the field.
- Use fakes to unbalance the opponent.

Score Your Success

Best of five games winner = 10 points

Best of five games loser = 0 points

Your score ___

BALANCED DEFENSIVE STANCE

A hockey defender, whose main objective is to take the ball from the opponent, must be able to instantly move in any direction and to change direction while sustaining body balance. Before you attempt to tackle the ball, you must control the space and you must block the forward space to the goal. This requires a well-balanced stance, which is fundamental to learning how to play defense role 1 (defender closest to the ball). The balanced, defensive stance (figure 1.8) resembles the basic attack stance with very bent knees and with an additional emphasis on effectively positioning the feet and body to force the opponent to move in the direction you want her to go. You must establish a more pronounced lead foot and refuse to allow the ball to pass that lead foot. To force the opponent with the ball to your left side, establish your right foot as the lead foot. Place your left foot directly opposite and in line with the opponent's left foot. A role 1 defender will most often use her left foot as the lead foot because it is most comfortable to make a forehand reach with the hockey stick from the right side of the body. To force the ball carrier to your right side, establish your left foot as the lead foot and place your right foot opposite the attacker's right foot.

Misstep

You easily lose balance.

Correction

Keep your heels off the ground and stagger your feet (establish a lead foot) shoulder-width apart. Distribute body weight evenly on the power points of your feet. Keep your knees bent and maintain proper body balance with head, feet, and hands.

Figure 1.8   Balanced Defensive Stance

1. Shoulders and feet face ball
2. Hands are in a separated shake-hands grip
3. Lead foot and shoulder should be aligned outside the opponent's body (left foot and shoulder aligned outside opponent's right side) in DR1
4. Align your back foot with the forcing direction
5. Feet are shoulder-width apart, weight on the power points, knees flexed
6. Head is steady over the knees
7. Stick head is moving to the ground in front of your feet, flat side facing the ball

Your head leads the upper body, with your feet staggered and shoulder-width apart or wider. Keep one foot (usually the left) in front of the other at all times, hips facing forward, and evenly distribute your weight on the power points (balls) of your feet. Flex your knees so that your body is low and coiled, ready to move or react in any direction. Grip your stick in both hands using the basic receiving grip. Keep your hands away from your body with your left hand positioned away from your left knee. It is important to keep the head of your stick on the ground in front of your feet and legs in order to prevent the opponent from pushing the ball into your feet. A well-balanced, defensive stance and a low stick are important because they allow you to better judge distance; you will therefore know when to tackle and when not to.

Misstep

You fail to protect the lead foot because you overreact to the ball's movement.

Correction

Know what direction you want to force the dribbler and establish a lead foot early.

Misstep

You are easily faked by your opponent's stick and ball movement.

Correction

Keep your eyes focused on the ball. Maintain a controlled playing distance from the ball and remain in balance when tackling the ball.

DEFENSIVE FOOTWORK

If you stop your feet, you're beat! To perform defensive footwork well, which is necessary in the three defense roles, you must have desire, discipline, anticipation, and superb fitness so that you can keep your feet moving! The key is to move your feet with balance so that you can react to your opponent's attack moves and block the forward space to the goal.

Defensive footwork requires short, quick steps with your weight evenly distributed on the power points of the feet. Avoid crossing your feet. Push off the back foot and continue adjusting with the lead foot. The only time you change your lead foot is when your opponent moves by your lead foot and gets behind you. In that case, execute a drop step to recover your defensive position. Otherwise, if the ball is still in front of you, always maintain your lead foot and push back away from the ball to recover your alignment.

Your feet are staggered shoulder-width apart so that you can instantly move laterally, forward, or backward. Keep your hips low, and lean your upper body forward with your head. Keep your eyes focused on the ball so that you can become a better judge of the distance between your probing stick and the ball. Hold your stick in both hands out in front of your feet. Defensive footwork calls for an active stick and for keeping the stick head close to the ground and then inching it closer to the ball as you time the moment to tackle.

Push-Back Footwork

In the basic defensive stance, the feet are staggered while one foot inches in front of the other. The front foot is called the *lead foot*. Establishing a lead foot enables you to push back easily in the direction of the rear foot. Moving or pushing back requires only a short step with the back foot as you push off the lead foot. The action resembles pushing away from a wall. To move in the direction of the lead foot requires using the *drop step*, a more difficult skill than protecting the lead foot. (The drop step will be covered in more detail later.) Keep your hips forward, square to the ball in front of you.

You must protect your lead foot as you establish your balanced, defensive stance. It is vital that you have a purposeful plan to force the opponent to either side so that a lead foot is immediately established and then protected (figure 1.9).

Misstep

Attack role 1 player moves the ball successfully past your backhand side.

Correction

Stay at least 4 yards (3.5 m) from the ball and get in position to keep the ball outside your right shoulder.

| Figure 1.9 | **Protect the Lead Foot** |

1. Shoulders and feet face ball
2. Position yourself at least 4 yards (3.5 m) from the ball in order to keep the ball outside your right shoulder
3. Hands are on the stick in a separated shake-hands grip
4. Lead foot and shoulder should be aligned outside the opponent's body (left foot and left shoulder aligned outside the opponent's right side)
5. Align your back (right) foot with the forcing direction
6. Feet are shoulder-width apart, on the power points, with knees flexed
7. Head is steady over the knees

Misstep

Attack role 1 player is able to dribble the ball either right or left, then in and behind you.

Correction

Maintain playing distance in order to keep the ball in front of you. Stagger your feet with a pronounced lead foot (left lead foot directs the ball to the right) and with your right shoulder and foot in line with the ball.

Misstep

Attack role 1 player fakes laterally and successfully penetrates with the ball by accelerating forward.

Correction

Maintain distance from the ball with your right shoulder aligned to the ball. Stay on power points and push back with the lead foot while sliding the rear foot back. Keep the ball in front of your right shoulder and foot.

Slide or Shuffle

Maintain a balanced, defensive stance between your opponent and the goal by sliding or shuffling. If the opponent moves to the side, quickly move your feet by sliding or shuffling laterally. Your feet remain staggered, with an established lead foot (figure 1.10). Use short, quick steps with your weight evenly distributed on the balls of your feet. To slide forward, push off the back foot and step forward with the lead foot. To slide back, push off the lead foot and step with the back foot. To slide laterally, push with the lead foot in order to slide. Keep your stick head on the ground and judge your distance from the opponent and the ball.

| Figure 1.10 | Slide or Shuffle |

PREPARATION

1. Use short, quick steps close to the ground
2. Shoulders and feet face the ball
3. Hands are on the stick in a separated shake-hands grip
4. Lead foot and shoulder should be aligned outside the opponent's body (left foot and shoulder are aligned outside the opponent's right side)
5. Align your back foot with the forcing direction
6. Feet are shoulder-width apart, on power points, with your knees flexed
7. Head is steady over your knees

a

b

c

EXECUTION

1. Push off the foot that is farther from the desired lateral position
2. Step with the foot that is closer to the desired lateral position
3. Stick head is on the ground in front of your feet, with the flat side facing the ball
4. Keep your arms away from your body
5. While sliding, pressure the ball with quick-stick probes

FOLLOW-THROUGH

1. Maintain a balanced, defensive stance
2. Patiently judge the distance from the ball
3. Head is up to see the field

Misstep

You cross your feet, preventing a quick change of direction.

Correction

Always keep your feet shoulder-width apart, and maintain a lead foot.

Misstep

You lean or reach too far with your stick, losing your balance.

Correction

Keep your head steady and slightly forward, basic grip on your stick, and keep your stick out in front of your feet on the ground.

Drop Step

The *drop step* (figure 1.11) is a defensive footwork technique that is used when you fail to protect the lead foot. The opponent has forced you to move back in the direction of your lead foot, which is a more difficult skill than moving in the direction of your back foot.

Drop step, or move the lead foot back, while pivoting on your back foot as you begin to move. After making the drop step in the direction of the opponent's move, use quick slide steps in order to reestablish your defensive stance with a lead foot forward. Keep your head up to see the field, and keep your eyes focused on the ball. Avoid turning your back to the ball or to your opponent. Aggressively push off your back foot in the direction of your drop step. Drop step straight back, moving your feet low along the ground.

Misstep

Your drop step lacks explosiveness and is too slow.

Correction

Execute your drop step straight back and low to the ground. Avoid circling your lead foot or lifting the lead foot.

Figure 1.11   Drop Step

a

b

c

PREPARATION

1. Shoulders and feet face the ball
2. Hands are in a shake-hands grip

EXECUTION

1. Reverse pivot on your back foot
2. Drop step with your lead foot straight back
3. Protect the space between your feet using your stick
4. Eyes are focused on the ball; maintain distance from the ball
5. Reestablish a defensive position by giving or running
6. Hips face the ball to reestablish the lead foot

FOLLOW-THROUGH

1. Protect your lead foot
2. Maintain a balanced, defensive stance
3. Prepare to change direction and to judge distance

Misstep

When your opponent moves, you turn your back, temporarily losing sight of your opponent and the ball.

Correction

Drop step in the direction of the opponent's move, keeping your eyes on the ball and the opponent.

Misstep

After the drop step, you use give steps rather than reestablish a defensive position. The opponent runs by and behind you.

Correction

Reestablish a defensive position by using slide steps or by running. Turn into position with your lead foot forward. Evaluate the opponent's speed and distance in order to make a good judgment.

Backward Run

A somewhat common movement pattern, the backward-run footwork is challenging but useful in the three defense roles. Backpedaling, or running backward, for a short distance allows you to see the field in front of you. You can better judge your distance from the ball, your opponent's speed of attack, and your teammates' movements.

To execute the backward run, drive back off the power points of the feet, keeping your head slightly forward to maintain balance. Knees remain flexed. Keep one or both hands on your stick, ready to reposition yourself in a balanced, defensive stance. Your feet stay low to the ground during the quick, short, backward running stride. Concentrate on swinging your lower legs back in order to land and push off the balls of the feet. Backpedal for only a short distance, while preparing to get into a balanced, defensive stance.

Misstep

You lose your balance and fall backward.

Correction

Stay on the power points of your feet and keep the head slightly forward while backpedaling.

Defensive Footwork Drill 1. *Body Control*

Partner with a teammate who has a tennis ball. Set two cones 5 yards (4.5 m) apart. Position yourself forward of the center area of the cones and face your partner, who should be 3 yards (2.8 m) in front of you with the tennis ball. Start in a balanced, defensive stance with your left foot in the lead position, and be ready to receive the ball. Your partner rolls the ball to the outside of one of the cones, both of which are behind you on your left and right sides. When you see the ball's path, immediately push back into the space between the cones and slide in the direction the ball is rolling and keep the ball directly in front of your body. Maintain your left lead foot and keep your hips and shoulders facing the rolling ball as you execute the footwork on the power points of your feet. Your body must be in control as you receive the ball in front of your feet with both hands. Pick up the ball with both hands and toss the ball to your partner. Return to the start area and take the ready position again. Repeat 10 times. Exchange roles with your partner.

Errors include picking up the ball while on one foot, turning shoulders and hips sideways instead of toward ball, not maintaining a left lead foot, allowing your heels to touch the ground during footwork, and reaching with one hand to pick up the ball. Award yourself a point for each ball you pick up in front of you.

To Increase Difficulty

- Increase the distance between the cones.
- Increase the number of repetitions.
- Quicken the pace.
- Use a hockey stick and hockey ball.
- The passer dribbles a hockey ball and the defender positions to block.

To Decrease Difficulty

- Decrease the distance between cones.
- Reduce the number of repetitions.
- Slow the pace.

Success Check

- Maintain balance and body control with your feet shoulder-width apart.

- Use the power points of the feet during movement.
- Maintain the lead foot in all directions during movement.
- Position your body perpendicular to the ball's path to keep the ball in front of you.
- Keep your head and eyes up, and look out at the field.

Score Your Success

Nine or ten pick-ups = 10 points

Seven or eight pick-ups = 8 points

Five or six pick-ups = 6 points

Three or four pick-ups = 4 points

One or two pick-ups = 2 points

Your score ___

Defensive Footwork Drill 2.
Power Steps With Mini-Bands

Use cones to set up a 2-by-2-yard (1.8 by 1.8 m) square. Partner with a teammate. Place a mini-band around your ankles and hold your hockey stick in both hands in a receiving grip. Stand in the center of the square in a balanced, defensive stance, with your left foot as the lead foot. Maintain a balanced, defensive stance on the power points when moving forward, left, right, or back. Both feet must move outside the square and return to the starting position in the middle before you move in another direction. Your partner stands outside the square facing you, and she uses her stick to point you in the direction you should go. Your partner does five directional points before you switch to the pointer role. Be sure to maintain your lead foot no matter what direction you are pointed, while keeping your stick head on the ground. With your body weight centered, keep your head steady and the mini-band taut at all times.

Balance errors include bearing your body weight on the heels of your feet or on only one foot, moving your head or feet outside the width of your shoulders, and positioning your feet too close together so that the mini-band becomes slack. Stick-handling errors include incorrect grip, stick head more than 2 inches (5 cm) above the ground, and flat side of the stick not facing forward toward the imaginary ball. Award yourself 1 point for each correct directional power step move without a balance error or stick-handling error. Repeat two sets of five repetitions.

To Increase Difficulty

- Increase the area to a 5-by-5-yard (4.5 by 4.5 m) square.
- Increase the number of repetitions.
- Quicken the pace.

To Decrease Difficulty

- Decrease the distance between the cones.
- Reduce the number of repetitions.
- Do not use the mini-band.

Success Check

- Maintain balance and body control with your feet shoulder-width apart.
- Use the power points of the feet during movement.

- Keep the head and shoulders aligned above the hips.
- Use the receiving hockey grip with the flat side facing forward near the ground.
- Keep your head and eyes up, and look out at the field.

Nine or ten correct power steps = 10 points

Seven or eight correct power steps = 8 points

Five or six correct power steps = 6 points

Three or four correct power steps = 4 points

Zero to two correct power steps = 2 points

Your score ___

Defensive Footwork Drill 3. *Lead-Foot Ladders*

Lay an agility ladder on the ground horizontally in front of you. Hold your stick in a receiving grip. Start with your left foot as the lead foot. Face the horizontal agility ladder on the left end and position yourself behind the first 24-inch (61 cm) ladder space. Establish a low, defensive stance and get ready to move. To start, push off your rear (right) foot and place your lead foot into the first ladder space, followed immediately by your right foot. Maintain balance with the lead foot as you immediately push with your right foot and thereby move the left lead foot out in the front of the first ladder space. Immediately push off the left lead foot in order to move your right foot into the second ladder space, followed immediately by your left lead foot into the second space. Use your left lead foot to push your right foot out of the back of the second space. Always maintain the left foot as the lead foot as you move through the spaces of the agility ladder. Keep a shoulder-width distance between your feet, and maintain your balance, with your body weight centered between your feet. Move up the right side of ladder, then move back down the left side for one repetition. Complete 10 repetitions. Errors include stepping on the ladder rungs, having your feet too close together or too far apart, touching the ground with the heels of your feet, or watching your feet instead of looking out at the field. Award yourself a point for each ladder repetition that you complete without an error.

To Increase Difficulty

- Increase the number of repetitions.
- Increase the ladder length.
- Quicken the pace.

- Add a short sprint or a change of direction after last ladder space.
- Add mini-band on ankles.
- Use the right foot as the lead foot.

To Decrease Difficulty

- Decrease the ladder length.
- Reduce the number of repetitions.
- Slow the pace.

Success Check

- Maintain balance and body control with your feet shoulder-width apart.
- Use the power points of the feet during movement.
- Keep the head and shoulders aligned above the hips.
- Use the receiving hockey grip, with the flat side facing forward near the ground.
- Keep head and eyes up, and look out at the field.

Nine or ten correct lead-foot ladders = 10 points

Seven or eight correct lead-foot ladders = 8 points

Five or six correct lead-foot ladders = 6 points

Three or four correct lead-foot ladders = 4 points

One or two correct lead-foot ladders = 2 points

Your score ___

Defensive Footwork Drill 4.
Push-Back-and-Up Footwork

Use cones to set up a 5-by-5-yard (4.5 by 4.5 m) area. Grip your hockey stick and begin at the top of the square in a balanced, defensive stance with a left lead foot. While maintaining a low, defensive stance with a lead foot, move back by pushing from the front lead foot. When both feet move outside the back of the square, immediately go forward by pushing from the rear (right) foot to the top of the square. Maintain the left lead foot and keep a low, defensive stance with your feet shoulder-width apart. Center your body weight between your feet and execute the footwork on the power points of the feet. Repeat the push back and forward footwork five times. Errors include bearing your body weight on the heels of the feet, turning hips and chest sideways instead of facing them forward, changing the lead foot or squaring the feet, not maintaining a shoulder's-width distance between your feet, and using an incorrect grip on the stick (one that fails to keep the flat side of stick facing the attack player or ball). Award yourself 1 point for each correct push-back-and-up trip without an error.

To Increase Difficulty

- Increase the size of the playing area.
- Increase the number of repetitions.
- Quicken the pace.
- Push back in a diagonal direction.
- Move laterally, then diagonally back and laterally in a Z pattern.
- Add attack role 1 player to compete against.
- Wear a mini-band.

To Decrease Difficulty

- Decrease the size of the playing area.
- Reduce the number of repetitions.
- Slow the pace.

Success Check

- Maintain balance and body control with your feet shoulder-width apart.
- Use the power points of your feet to push back quickly.
- Shoulders and hips face forward in the direction of ball.
- Keep the stick's head on the ground.
- Use the receiving hockey grip with the flat side facing forward.
- Keep head and eyes up, and look out at the field.

Score Your Success

Zero errors = 10 points

One error = 8 points

Two errors = 6 points

Three errors = 4 points

Four errors = 2 points

Five errors or more = 0 points

Your score ___

SUCCESS SUMMARY OF BALANCE AND FOOTWORK

Success in field hockey is often associated with speed, but balance and quick feet, or agility, are the most important physical attributes. Little can be done to improve innate sprint speed, but balance and agility can be improved significantly through proper training. The head, feet, and hands, along with the stick, control balance. When these extremities are in balance, your body is ready to move quickly and skillfully. Place a priority on having physical control of your body, feet, and stick before attempting to perform skills rapidly. Rushing your execution of hockey techniques will only promote mistakes and bad habits, which reflect a lack of emotional control as well as a lack of balance. Quickness is specific to the hockey skill being performed. The successful hockey player must seek an absolute point of balance in her relationship to the ball with every offensive and defensive technique.

Balance and Footwork Drills

1. Mini-Bands for Lateral Balance	___ out of 10
2. Breakaway for Quick First Step	___ out of 10
3. 10-Yard (9 m) Weave Run	___ out of 10

Attack Footwork

1. Fake and Accelerate	___ out of 10
2. Change of Direction With Agility Rings	___ out of 10
3. Change-of-Direction Races	___ out of 10
4. Agility Change-of-Direction Game	___ out of 10
5. Chicken Tag Game	___ out of 10
6. Capture-the-Ball Team Game	___ out of 10

Defensive Footwork Drills

1. Body Control	___ out of 10
2. Power Steps With Mini-Bands	___ out of 10
3. Lead-Foot Ladders	___ out of 10
4. Push-Back-and-Up Footwork	___ out of 10
Total	___ *out of 130*

A combined score of 104 points or more suggests that you have satisfactorily mastered the balance and footwork skills and that you are prepared to move to step 2. A score in the range of 91 to 103 is considered adequate. You can move on to step 2 after additional practice of the balance and footwork skills that you find most difficult. A score of 90 points or less indicates insufficient control of various movements. Review and practice the techniques discussed in step 1 again before moving on to step 2.

Passing and Receiving

The truly sophisticated aspect of field hockey is the team passing game. Unfortunately, many players are remembered for their dribbling skills instead of for their passing skills because dribbling appears to be more spectacular. Bad passing will destroy a team's chances of success, no matter how much stick work and dribbling ability the players have. Hence, passing and receiving skills are most important. To master passing and receiving, you must develop the attack role 1 techniques of pushing, hitting, and lifting.

All team sports demand interaction among players, so passing is a priority in all basic skills. Passing and receiving the hockey ball require that players work the ball in combination. The key to creating a steady flow of passing options is the effective movement of players who do not have the ball.

Depending on the game situation, you may choose to pass the ball along the ground or to lift it into the air. As a general rule, a pass that is moving along the ground is easier to receive and control than a ball that drops from the sky.

Winning team play depends on effective passing combinations and on solid receiving skills. Failing to accurately pass the ball or to receive and control it will cause a team to lose possession of the ball. The critical elements of passing include correct timing, correct pace or speed, and the ability to read a play and thereby to judge distances accurately. Every player and team can improve if adequate attention is given to timing, accuracy, and power.

You will improve your skill level by passing the ball on the ground whenever possible. In the information that follows, you will first learn about the attack role 1 techniques that are used to pass the ball along the ground and then learn how to practice the proper methods of receiving and controlling passes on the ground.

PASSING GROUND BALLS

Always have a target. The two requirements of a good pass are *accuracy* and *timing*.

The factors that govern an accurate pass are its accuracy and its speed. The position of the target (either a receiver's stick or free space, both of which enable the receiver to run to the pass) and the width of the passing lane determine the direction of the pass. The passing lane must allow the ball to clear the opponent's stick. The shorter the pass, the more precise it must be. Short, direct passes must be firm and fast, leading a successful ball trap. A longer pass permits the receiver more time to move into position if the direction of the pass is wrong.

The speed of the pass is determined by the distance between the passer and receiver, the width of the passing lane established by the opponent's position, and the ground or surface conditions. Every pass has a correct speed. A ball hit firmly to the receiver's stick or one that leads the receiver into open space is easier to stop than a ball poking along the ground. A common error is to underhit a short pass.

For the timing of a pass to be right, the receiver must be free, or at least prepared, to receive the ball. Hence, the passer must hold the ball and look up before passing. The pass should arrive when the receiver wants the ball.

Push Pass

The push pass is the most common field hockey pass. The push pass, which is primarily used to play the ball over a 5- to 15-yard (4.5 to 13.8 m) distance, provides accuracy, quicker release time when needed, and excellent control over the pace of the ball. Although a push pass does not generate the same ball speed as a hit, it is still effective and accurate. A good push passer

can predict when and where the ball will stop rolling. The essential elements of the push pass are accuracy, a quick release, and a varied pace. Accuracy depends on the correct position of the feet, which balance the body.

To execute the push pass on the forehand side (figure 2.1), point your left shoulder at your target and use the shake-hands (receiving) grip. Placing your body sideways to the line of the pass enables you to transfer your body weight through the front leg. Your center of gravity is lowered during the pass, with your feet a little more than shoulder-width apart. Your head is down and your hands are apart on the stick and in the shake-hands grip. There is no backswing, so your stick must start next to the ball. Keeping the stick next to the ball helps disguise direction and time of release. The face of the stick is closed slightly to keep the ball on the ground. The ball is positioned under your eyes, with your weight evenly distributed.

Push the ball using the head of the stick as you transfer your body weight to the left or front leg. You should feel as if you were pushing through the ball while controlling the stick with mainly your right hand. The left hand starts the push and the right hand provides direction. With your hands and stick away from your body, follow through with your stick along your target line.

| Figure 2.1 | **Forehand Push Pass** |

PREPARATION

1. Ball is positioned in your control box
2. Left shoulder points to the target
3. Weight is balanced over the balls of your feet, 12 inches (30.5 cm) apart
4. Head is steady over the ball
5. Stick is next to the lower half of ball
6. Use a shake-hands grip
7. Stick face is closed slightly

a

(continued)

(continued)

b

c

EXECUTION

1. Start weight transfer forward
2. Keep the stick next to the ball
3. Push your stick through the lower half of the ball
4. Left hand pulls the stick forward
5. Right hand exerts pressure and direction
6. Keep your head steady over the path of the ball
7. Extend your arms as your left hand passes your left foot

FOLLOW-THROUGH

1. Generate momentum through the ball
2. Finish your weight transfer through the front leg
3. Extend your stick and arms toward the target
4. Return to a ready position

Misstep

The push pass comes off the ground.

Correction

Slightly close the face of the stick so that the top of the stick blade is ahead of the underside of the hook. Follow through with the head of the stick low along the ground.

Misstep

You slap at the ball.

Correction

Start with the ball next to the stick.

The push pass on the backhand side, also called the reverse push pass, is used to pass the ball over short distances when there is neither time nor space to move into a forehand position. To execute the reverse push pass, point your right shoulder at your target and grip the stick in a reverse grip position (figure 2.2a). The ball should be near the front foot so that the stick will be at a 45- to 60-degree angle to the ground when it strikes the ball (figure 2.2b). The power of the reverse stick push comes from pulling firmly with the right hand. Your head should remain over the ball as you make the pass (figure 2.2c).

Figure 2.2   Reverse Push Pass

a

b

c

PREPARATION

1. Ball is in your control box
2. Right shoulder points toward the target
3. Weight is balanced over the balls of your feet, 12 inches (30.5 cm) apart
4. Head is steady over the ball
5. Stick is next to the lower half of the ball
6. Stick is held in a reverse grip
7. Stick face is slightly closed

EXECUTION

1. Start your weight transfer forward
2. Keep your stick next to the ball
3. Right hand pulls the stick forward
4. Push through the lower half of the ball using both hands
5. Right hand exerts pressure and direction
6. Head is steady over the path of the ball

FOLLOW-THROUGH

1. Extend your arms as your left hand moves past your right foot
2. Generate momentum through the ball
3. Transfer your weight through your front leg
4. Finish with your stick and arms extended toward the target
5. Return to a ready position

Misstep

The push pass is inaccurate.

Correction

Feet must be shoulder-width apart in order to establish balance, with the left (forehand) or right (backhand) shoulder pointing to the target. Using a shake-hands grip (reverse for backhand), keep the stick next to the ball, and use the head of the stick to push the ball as you transfer your body weight to the front leg.

Push Passing Drill 1.
7- and 15-Yard Partner Push Pass

Partner with a teammate and use a 15-yard-long (13.8 m) area. Position yourself 7 yards (6.4 m) from your partner. From a side-on position (the left side of your body faces your partner), start with the ball in your control box and push pass the ball to your partner's stick. Your partner receives and immediately push passes the ball back to your stick. Complete 15 forehand push passes without error. Next, position the ball on your left side and execute a backhand push pass to your partner's stick. Complete 15 backhand push passes to your partner without error. Next, position 15 yards (13.8 m) from your partner and complete 15 forehand push passes without error. Finally, complete 15 backhand push passes without error. Push pass errors include pushing a bouncy pass because of improper stick angle, pushing an inaccurate push pass in which the receiver has to move his or her stick more than 12 inches (30.5 cm) from the initial target, slapping the ball instead of keeping the stick close to the ball and pushing it, or pushing a slow, pokey pass. Award yourself 1 point for each completed push pass without an error.

To Increase Difficulty

- Increase the number of repetitions.
- Quicken the pace with the added pressures of time or competition. (Winner is the pair that completes 15 passes each.)
- Receiver must move her stick (target) before each pass.

To Decrease Difficulty

- Decrease the distance.
- Perform fewer repetitions.

Success Check

- Look up at the target before push passing.
- Make certain the ball is in your control box and your stick is next to the ball.
- Take a balanced side-on position to the ball, with feet 12 inches (30.5 cm) apart.
- Maintain the shake-hands grip.
- Follow through into a ready position to receive the ball.

Score Your Success

15 7-yard forehand push passes = 5 points

15 7-yard backhand push passes = 5 points

15 15-yard forehand push passes = 5 points

15 15-yard backhand push passes = 5 points

Your score ___

Push Passing Drill 2. Shuttle Push Passing

Divide into groups of five players. Divide each group into two shuttle lines—one with two players and one with three players—and stand in two lines 25 yards (23 m) apart. The front player in the three-player shuttle line starts with the hockey ball, pushing it 3 to 4 yards (2.8 to 3.7 m) directly in front of herself and then accelerating after it. After regaining control of the ball, she push passes the ball to the first player in the opposite shuttle line who repeats the exercise—receive, self-push, accelerate, and push pass to the opposite shuttle line. Turn your left shoulder to the target before executing the forehand push pass, and accurately pass the ball onto your teammate's stick. After you push pass the ball, follow your pass and run to the back of the opposite shuttle line. Each player completes five forehand push passes from each line. To finish the drill, push to your left, regain the ball next to your stick, and execute a reverse push pass to the player in the opposite line. Each player completes five reverse push passes. Award a point for each forehand and backhand push pass without an error. Errors include poor accuracy, inadequate timing, and slow passes.

To Increase Difficulty

- Increase distance between shuttle lines.
- Increase the number of repetitions.
- Quicken the pace with the added pressures of time or competition. (First group to complete 25 passes without error wins.)
- Place obstacles in the passing area.

To Decrease Difficulty

- Decrease the distance.
- Perform fewer repetitions.

Success Check

- Look up at the target before push passing.
- Make certain the ball is in your control box, with your stick next to the ball.

- Turn your front shoulder to the target before passing.
- Maintain a balanced side-on position to the ball, with feet 12 inches (30.5 cm) apart.
- Maintain the shake-hands grip.
- Follow through and prepare your body and stick for the next action.

Score Your Success

13 to 15 correct push passes = 5 points

10 to 12 correct push passes = 3 points

0 to 9 correct push passes = 1 point

Your score ___

Push Passing Drill 3. *Fives Downfield*

Divide into groups of five players. Use a vertical lane 50 yards (46 m) long by 20 yards (18.5 m) wide. Start the ball on the endline. While push passing the ball to each other, progress down the field to the 50-yard line. After pushing a ball to a teammate, move to a position in front, behind, or alongside the ball. Always have a player in front of the ball and a player behind the ball. The aim is to progress without error all the way down to the 50-yard line and back to the start using push passes. Push passing errors include a slow ball speed, poor accuracy, and poor timing of the pass release. If your group commits more than one error while progressing down the field and back, you must restart from the endline. Complete three down-and-back trips.

To Increase Difficulty

- Increase the distance.
- Require that all trips be executed in six passes without error.
- Quicken the pace with the added pressure of time.
- Race against another group.
- Add obstacles or defenders in the vertical lane.
- End with a shot at goal.

To Decrease Difficulty

- Decrease the distance.
- Use only three players.

Success Check

- Look up at the target before push passing.
- Make certain that the ball is in your control box, with your stick next to the ball.
- Take a balanced side-on position to the ball, with feet 12 inches (30.5 cm) apart.
- Maintain the shake-hands grip.
- Follow through and move into a ready position to receive the ball.

Score Your Success

Three trips with zero errors = 10 points

Three trips with two errors = 5 points

Three trips with three errors = 1 point

Your score ___

Hit

The hit is the best option for moving the ball quickly over longer distances and for scoring simply because of the ball speed. The hit, or drive as it is sometimes called, is a significant strike in hockey because

1. the hit is a one-ball touch that can beat opponents in an instant;

2. the hit uses more field area when changing the point of attack from sideline to sideline and from backline to backline;

3. the hit provides enough power to determine the pace and speed of play, which is vital in transition;

4. the hit extends the time that teammates share the ball, which is essential for team play; and

5. the hit is used to score more often than any other hockey technique.

The hockey player must be able to perform all kinds of hits while running or while in a free-hit situation. The most important aspect of the hit is to pass the ball accurately with the proper speed. The hitter must pass to a selected target and not be afraid to hit short passes firmly. Every hit should have a planned destination and particular target. Therefore, the mechanics of the hit become as important to the player who receives the ball as to the player who hits it.

During a hit (figure 2.3), the hips move slightly laterally, not rotationally, as with a sweep hit or a golf swing. The hit also requires correct foot spacing from the ball, with the left shoulder pointing in the direction of the hit. The hitter must sustain the footwork speed and balance in order to change direction and to move into position for hitting. If you are able to consistently establish the proper foot-to-ball distance before striking the ball, you will be well on your way to executing hits and outperforming your opponent. After you prepare your feet in relation to the ball, perform a fluid swing using the four action phases of the hit: grip, backswing, weight transfer and contact, and follow-through. Remember to look at the target before passing.

Figure 2.3   Hitting

PREPARATION

1. Left shoulder points toward the target
2. Head is down and over the ball
3. Control the ball
4. Feet are 12 inches (30.5 cm) apart
5. Ball is in line with your left foot
6. Knees are bent and your weight is evenly distributed on the balls of your feet
7. Hands are together at the top of the stick

a

b

c

EXECUTION

1. Body weight is centered between your feet

2. Keep your head down and over the ball

3. Keep your knees bent and your feet shoulder-width apart

4. Left arm is nearly straight and the right elbow is tucked

5. Transfer your weight to your front leg and hip on the downswing

6. Align your hands with your wrists before contact

7. Flat stick head squarely strikes the lower half of the ball

FOLLOW-THROUGH

1. Fluidly transfer your weight through your front leg

2. Knees remain relaxed and bent

3. Keep your head down and watch the ball leave your stick

4. Arms and stick finish in line with the target

5. Return to a ready position

Misstep

You miss the ball.

Correction

Keep your eyes focused on the lower half of the ball instead of on the target. Maintain bent knees.

Start with a controlled ball about 9 inches (23 cm) in front of and in line with the front foot. The first phase of the hit is the grip. The grip is the same as the receiving grip (shake-hands grip) except that you bring the hands together so that they can act in unison to strike the ball. With the hitting grip, make certain the forefinger of the left hand is in contact with the little finger of the right hand. There are three methods to bring the hands together for the hit:

1. The left hand remains near the top of the stick and the right hand moves up. This method is the most commonly used and it provides the most leverage for the swing.

35

2. The right hand remains in its original receiving grip and the left hand moves down to join the right. This method restricts leverage and it requires wrist action during the swing.

3. The left hand is moved down and the right hand is moved up to meet in the middle of the handle. This method combines power and control.

The second action phase of the hit is the backswing. Shift your body weight slightly to the back foot, leg, and hip as you take your stick back and away from the ball. Keep your head down and look at the bottom half of the ball. Your body remains low, with your knees bent and feet shoulder-width apart. The left arm is nearly straight but not rigid on the backswing, with the right elbow bent almost to 90 degrees. The arms swing freely away from your body, coordinating the shoulders and legs for the third phase of the hit.

During the third phase of the hit, the weight transfer and contact, transfer your body weight to the front leg as your stick sweeps down and through the lower half of the ball. Pull with your left hip and push from the rear foot to the front foot in order to initiate the transfer of body weight. This hip pull will fluidly bring the straight left arm forward, directing the stick down into the ball. Your right hand and arm follow the momentum of the hip pull and the relatively straight left arm. Eyes and head stay down to see the base of your stick strike the lower half of the ball. The knees are relaxed and bent while your arms swing freely through the ball. At contact, the flat face of the stick is at a right angle to the ground and your hands are aligned with your wrists. Inches before contact, the right hand, working in unison with the left, snaps at the ball. The flat part of the stick makes solid contact on the back lower half of the ball. The speed of the wrists and hands is crucial during this action. Although the hips and legs move first to initiate speed, the arms, wrists, and hands freely follow and they transfer that speed through the hit, which imparts force to the ball.

Misstep

You undercut or slice the ball.

Correction

Set your feet 12 inches apart (30.5 cm), knees bent, and position the ball 9 inches (23 cm) away from, but in line with, your front foot. The face of the stick must be flat at the moment of impact.

Misstep

You top the ball, causing it to bounce.

Correction

With bent knees, position the ball farther from your left (forehand) or right (backhand) foot. Strike the lower half of the ball center with the blade square.

In the follow-through phase, body weight is relocated to the front leg, with the hands extended out toward the target. After contact, continue to extend the stick down the target line during those few inches after the ball leaves the stick. The ball will follow the path of your stick head after those few critical inches from the ball. Continue to finish the follow-through until the stick and hands are out in front of the left leg.

Misstep

Your hit is choppy.

Correction

Position the ball in your control box, and align it with the front foot instead of with the back foot. Follow through after impact.

Misstep

Your hit has little power or accuracy.

Correction

Make sure your hands are together and that there is no space between them. Coordinate and lead the left (forehand) or right (backhand) hand and arm on the downswing and on the weight transfer through the front foot.

Hit Drill 1. *Hit the Boards*

Select a teammate. Obtain two 4-by-4-inch-thick (10 by 10 cm) boards that are at least 1 yard (0.9 m) long. Place one board on the ground 15 yards (13.5 m) in front of your selected start area. Place the second board on the ground 15 yards to the left of the start area. The long sides of both boards should face the start area. Your teammate times you for a period of 30 seconds. Award yourself a point each time you successfully hit the ball against the boards from 15 yards away. You may not attempt to hit the same board twice in succession. Record your best score from five 30-second rounds.

To Increase Difficulty

- Increase the hit distance.
- Score only consecutive hits on the boards.
- Reduce the time period.
- Race against another player.
- Make the target smaller.

To Decrease Difficulty

- Move closer to the boards.

- Increase the amount of time.
- Increase the size of the target.

Success Check

- Look up at the target before hitting the ball.
- Make certain the ball is in your control box and in front of your left foot when hitting forehand.
- Take a balanced side-on position to the ball, with feet 12 inches (30.5 cm) apart.
- Maintain the shake-hands grip with hands together.
- Follow through and move into a ready position to receive.

Score Your Success

More than nine hits in 30 seconds = 5 points

Seven to nine hits in 30 seconds = 3 points

Fewer than seven hits in 30 seconds = 1 point

Your score ___

Hit Drill 2. *Square Passing With Quick Hits*

Divide into groups of four. Use one ball for each group. Position one player at each corner of a 7-by-7-yard (6.4 by 6.4 m) square. Start the drill by passing the ball to the player on your left (clockwise). Each player receives the ball and hit passes the ball to his or her left. Because the ball is to travel only 7 yards (6.4 m), use the short shake-hands grip to quickly strike the ball from a very small backswing. (For the short shake-hands grip, bring your hands together and move them about 12 inches (30.5 cm) down the stick handle after you receive the ball.) Set your body by turning

your left shoulder to the target and position your feet to keep the ball in your control box. Pass the ball to your left around the square three times, then switch the pass direction to the right (counterclockwise). When receiving from your left and passing right, allow the ball to travel across your body before turning your left shoulder to the target on your right. Pass the ball counterclockwise around the square three times. You must start and finish with the same ball. Award yourself a point for each accurate quick hit that travels smoothly to your teammate's stick.

To Increase Difficulty

- Increase the size of the square.
- Use the reverse quick hit to the right.
- Quicken the pace with the added pressure of time.
- Race against another group.
- Use two balls and pass to anyone. Compete against time or another group to see who can keep both balls in play the longest.
- Add a defender in the middle. Passes must be deceptive and may go clockwise, counterclockwise, or diagonally.

To Decrease Difficulty

- Decrease the distance.
- Reduce the number of repetitions.
- Use only three players.

Success Check

- Look up at the target before the backswing.
- Make certain the ball is in your control box, with your stick next to the ball.
- Take a balanced side-on position to the ball, with feet 12 inches (30.5 cm) apart.
- Use the short shake-hands grip to quick hit.
- Front shoulder points to target.
- Follow through and maintain a balanced position to receive and quick hit the ball.

Score Your Success

Nine passes without error = 10 points

Nine passes with one error = 8 points

Nine passes with two errors = 6 points

Nine passes with three errors = 4 points

Nine passes with four errors or more = 2 points

Your score ___

Sweep Hit

Modern hockey, which is often played on watered artificial turf, has showcased the sweep hit for the game's long passes. Top players use the sweep hit because it generally is more accurate due to a much wider impact zone (the zone of the stick shaft or label instead of the curved stick head). Because of the wide impact zone, you do not have to focus only on the ball and you can read the game while executing the sweep hit. You also have the advantage of changing the direction of the hit at the last moment. The sweep hit is especially important during games played on artificial turf. A sweep hit creates a smooth running ball along the ground without any bounce, which results in a better chance of receiving and controlling the ball. The ball can be hit with more speed because of the longer-swing follow-through and an increased velocity of the curve without any pauses in the backswing and forward swings. To impart a great deal of power to the sweep hit, both hands must be so close together at the top of the stick that the index finger of the upper left hand touches the little finger of the lower right hand. The sweep hit can be executed faster than the upright hit because it generally requires a shorter backswing.

The sweep hit can start with a lifted stick or with the stick on the ground. To develop maximum speed of the curve and powerful passes, start with your stick lifted far back from the ball. For a less powerful pass but more accuracy, keep the stick on or close to the ground at the start and at impact. In both sweep-hit styles, the impact zone is on the label near the upper portion of the stick curve.

Similar to the upright hit, the sweep hit is used to pass the ball over longer distances and to score goals, but the forehand sweep hit (figure 2.4) has its own distinguishing characteristics:

- It is a deceptive hit.
- It requires quick wrist movement.
- The player is farther than control-box distance from the ball so that the left arm can fully extend.
- Knees are bent 90 degrees in order to establish a low center of gravity.
- The sweep hit features continuous stick curve movement with a small loop back and down to the ball.

- The stick can start on the ground or from a lifted position.
- The sweep action increases the stick speed toward the ball.

- Ball contact is made on the label zone near the upper part of the curve of the stick while the stick is horizontal.
- After contact, the player continues to lower his or her center of gravity.

Figure 2.4 | Forehand Sweep Hit

a

b

PREPARATION

1. Take a side-on position from the ball, which is outside the control box
2. Look up and select a target
3. Left shoulder points toward the target
4. Both hands are together in a shake-hands grip at the top of the stick
5. Feet are more than 12 inches (30.5 cm) apart, with the knees bent 90 degrees
6. Ball is in line with your left foot

EXECUTION

1. Bend your knees 90 degrees
2. Approach the ball with a wide stride with your left foot
3. Push from your right foot to extend the right leg far away from your right hip
4. Breathe in as you lift the stick back
5. Use your wrists to move the curve of stick back in a semicircle loop
6. Continuous flow into the beginning of the downswing
7. Left foot steps down and into line with the ball
8. Keep your stick parallel to the ground when your wrists enter your hip line
9. Rotate hips and transfer your weight from your right leg to the left leg
10. Exhale
11. Head is above your hands, which are 8 inches (20 cm) above the ground
12. Strike behind the ball's center

(continued)

(continued)

FOLLOW-THROUGH

1. Continue to lower your center of gravity
2. Control the forward and curved movement of the stick in order to follow the ball's direction
3. Return to a ready position

c

Misstep

The ball travels in an unintended direction.

Correction

Maintain a side-on position to the ball.

Misstep

You fail to disguise the direction of the sweep hit.

Correction

Sweep from a side-on position instead of from a front position to the ball. To disguise the height of the sweep, control the stick angle by breaking your wrists either forward or backward at impact. Hit on the right or left side of the center of the ball in order to change the direction of the sweep hit at the last second.

The low reverse sweep hit (figure 2.5) is characterized by a very low body position, a wider stance, and the use of the inside edge of the stick. The stick is in an almost-horizontal position at the moment of impact. The right foot is in front in order to provide better balance during the reverse sweep. As with the forehand sweep, the stick can be lifted or it can be set on the ground at the beginning of the reverse sweep. The impact zone is the inside edge of the stick close to the upper section of the curve. At the moment of impact, the stick is parallel to the turf.

Figure 2.5   Reverse Sweep Hit

PREPARATION

1. Take a side-on position from the ball, which is outside the control box
2. Look up and select a target
3. Right shoulder points toward the target
4. Both hands are together in a reverse grip at the top of the stick
5. Feet are more than 12 inches (30.5 cm) apart, knees very bent
6. Ball is in line with your right foot

a

b

c

EXECUTION

1. Bend your knees 90 degrees
2. Approach the ball with a wide stride with the right foot
3. Push from your back left foot to extend the left leg away from left hip
4. Breathe in and lift the stick back
5. Use your wrists to move the curve of stick back in a semicircle loop
6. Continuous flow into the beginning of the downswing
7. Right foot steps down and into line with ball
8. Keep your stick parallel to the ground when your wrists pass the left hip
9. Rotate your hips and transfer your weight from the left leg to the right leg
10. Exhale
11. Head is above the hands, which are 8 inches (20 cm) above the ground
12. Strike behind the ball's center

FOLLOW-THROUGH

1. Continue to lower your center of gravity
2. Control the forward and curved movement of the stick in order to follow the ball's direction
3. Return to a ready position

Misstep

The sweep hit lacks speed and power.

Correction

Use a side-on position to the ball so that a greater stick-curve distance can be generated in the backswing and downswing. Keep the left arm (forehand sweep) or right arm (reverse) fully extended. Avoid striking the ground with your stick before or during impact.

Misstep

The ball pops dangerously into the air during the reverse sweep.

Correction

Maintain a low body position and strike the ball off your front right foot with the inside edge of the upper curve. Keep your stick parallel to the ground.

Learn the sweep hit after you have become proficient with the push and the hit. When first learning to sweep hit, focus on hitting through the ball in order to serve a level pass to the receiver. Practice with closed eyes in order to help you feel the proper movement and to train the physical and kinetic senses. Also practice hitting balls of different sizes and weights, as well as hockey balls, under pressure and while fatigued. After mastering the key elements of hitting a stationary ball, learn to sweep hit the ball on the run.

The sweep hit is a skill that requires the coordination of the entire body, especially of the core muscles and joints. Learn to coordinate all partial joint movements perfectly in order to execute a fluent and powerful sweep hit. A warm-up with dynamic functional exercise will help prepare the specific muscles and joints for passing. (See step 11 for more on the warm-up.) All hit drills can be modified to incorporate the powerful sweep hit.

Hit Drill 3. *Sweep Hit Through Targets*

Select one or two teammates. Use cones to set up five goals at various angles, 15 yards (14 m) away from two stacks of 10 balls. Set two cones 2 yards (1.8 m) apart that will serve as goals. Stand between the two stacks of balls with 3 yards (2.8 m) of space on your right and left sides. Run to a stack of balls and prepare to sweep hit one ball to any of the five targets. After sweep hitting a ball, run to the other stack of balls and hit to any of the targets. Continue for 15 seconds. Award yourself a point for each accurate pass through a target. Compare your point total with your partner's. Repeat for five rounds.

To Increase Difficulty

- Increase pass distance.
- Increase the time to 30, 45, or 60 seconds per round.
- Reduce goal width to 1 yard (0.9 m).
- Use reverse sweep hits.

To Decrease Difficulty

- Decrease the distance between the stacks of balls.
- Decrease the hit-passing distance.
- Reduce the number of rounds.
- Increase the goal width to 3 yards (2.8 m).
- Reduce the time per round.

Success Check

- Use short, quick footwork.
- Look up at the target before the backswing.
- Make certain that the ball is in your control box, with your stick next to the ball.
- Knees are very bent in a balanced side-on position to the ball, with feet 12 inches (30.5 cm) apart.
- Hands are together in shake-hands grip.
- Front shoulder points to the target.
- Stick is parallel to ground and the left arm is straight throughout the downswing.
- Strike the lower half of the ball on the label of stick.
- Follow through with your hands and stick toward the target.

Score Your Success

13 points or more = 5 points

8 to 12 points = 3 points

0 to 7 points = 1 point

Your score ___

Passing Drill 1. *Pass Inside and Outside*

Organize into groups of three. Place a rebound board on the 50-yard line. Sit the board parallel to the sideline. Use cones to set two areas 7 to 10 yards (6.4 to 9 m) wide, one 20 yards (18.3 m) to the outside of the field and the other 25 yards (23 m) to the inside of the field. Use seven cones set at 10-yard (9 m) intervals to represent the space occupied by a defender. Teammates stand behind each set of cones on the goal side. The server starts the drill by sweep passing the ball onto the board and then receiving the ball and sweep hitting to the outside teammate. The server takes another ball from a stack of 10 balls and repeats the short pass to the board. This time she passes to her teammate while standing inside the perimeter of the field. Both receivers start behind their respective sets of cones and cut to the outside of the cones (moving away from the defender) to arrive at the same moment as the pass from the server arrives. The server sweep hits a total of 10 balls and then rotates to take a turn at the other positions. The server receives 1 point for each accurate sweep hit to the receiver's stick.

To Increase Difficulty

- Increase the passing distance to the board.
- Increase the passing distance to the outside and inside areas.
- Use only sweep hits.
- Add the pressure of time, or place a defender 10 yards (9 m) from the server and between the receivers.
- Place a defender inside the square.
- Receive and pass with two touches.
- Increase the number of receiving attempts.

- Add another attack player in the shooting circle so that the inside or outside players can two-touch the ball and then finish with a shot on goal.

To Decrease Difficulty

- Decrease the pass distance to the board and to the receivers.
- Reduce the number of pass attempts.
- Receive and pass using three touches.

Success Check

- Use short, quick footwork.
- Look up at the target before the backswing.
- Make certain the ball is in your control box, with your stick next to the ball.
- Knees are very bent in a balanced side-on position to the ball, with your feet 12 inches (30.5 cm) apart.
- Hands are together in shake-hands grip.
- Front shoulder points toward the target.
- Keep left arm straight throughout the downswing.
- Strike the lower half of the ball.
- Follow through with your hands and stick toward the target.

Score Your Success

9 or 10 points = 10 points

7 or 8 points = 5 points

5 or 6 points = 3 points

Fewer than 5 points = 1 point

Your score ___

RECEIVING GROUND BALLS

Receiving the hockey ball means fielding the ball on the stick so that it is instantly brought under control without a rebound. Good receiving mechanics will place the receiver in a multiple-threat position to either hold the ball, elude an opponent, pass to a teammate, dribble to free space, or shoot. It is impossible to overemphasize the importance of sound receiving techniques because they are the prelude to ball possession, stick handling, good passing, shooting, and attacking.

Receiving means allowing the ball to come to the stick, even if you are running to meet the pass. Any forward movement or swing of the stick will cause a rebound. A receiver wants a ball passed accurately to the stick so that it can be trapped or bumped into open space and then be used immediately. Quality passes roll smoothly along the ground and they travel directly to the target. The best position for receiving a ball that is moving along the ground is to be facing parallel to the line of the ball.

Receiving ground balls requires that you learn to perform receiving techniques on the right side of the body (referred to as *forehand* receiving, figure 2.6) and on the left side of the body (*reverse*, or *backhand*, receiving, figure 2.7). Good forehand and backhand receiving techniques are the basic tools for a winning team effort. Backhand receiving follows the same receiving principles as forehand receiving but with a few differences. Because 90 percent of passing techniques originate from the right side of the body, after reverse receiving, control the ball to the right side of the body and establish a multiple-threat position with the ball.

Figure 2.6   Forehand Receiving

a   *b*   *c*

PREPARATION

1. Face the ball or point the left shoulder toward the oncoming ball
2. Move toward the ball using short, quick steps
3. Use a shake-hands grip
4. Weight is evenly distributed on the balls of your feet
5. Bottom of the stick head is on the ground
6. Stick wedge is 70 degrees forward toward the ground
7. Keep your receiving stick still
8. Head is steady and your eyes are focused on the ball

EXECUTION

1. Adjust your feet to receive the ball in your control box
2. Allow the ball to come to the stick
3. Receive the ball on left side of the stick and strike the lower half of ball on the stick blade
4. Head is steady over, and in line with, the ball
5. Steer the ball into space, away from nearby opponent

FOLLOW-THROUGH

1. Maintain your balance
2. Keep your head up and watch the field
3. Ball is next to the stick
4. Be ready to pass, shoot, or dribble

Misstep

The ball pops up in air off your stick.

Correction

Relax the separated shake-hands grip and bend your knees. Distribute weight on the balls of feet.

Misstep

The ball travels under your stick.

Correction

Keep your head down, stick head on the ground, and watch the ball come to your stick. Trap the lower half of the ball.

Forehand Receiving

- Point your left shoulder along the ball's line of direction.

- Always keep both hands on the stick and use the shake-hands grip or receiving grip. Lunge with only one hand when time and distance prevent using two hands.

- Balance your body with your knees bent and weight evenly distributed on the balls of the feet.

- Keep your head steady and your eyes on the ball.

- Hold the bottom of your stick head still along the ground in your control box.

- Put your left hand in front of your right and in line with your left knee.

- Incline the stick angle forward 70 degrees to the ground so that a wedge is made between the ground and stick so that the ball is allowed to come to the stick. The ball will rebound downward—toward the ground—from the flat surface of the stick if the stick is inclined forward. Grass surfaces or heavier grounds more readily absorb rebounds, so a more upright stick will suffice. On hard, fast ground or on artificial surfaces, a more acute angle of the stick to the ground will be necessary.

- At the moment of contact, use your hands as a pillow. Skillful receiving requires great sensitivity of touch. Underspin occurs if the ball comes to the stick; if you move your stick forward to the ball, you will create topspin.

- Keep your stick still and your head and shoulders over the ball. Stop the rolling ball in the control box in front of your right foot. Always receive the ball on the part of the stick where the straight blade of wood meets the ground, as if you were using a straight stick without a toe.

Figure 2.7   Backhand Receiving

1. Adjust your feet to receive the ball in your control box

2. Allow the ball to come to your stick

3. Receive the ball on left side of your stick and strike the lower half of the ball on the stick blade

4. Head is steady over, and in line with, the ball

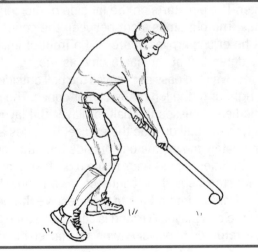

Misstep

The ball rebounds off your stick.

Correction

Keep stick still in line with your right foot. Angle stick forward to create a 70-degree wedge to the ground.

Misstep

Ball hits your feet.

Correction

Move your stick and hands away from your body.

Reverse (Backhand) Receiving

- Point right shoulder along the ball's intended line of direction.
- Grip the stick with both hands in a reverse position so that the stick's toe faces your feet and the flat side of the stick faces the ball. When time and distance prevent using the two-handed receiving grip, lunge with only the left hand gripping the stick.

- Balance your body as you would when forehand receiving.
- Place your left hand in front of your right and in line with your right knee.
- Once you receive the ball on your left side, move the ball immediately to your right side in a multiple-threat position.

Receiving Drill 1. *Pig in the Middle*

Use three pairs of cones (six total) and select two teammates to play with you. Place a pair of cones 7 yards (6.4 m) apart in the center of a 40-yard-long (36.5 m) vertical lane. Place the other two pairs of cones at each end of the 40-yard vertical lane. Player A begins with a hockey ball at the start end of the lane. Player B begins at the other end of the 40-yard vertical lane. The "pig," player C, starts in the middle, between the 7-yard cones. Player A starts the drill by moving the ball to the right, outside of the cone, and passes to the pig in the center. The pig starts on the far side of the center cones. The pig times a cut between the cones so that he or she arrives in area 1 (in front of imaginary defender) at the same time as the ball. The pig receives the pass and moves the ball outside to the right or to the left of the center cones. The pig Immediately passes the ball to player B. Player B receives the ball outside the end set of cones and immediately moves the ball outside the other side cone in order to pass back to the pig. The pig must always start behind the center cones and time her cut in front or into area 1 to then receive the pass from the end player. A round is complete when the ball is returned to player A, who has moved outside

her set of 7-yard cones to receive the pass from the pig. Complete five games of two rounds each, receiving and passing with the same ball. Compete against another threesome. Award your team a point for each game you win.

To Increase Difficulty

- Increase the passing distance.
- Add the pressure of time.
- Complete more rounds per game.
- Receive the ball using the backhand.

To Decrease Difficulty

- Decrease the passing distance.
- Reduce width of cones.
- Reduce the number of rounds per game.
- Reduce the number of games.

Success Check

- Face the ball path and receiving space.
- Make eye contact with the passer.
- Time your move toward the ball with short, quick steps.

- Use a receiving grip and keep a still stick head on the ground.
- Evenly distribute your weight on power points of your feet. Feet are shoulder-width apart.
- Bend your knees.
- Allow ball to come to your stick.
- Steer the ball into space away from the nearest defender.

- Prepare the body and ball to pass, shoot, or dribble.

Score Your Success

13 points or more = 5 points

8 to 12 points = 3 points

0 to 7 points = 1 point

Your score ____

Receiving Drill 2.
Receive and Transfer, Horizontal and Vertical

Organize into a group of three players, one ball per group. Use four cones to set up a 5-by-5-yard (4.6 m) square in the center of the field. Two players take positions approximately 20 yards (18 m) from both sides of the square (one on each side). Passer 1 starts with the ball 20 yards from the square. The target receiver starts along the opposite side of the square from passer 1. The target receiver starts the drill by cutting to the side of the square closest to the ball (passer 1) to arrive at the same time as the pass. After receiving the ball, the target player takes the ball to the other side of the square and passes the ball to the other outside player (receiver 2). The target receiver immediately pulls away to the other side of the square to initiate her cut toward passer 1. Upon receiving the ball from passer 1, the target receiver repeats the same sequence back in the direction of receiver 2. Award the target receiver 1 point for each time a passed ball is received without error on the other side of the square. After 10 receiving attempts, the target player rotates to a new position.

After all players complete turns at all three positions, set the 5-yard (4.5 m) target square near the sideline for vertical receiving. Position two players vertically, one player (passer) 20 yards (18.5 m) behind the square with the balls, and the other player (receiver 1) 20 yards in front of the square. The target receiver starts in front of the box and diagonally cuts to the back of the box, then receives and then passes the ball vertically forward to receiver 1. Award the target receiver 1 point for each time a passed ball is received and passed without an error.

To Increase Difficulty

- Increase the size of the square to create a rectangle.
- Increase the passing distance.
- Add the pressure of time or compete against another group.
- Receive and pass with two touches.
- Increase the number of receiving attempts.
- Play with two target players starting on opposite sides of the square.
- Receive the ball and then drop step out the back of the square.
- Receive the ball and then step out the front of the square.

To Decrease Difficulty

- Decrease the pass distance.
- Reduce the size of the box or square.
- Reduce the number of receiving attempts.
- Receive and pass using three touches.

Success Check

- Face the ball path and select a receiving space.
- Make eye contact with the passer.
- Time your move toward the ball with short, quick steps.
- Use a receiving grip and keep a still stick head on the ground.
- Evenly distribute your weight on power points of your feet. Feet are shoulder-width apart.

- Bend your knees.
- Allow the ball to come to the stick.
- Control the ball while changing horizontal direction to pass the ball.
- Ready the body and ball to pass.

Receiving Drill 3. *Mimi Drills*

Four players assume the roles of one center passer, two end passers, and one target receiver. Place two cones 7 yards (6.4 m) apart and 15 yards (14 m) in front of the center passer. The 7-yard area represents the receiving space. On the outside of each 7-yard cone, place four more cones (two on each side) 2 yards (1.8 m) apart in a horizontal line. The target player starts at one of the 7-yard cones and cuts into the 7-yard receiving space to receive a pass from the center passer. The target receiver controls the ball and passes to one of the end passers who receives the ball and passes it back to the center passer. The target receiver repeats a move into the 7-yard (6.4 m) free space to receive another pass from the center passer. Upon receiving and controlling the ball, the target player passes the ball in the other direction to the other end passer who receives the ball and sends it back to the center passer. After attempting to receive a round of 10 balls, players rotate clockwise. The target receiver earns 1 point for each ball received, controlled, and accurately passed to the end passer.

Variation: The target receiver controls the pass from the center passer and weave dribbles the ball through the 7-yard (6.4 m) cones.

To Increase Difficulty

- Increase the pass distance.
- Add the pressure of time or use a defender who attempts to tag the target receiver when the target player first touches the ball. The tag player starts 5 yards (4.5 m) from the target receiver and can only move when the target receiver touches the ball.
- Attempt more balls per round.
- Receive and pass using two touches.
- Receive using backhand.

To Decrease Difficulty

- Decrease the pass distance.
- Reduce the distance between the 7-yard (6.4 m) target cones.
- Reduce the number of receiving attempts.
- Permit three touches to receive and pass.

Success Check

- Face the ball path and select receiving space.
- Make eye contact with the passer.
- Time your move into the receiving space and toward the ball with short, quick steps.
- Use a receiving grip and keep a still stick head on the ground.
- Evenly distribute your weight on power points of your feet. Feet are shoulder-width apart.
- Bend your knees.
- Allow the ball to come to the stick.
- Receive and control the ball with one touch.
- Look up to see your target and pass to it with the second touch.
- Ready your body to receive the ball.

PASSING AERIAL BALLS

Although the best field hockey is played on the ground, an aerial ball is effective in some situations. For example, an opponent may be blocking the passing lane between you and your teammates who are away from the ball in attack roles 2 and 3. Or you may decide to lift a ball so that it drops into an open space behind the opposing defender. You may even use a lifted pass to score a goal when the opposing goalkeeper drifts too far forward from her goal line or in a penalty-stroke situation. On artificial surfaces, a low aerial pass below the knee is used more often to beat an opponent who plays with his stick low in a horizontal block. Also the lofted ball can be useful on heavy, waterlogged, grass fields. To take advantage of any situation in which the aerial ball is used, you must become skilled at one basic aerial technique, the flick. Do not confuse the flick with the nearly obsolete scoop pass, which was used years ago on slow, rarely mowed, grass fields before the proliferation of artificial playing surfaces. In the mid-1980s, FIH outlawed lifting a free hit.

Skillful players rarely use the aerial pass as a means of attack because the hang time of an aerial pass allows more time for an opponent to reposition and defend. Aerial balls can be used only during open play. A player using the aerial pass will be penalized if she lifts the ball in a manner that causes danger (for example, hitting an aerial ball into the shooting circle). When the aerial ball is passed to an occupied area in which possession is contested by the defender and attacker, the umpire will penalize the passer of the lifted ball for hitting a dangerous pass and will award a free hit to the opponent. To avoid the free-hit penalty on a high lifted ball, the receiver of the lifted ball must be given 5 yards (4.5 m) by the defender to safely bring the ball down to the ground.

For the aerial flick, or overhead pass, the player uses the stick to shovel the ball into the air. If enough strength is exerted for the lift, the ball may be hurled 50 yards (46 m) or more. Remember, aerial passing is not a substitute for stick work or on-the-ground passing. Keep your lifting distance within your ability in order to achieve success.

The flick is a push pass lifted into the air. The flick technique is used to lift the ball at various heights into the air for long or short distances and at greater speed. Use this technique to play the ball to a teammate over an opponent who is blocking the passing lane. Or use the flick through a narrow gap to surprise an opponent who is expecting to intercept a ground pass. The high flick can be used to lift the ball into the air in order to make plays for tightly marked attack wings. The high flick pass can be dropped into the space behind the opponent where the attack wing can use her speed to get to the ball. The most important use of the flick is for penalty strokes or when shooting powerfully at goal.

Differences between the flick and the push pass are that, for the flick, the face of the stick is open, the right shoulder is lower, the ball is slightly ahead of the left foot, and the stick follow-through varies with the height of the aerial. The shake-hands grip is used and the body can be in front of or parallel to the line of the ball. The parallel position is better for weight transfer. While keeping your head over the ball, drop your right shoulder and insert the lower part of your stick face under the lower half of the ball in order to prepare to throw the ball into the air. Your right arm exerts power as you transfer your body weight from your right leg to your left leg.

Misstep

Pass is too low.

Correction

With bent knees, strike the lower half of the ball with the face of the open stick and lift the ball. Follow through with the stick lifted high.

For the aerial flick (figure 2.8), keep your body low until the ball leaves your stick. The right hand controls direction and speed. Throw or whip the ball with the face of the stick from an open stick blade to left stick-blade rotation. This whiplike action imparts rapid side topspin to the ball. Follow through with your hands and raise your stick forward and up, imparting height, distance, and speed to the ball. If you want the ball to rise to knee height, follow through with the right hand to a knee-height position. For an overhead height, transfer your weight and follow through higher.

Figure 2.8 | Aerial Flick

a

b

c

PREPARATION

1. Left shoulder points to the target
2. Use a separated shake-hands grip
3. Knees are bent and your weight is balanced on the power points of your feet
4. Ball is in center of your control box or is in line with your left foot
5. Head is steady over the ball; eyes are focused on the ball
6. Open stick is next to the bottom half of the ball

EXECUTION

1. Drop your right shoulder and transfer your weight forward
2. Maintain an open stick next to the ball
3. Left hand pulls the stick forward
4. Lift through the lower half of the ball
5. Right hand exerts pressure and direction
6. Head is steady over the ball
7. Extend your arms as the left hand goes past your left foot
8. Use open-to-left stick rotation

FOLLOW-THROUGH

1. Generate momentum through the ball
2. Transfer your weight through your front leg
3. Finish with the stick toe up
4. Arms extend toward the target
5. Return to a ready position

Misstep

Pass is inaccurate.

Correction

Make sure that the left shoulder points to the target and that your stick follows the line of the ball toward the target.

Misstep

The pass is too short.

Correction

Keep your head over the ball as you generate the lifting action. Keep knees deeply bent. Extend your arms and stick forward and up, and use a complete follow-through toward your target.

RECEIVING AERIAL BALLS

You must be able to receive and control aerial passes while facing the ball and while running forward. Field hockey rules require that the ball be below shoulder height when it is played with the stick. Keep your eyes focused on the ball and your stick below shoulder level as you use short, quick steps to move into line with the ball. If an aerial ball is approaching, receive the ball in a position similar to a baseball outfielder who readies to catch a fly ball (figure 2.9). When running forward, away from where the lifted pass came, look over your shoulder on the side from which the ball is approaching, catch the ball on your forehand or reverse, play it down, and go! Play the ball down so that it lands close to the right foot, thus making you a multiple-attack threat. Use a shake-hands or receiving grip with all aerial receptions.

Figure 2.9	Aerial Pass Reception

PREPARATION

1. Position yourself behind the descending ball
2. Use a shake-hands grip
3. Raise the stick below head level
4. Be in a balanced stance with your knees bent
5. Determine the ball's aerial line and prepare a horizontal or vertical stick
6. Stick wedge is 70 degrees forward to ground
7. Keep the receiving stick steady
8. Left foot is in front of your right
9. Head is steady and eyes are focused on the ball

a

(continued)

51

(continued)

b

c

EXECUTION

1. Transfer your weight to the side from which the aerial pass is coming
2. Receive the ball on the stick shaft, below shoulder level
3. Direct the rebound downward
4. Place the stick behind the ball
5. Control the ball to the right side of your body

FOLLOW-THROUGH

1. Steer the ball into a space away from a nearby opponent

Misstep

The ball bounces forward off your stick and out of your range of control.

Correction

Keep your stick still and incline the shaft of the stick forward to rebound the ball down to the ground at your feet. Ball-to-stick contact is above the stick's head and below the right hand at knee height.

Misstep

The ball pops up and over your body or it hits your body or stick handle.

Correction

Prepare your feet using quick, short adjustment steps. Transfer weight to the side of the approaching aerial pass. Watch the ball drop below your waist and onto the shaft-to-head portion of the stick.

When a lifted pass is approaching your right side, lift your left elbow up, keeping the blade of the stick horizontally straight and your right elbow pointing back, not tucked. Knees are bent, with most of your body weight on your right foot. Right shoulder is in line with the approaching ball. The shaft and face of your stick are inclined forward so that the rebound is directed vertically to the ground. Always position yourself behind the dropping aerial pass so that you can let the ball hit your stick on the shaft below the right hand, at knee height or lower. The faster the pass, the more inclined the stick should be. Grip is relaxed. Immediately bring the ball under control near your right foot.

For an aerial ball approaching the left side, the stick is held vertically. Body weight is shifted to the left foot, and the stick is taken across the front of the body with the left elbow well up. The right elbow points across the body to the right. If a ball is lifted far to your left, use a reverse stick in a horizontal position. Once the aerial ball is directed down, use your stick to check and control the ball before making your next move.

Misstep

Body is too close to the ball, and the ball bounces out of control upon contact.

Correction

Break down your run into short, quick steps in order to balance your attack stance. Ready a horizontal or vertical stick using a shake-hands grip.

SUCCESS SUMMARY OF PASSING AND RECEIVING

The ultimate goal of every field hockey team is to play as a unit. The game becomes far more enjoyable when a team's players can perform quality skills. To achieve this goal, each team member must have good passing and receiving skills. Receiving remains the most rehearsed technique in hockey because you cannot pass, shoot, or dribble unless you first receive the ball.

Beginners should practice passing and receiving without the pressures of time or opponents, and without the restriction of space. This will allow you to concentrate on the performing the skill correctly. It takes time to master the passing and receiving techniques that field hockey demands, especially aerial balls. Passing and receiving require confidence, proper technique, and a great deal of practice. As your technical skills improve, progress to more game-related training by adding the pressures of time and opponents, and begin to restrict space for passing and receiving. Eventually you will be able to execute the attack role 1 techniques of passing and receiving in a real game.

Push-Passing Drills	
1. 7- and 15-Yard (6.4 to 13.8 m) Partner Push Pass	___ out of 20
2. Shuttle Push Passing	___ out of 5
3. Fives Downfield	___ out of 10
Hit Drills	
1. Hit the Boards	___ out of 5
2. Square Passing With Quick Hits	___ out of 10
3. Sweep Hit Through Targets	___ out of 5
Passing Drill	
1. Pass Inside and Outside	___ out of 10
Receiving Drills	
1. Pig in the Middle	___ out of 5
2. Receive and Transfer, Horizontal and Vertical	___ out of 10
3. Mimi Drills	___ out of 10
Total	___ *out of 90*

A combined score of 74 points or more suggests that you have satisfactorily mastered the skills of passing and receiving and that you are prepared to move to step 3. A score in the range of 63 to 73 is considered adequate. You can move on to step 3 after additional practice of the passing and receiving skills that you find most difficult. A score of 62 points or fewer implies insufficient control of various movements. You should review and practice the techniques discussed in step 2 before progressing to step 3.

Controlling the Ball and Dribbling

After receiving the ball from a teammate or after intercepting an opponent's pass, you must use good ball-possession skills that will give your team more time and space to be successful. The next attack role 1 techniques to learn are ball control and dribbling. To be a successful field hockey player, you must coordinate your balance and control to quickly move the ball with your stick, because stick work is the essence of these skills.

Ball control must not be confused with receiving and passing. Ball control refers to skilled ball movements that accompany footwork, change of direction, and body swerve and balance. Most important, ball control is the ability to keep the ball close to your stick. Losing control of the ball adversely affects the execution of your next move. Your next move may be a pass, dribble, or shot on goal depending on the situation and on your ability to control the ball.

The two basic ball-control techniques are the ball check and the drop step. The ball check brings the ball back under control when it moves outside your control box. It is used to slow or stop the ball from rolling away or to change directions during dribbling. The drop step moves the ball back and away from an opponent while keeping the ball next to your stick. A successful drop step creates more space between the attack role 1 player and the nearest defender, which provides more time for the next attack move. The attack role 1 player is constantly moving her control box and the ball within it away from the nearest opponent.

Dribbling is basically stick work on the run. Running with the ball, or dribbling, serves the same purpose as dribbling in soccer or basketball; it allows you to keep possession of the ball by moving into open areas of the field and away from opponents, it creates space for teammates to use, and it leads to goal-scoring opportunities. Use the dribble to beat an opponent in the attack zone near the opponent's goal. Penetrating this area of the field while maintaining ball possession will give you a numbers-up advantage (more teammates than opponents) and more goal-scoring chances. Keep in mind that excessive dribbling does not promote team play. Resist dribbling to take on opponents in the defensive zone nearest your own goal. Losing possession in this area can lead to a scoring opportunity for the opponent.

Four dribbling techniques are important in game situations—the power dribble, speed dribble, Indian dribble, and spin dribble. The power dribble is used to maintain possession of the ball in tight, crowded spaces. The speed dribble is used to advance the ball into open spaces along a straight or diagonal line. The most effective element in speed dribbling is to cut with the ball along a diagonal line to the open space, which moves the opponent laterally. The most advanced dribbling skill is the Indian dribble, which is used to disguise the dribbler's next move. When executed correctly with control and speed, the Indian dribble unbalances the opponent with its back-and–forth, forehand-to-reverse stick movement. The spin dribble is used to protect the ball as you move away from the nearest opponent, who is blocking the forward space you want to move to.

The best means of attack is to have the ball. The ability to control the ball so that you can execute a multiple-threat attack and beat opponents in one-on-one situations—particularly in the attacking half of the field—and the ability to prevent defenders from getting the ball are crucial to individual and team success.

The purpose of ball control is to maintain possession by using sidesteps to go around an opponent. Getting the ball in position in the shortest amount of time requires a consistent relationship with the ball, your feet, and the stick. For good ball control, the ball must be next to your stick head, which is on the ground in a push position. This position will enable you to easily scan the field to pass or dribble or to elude an advancing opponent. In field hockey, it is difficult to isolate the relationships that exist among footwork, body balance, running speed, and ball control. Good ball control and dribbling demand daily attention. There is no shortcut to learning efficient stick work for ball control and dribbling, which demand the coordination of footwork, balance, concentration, and the light touch of your stick on the ball. Make time to play the ball with your stick, and enjoy developing a comfortable coordination of your feet, hands, stick, and the ball.

BALL CONTROL

The basis of ball control and stick work is moving the ball from left to right by means of a reverse stick. This requires that the stick be turned over the top of the ball. You must learn to turn the stick because field hockey rules prevent the use of the rounded side—right side—to control or pass the ball. The two ball-control techniques—the ball check and drop step—use a split grip with a changeable V of the left hand. The left hand turns and controls the stick. The right hand's function is to allow the stick to be turned by the left hand and to occasionally add power.

Before learning how to dribble, hockey players should practice sidestepping to the left and right, diagonally forward to the right, and diagonally back to the right and left—the drop step. When your ball-control techniques improve, practice against an opponent. The greater the speed of an approaching opponent, the smaller the sidestep. If the opponent is more cautious, your stick work and sidestep distance must increase.

Ball Check

Never move the ball into a position that makes it more readily available to your opponent than to you. The ball check, or sudden stop, is a ball-control technique that prevents the ball from running away from your control box and into the opponent's reach. It is also useful to the attack role 1 (AR1) player, who uses the ball check to control a through ball and to stop and go with all dribbling techniques.

Whether you are standing still or running, the ball check can be executed from various directional ball movements. The left-to-right and right-to-left ball movements are coordinated with sidesteps, body swerves, weaves, and hesitations, and they are constantly integrated with the ball check. The ball check also accompanies the drop step ball-control movement in which the ball and stick follow a diagonal line backward.

To execute the ball check (figure 3.1), position the ball in your control box. Keep your stick near the lower half of the ball and prepare to change your left hand from the shake-hands grip to the back of the stick. When the hands are in the shake-hands grip and the toe of the stick is pointing up, the forefinger and thumb of both hands form a V shape that points down along the edge of the stick. For good ball control and dribbling, the V of the left hand adjusts a quarter turn to the right so that it runs down the back of the stick. To momentarily stop the roll of the ball, place the face of the stick on the lower half of the ball while maintaining a 12- to 18-inch (30.5 to 46 cm) ball-to-feet distance. A ball check on the reverse side should be immediately followed by a ball-control movement to the right side so that you are ready to pass, dribble, or shoot.

Misstep

The ball moves outside your control box and you lose control.

Correction

Move your hands farther apart and bend your knees. Move the ball away from your feet about 12 to 18 inches so that you can see it in your control box. Your left hand controls and turns the stick. Keep your head steady over the ball and your eyes focused on the ball.

Figure 3.1 | Ball Check

a   b   c

PREPARATION

1. Receive the ball with short steps and quick footwork
2. Use a split grip, with your left hand adjusted
3. Ball is in your control box, next to your stick
4. Be in a crouched position, with your knees bent
5. Maintain balance and body control on power points
6. Be aware of options

EXECUTION

1. Left hand turns the stick
2. Allow the stick to rotate in your right hand
3. Ball is 12 inches (30.5 cm) from left or right foot
4. Check the ball movement—speed, direction, or both

FOLLOW-THROUGH

1. Move the ball to the right side of your body
2. Change Vs to a shake-hands grip
3. Maintain close control of the ball
4. Move away from pressure
5. Be ready to pass, dribble, or shoot
6. Return to ready position

Misstep

You snatch at the ball on the upper half of the ball.

Correction

Move the ball away from your feet and keep the ball in your control box, in line with and in front of your feet. Focus on keeping the stick head in contact with the lower half of the ball.

Misstep

You lose the ball on your reverse side.

Correction

The ball must be within your control box. Do not allow it to pass your left foot. Keep your stick head a few inches from the ball when placing the stick on the left side of the ball. Use your left hand to turn the stick counterclockwise.

Drop Step

The drop step is an individual ball-control technique that coordinates ball movement in a forward-to-back direction away from the opposing defender. The ball carrier (AR1) uses the drop step to make space. The more space you have between you and your opponent, the more time you have to execute the pass.

You must time the drop step (figure 3.2) with a hip turn to the left or right to coincide with the defender's forward commitment. If the opponent has time to change direction and tackle the ball, you have executed the drop step too soon. The key to successfully performing any ball-control skill that involves a change of direction and change of pace is moving the ball along with the foot and maintaining consistent ball-from-feet distance.

As with the ball check, you must change the V of your left-hand grip so that the left hand turns your stick. Keep your knees bent and your feet shoulder-width apart for balance. Your head stays over the ball in your control box, in line with the right or left foot, and your stick remains next to the lower half of the ball. If drop stepping to your right, move your right foot and the ball diagonally backward simultaneously by transferring your body weight from your left to right foot. For the left drop step, transfer your weight from your right foot to your left. Follow the drop step with a ball check to prevent the ball from going beyond your foot. When executing a left drop step, immediately move the ball to the right side of your body. Getting into this position will make you a multiple-attack threat.

Misstep

Approaching opponent has time to change direction and tackle you.

Correction

Your foot and the ball must move at the same time in order to coincide with the defender's forward commitment to tackle.

Slight errors in judgment or technique can cause you to lose control of the ball while in a restricted space. Most ball-control errors are due to incorrect stick handling when changing grips, poor body balance, inadequate footwork, the inconsistent relationship of the ball to the feet, and poor judgment of the opponent's positioning. Maintain as much space as possible between the ball and your nearest opponent. To do so, you must constantly adjust your position in response to the challenger's movements.

Figure 3.2	Drop Step

PREPARATION

1. Receive the ball in your control box with short steps and quick footwork
2. Use a split grip with your left hand adjusted
3. Ball is in control box
4. Stagger your feet shoulder-width apart
5. Knees are flexed; body is slightly crouched
6. Be aware of options; eyes see the ball and the space between you and DR1
7. Stick is next to the lower half of the ball

a

(continued)

(continued)

b

c

EXECUTION

1. Make quick glances at the approaching opponent
2. Simultaneously push the ball and transfer your weight to your back foot
3. Left hand turns the stick; allow the stick to rotate in your right hand
4. Keep the ball 12 inches (30.5 cm) from your feet and within the control box
5. Stick is on the lower half of the ball
6. Check the ball's movement

FOLLOW-THROUGH

1. Move the ball to the right side of your body
2. Keep the stick on the lower half of the ball
3. Use a shake-hands grip
4. Be ready to pass, dribble, or shoot

Misstep

The stick is slower than the ball.

Correction

Control is of primary importance and speed is secondary. Keep your stick close (less than 1 inch, or 2.5 cm) from the lower half of the ball. Use your left hand to turn the stick; the right hand allows stick to turn.

Misstep

The ball gets too close to your feet or outside your control box.

Correction

Keep the ball in your control box about 12 to 18 inches (30.5 to 46 cm) from your feet and aligned with your feet. Move your foot first to start the ball moving.

Ball Control Drill 1.
North-South Ball Check With Pipe

Obtain 1 1/2-inch plastic piping (PVC) at your local hardware store and cut a 6-inch (15.3 cm) long piece to fit down the handle of your stick. You can substitute a small toilet paper roll for the plastic piping. Grip the tube with your right hand and your stick with your left hand. The pipe or toilet paper roll trains your left hand to handle the constant stick grip changes used in ball control. The right hand stays in the V-grip position and does not get involved in the stick turning movement. Set three cones 3 yards (2.8 m) apart in a line. Stand 1 yard (0.9 m) behind and to the right of the first cone and face forward with a ball on your stick. Move the ball to the first cone and check the forward roll of the ball. Move the ball quickly to the second cone with a ball check and to the third cone followed by a ball check. Turn your body to the right in a sideways position and execute ball checks on the way back to each of the cones until you have reached the start. Have a teammate time you. Repeat the exercise for 30 seconds. Award yourself 1 point for each successful ball check during the time period. A successful ball check keeps the ball in your control box next to your stick and temporarily stops the ball. Rest and time your teammate doing the same exercise. Complete five 30-second rounds and score your best round total.

To Increase Difficulty

- Increase the number of repetitions.
- Quicken the pace and add the pressure of time or competition (first player to go up and back wins).

- Decrease the distance between the cones in order to reduce the available space.
- Move the ball backward along the left side of your body.

To Decrease Difficulty

- Increase the distance between cones.
- Reduce the number of repetitions.

Success Check

- Maintain close control of the ball in your control box.
- Bend your knees and maintain a low center of gravity.
- Maintain the shake-hands grip, using your left hand to change stick positions.
- Maintain balance on the power points of your feet. Feet remain shoulder-width apart.
- Combine sudden changes of speed with changes of direction.

Score Your Success

15 ball checks or more = 5 points

12 to 14 ball checks = 3 points

8 to 11 ball checks = 1 point

7 ball checks or fewer = 0 points

Your score ___

Ball Control Drill 2. *Lateral Ball Check*

Select a teammate to time and to compete against. Use chalk to mark three lines 24 inches (61 cm) apart on the artificial turf. If playing on grass, set up three cones 24 inches apart in a line. With the three lines in front of you, start with the ball next to your stick outside the first line on the left. Your teammate will time you for 30 seconds and count your successful lateral ball checks. While keeping the stick next to the ball, move the ball over the first line and back, the second line and back, and the third line and back. Execute a ball check each time you change direction to the right and back to the left. Maintain good balance and focus on quality footwork. Earn 1 point for each successful ball check during the 30-second time period. For a successful lateral ball check, the ball should travel entirely over the line and remain on the stick. After each 30-second period, switch roles with your teammate. Complete five 30-second rounds and score your best round total.

To Increase Difficulty

- Increase the time period.
- Use the PVC piping on the stick handle for the right hand.
- Quicken the pace with the added pressure of competition (first player to the right and back wins, first player to receive 30 successful ball checks, and the like).
- Increase the distance between the lines or cones.

To Decrease Difficulty

- Decrease the distance between the lines or cones.
- Reduce the number of repetitions.

Success Check

- Maintain close control of the ball in your control box.

- Bend your knees and maintain a low center of gravity.
- Maintain the shake-hands grip, using the left hand to change stick positions.
- Maintain your balance on the power points of your feet. Feet remain shoulder-width apart.
- Maintain agile foot movements.
- Combine sudden changes of speed with changes of direction.

Score Your Success

20 ball checks or more = 5 points

15 to 19 ball checks = 3 points

10 to 14 ball checks = 1 point

9 ball checks or fewer = 0 points

Your score ___

Ball Control Drill 3. Box Exercise for Drop Step

Use four cones to set up a 3-by-3-yard (2.8 by 2.8 m) square. Start with a ball on the outside of the box and move it to the middle of the box. Keep your stick on the ball as you move your feet in coordination with the ball. The object is to move the ball and both feet to the inside of the box and back out on a different side. Do 20 sides and score 1 point for each successful ball-control movement through the sides of the box without error. An error occurs when you lose control of the ball.

To Increase Difficulty

- Increase the number of attempts.
- Quicken the pace with the added pressure of time.
- Decrease the size of the box.
- Add a defender who pressures from outside or inside the box.

To Decrease Difficulty

- Increase the size of the box.
- Reduce the number of attempts.

Success Check

- Maintain close control of the ball in your control box.
- Bend your knees and maintain a low center of gravity.
- Maintain your balance on the power points of your feet. Feet remain shoulder-width apart.
- Combine sudden changes of speed with changes of direction.

Score Your Success

16 points or more = 5 points

12 to 15 points = 3 points

8 to 11 points = 1 point

7 points or fewer = 0 points

Your score ___

Ball Control Drill 4. *Ball in the Playground*

Set up a 10-by-10-yard (9 by 9 m) area with obstacles such as cones, hockey sticks, rebound boards, or anything else. Start with a ball on the inside of the playground and dribble the ball to avoid the obstacles. Keep your stick on the ball as you move your feet in coordination with the ball. The object is to maneuver the ball with control through the playground. Do five 20-second periods, alternating turns with a teammate. Give yourself 1 penalty point each time you lose control of the ball or when you touch an obstacle.

To Increase Difficulty

- Decrease the size of the playground.
- Increase the duration or number of periods.
- Add a defender who pressures from inside the playground.
- Place the playground inside or outside the shooting circle and break out to score.

To Decrease Difficulty

- Increase the size of the playground.
- Reduce the number of obstacles.
- Reduce the number of periods.

Success Check

- Maintain ball control in your control box.
- Bend your knees.
- Maintain your balance on the power points of your feet. Feet remain shoulder-width apart.
- Combine sudden changes of speed with changes of direction.

Score Your Success

2 penalty points or fewer = 5 points

3 or 4 penalty points = 3 points

5 or 6 penalty points = 1 point

7 penalty points or more = 0 points

Your score ___

Ball Control Drill 5. *Ball Control and Vision Game*

Use a circle with a 10-yard (9 m) radius and use four cones to set up a 5-by-5-yard (4.5 by 4.5 m) square in the middle. Place three defenders without sticks inside the circle to tag the attackers. Have eight attackers around the outside of the circle. Each attacker has a ball and is ready to dribble. The attackers must successfully dribble and control their own balls into the square and back outside the circle without being tagged by a defender. The attacker is out of the game if tagged. The attacker can be tagged only while inside the circle. The attacker is safe when inside the middle square or outside the circle. The attacker may go in and come out of the circle, but she must keep control of the ball. Award a point to the attacker who penetrates inside the square. Award another point when the attacker controls the ball and then safely travels to the outside of the circle. When all attackers are tagged or lose control of their balls, total the scores. Play three games, rotating in three new defenders for each game.

To Increase Difficulty

- Decrease the size of the square.
- Increase the number of games.
- Add the pressure of time.
- Add another defender to tag.
- Allow defenders to use their sticks to knock the ball away from attackers.

To Decrease Difficulty

- Increase the size of the circle.
- Increase the size of the square.
- Reduce the number of games.

Success Check

- Maintain ball control in your control box.
- Bend your knees.
- Maintain your balance on the power points of your feet. Feet remain shoulder-width apart.
- Move into open space in order to maintain ball possession.
- Combine sudden changes of speed with changes of direction.

DRIBBLING

Although passing is the most effective way to beat an opponent, the individual attack role 1 technique of dribbling is used to set up attack play. Dribbling is easier than passing for many players to learn and for many coaches to coach. The close ball control and efficient stick work required for efficient passing will enhance dribbling.

Dribbling techniques share much in common with ball control. In addition to the close control of the ball, these elements include sudden change of direction and speed, body swerves and fakes, and deceptive sidesteps. Inside attack players need closer stick work and dribbling techniques because they are frequently in tight spaces. Outside attack players have more open space, so dribbling speed and a good ball check must be developed.

The most effective way to acquire dribbling skills is to practice. With practice, you will learn to keep the ball at the base of the stick and you will develop control. You will need strong back and leg muscles in order to crouch down while running. Your weight should be on the power points of your feet so that there is a lightness of movement. Keep your head down and your eyes on the ball, but make quick glances at the opponent to evaluate her distance, balance, and position. To keep the ball close to your stick in the control box, you must run with a low center of gravity. Coordinating stick work with changes of direction while running with the ball requires you to improve footwork. Remember, your dribbling speed will improve as your ball control improves.

The two basic levels of dribbling are the fundamental level and the advanced level. The fundamental level consists of one dribbling technique called the speed dribble, which is used for open field runs with the ball. The advanced level consists of four dribbling techniques—the power dribble, Indian dribble, spin dribble, and lifted dribble—that use both the forehand and the reverse stick positions to put the ball into an open space or over a defender's stick.

Speed Dribble

The speed dribble (figure 3.3) is sometimes called the open field, or forehand, dribble. The object of the speed dribble is to run with the ball into open field space in order to gain ground and move the opponent. The speed dribble can be used during a straight-line run or, more effectively, the player can cut diagonally by using small push passes. Cutting with the ball or dribbling diagonally will move the opponent laterally, which allows the attacker to penetrate through spaces closer to goal.

Figure 3.3   Speed Dribble

a   *b*   *c*

PREPARATION

1. Receive the ball
2. Body is slightly crouched
3. Use a shake-hands grip
4. Ball is on the right side of your body
5. Stick is behind and close to the lower half of the ball
6. Glance up and then look back down to the ball

EXECUTION

1. Focus on the ball
2. Strike the lower half of the ball
3. Use a sudden change of direction and speed
4. Push the ball ahead, outside of your right foot

FOLLOW-THROUGH

1. Head is up for good field vision
2. Accelerate with the ball on your right side
3. Push the ball ahead

Misstep

You are chasing after your uncontrolled, rolling dribble.

Correction

Lower your body posture so that you can keep your stick head close to the lower half of the ball.

Misstep

The ball gets too close to an opponent, who then successfully block tackles the ball.

Correction

Keep the ball close to your stick and your eyes downfield. Execute a quick turn (change of direction) at least 5 to 7 yards (4.5 to 6.4 m) from an opponent's stick reach.

The first step to speed dribbling effectively is to execute the change of direction with a burst of speed. To change the direction of the ball, use your right hand (shake-hands grip) to push the ball out into free space. This small, aggressive push pass to yourself enables you to break out into a good run. During the speed dribble, keep the ball at the forehand or right side of the body 3 to 4 inches (7 to 10 cm) outside the right foot so that your running action is not impeded. (Advanced speed dribblers can also execute the speed dribble from outside the left foot.) Use the shake-hands grip and keep the stick head close behind or next to the ball. When dribbling on an artificial surface, always keep the stick blade on the lower half of the ball and the stick head on the ground, which requires a crouched running posture. On rough grass surfaces, the stick must be more vertical, with the left hand slightly inclined in front of the right. From this stick position, push the ball forward with small push passes as you run. It is very important to maintain a low running position to avoid losing contact with the ball. Running at maximum speed naturally places your body in a more upright position, which may force your stick too far from the ball, resulting in losing control of the ball.

To pass to the left from the speed dribble, move the ball to the front of the left foot or the center of your control box. When you pass from the speed dribble, reduce the speed of the dribble or move the ball into your control box in order to execute a quality pass. Always practice using various speeds, but remember, skill is of primary importance and speed is secondary. If speed is emphasized as more important, your skill level will be reduced.

Speed Dribble Drill 1. *Change of Direction*

Place two cones 24 inches (61 cm) apart. Start with a ball 7 yards (6.4 m) behind the first cone. Push the ball forward using a short push pass to yourself, and accelerate into a speed dribble to the left side of the first cone. Push the ball to the right between the cones to change direction. Turn your shoulders, head, and hips as you execute a quick stick turn with your right hand. Run outside the cones as the ball travels between the cones when changing direction to your right. End with a shot or pass to a target. Complete 10 repetitions to the right, resting briefly between each repetition. Then execute 10 changes of direction to your left. Award yourself 1 point for each successful change of direction without an error. Errors include a lack of body control (e.g., knocking over the cones); feet entering the space between the cones; ball not traveling between the cones; ball being too far from your stick; moving at a slow, deliberate pace instead of changing direction or pace; and tapping or hitting the ball instead of pushing it.

To Increase Difficulty

- Increase the distance from start to cones.
- Reduce the distance between the cones.
- Receive a pass and go.
- Increase the number of attempts.
- Add another set of cones so that two changes of direction are executed before the shot.
- Add the pressure of time or compete against another player.

To Decrease Difficulty

- Increase the distance between the cones.
- Reduce the number of attempts.
- Decrease the distance from the starting line to the first cone.

Success Check

- Maintain ball control in your control box.
- Bend your knees.
- Maintain your balance on the power points of your feet. Feet remain shoulder-width apart.
- Combine sudden changes of speed with changes of direction.
- Push the ball when dribbling.

Score Your Success

16 points or more = 5 points

12 to 15 points = 3 points

8 to 11 points = 1 point

7 points or fewer = 0 points

Your score ___

Speed Dribble Drill 2. *25-Yard (23 m) Race*

Divide into two equal teams. Set two identical areas for team 1 and team 2. Each area is 25 yards (23 m) long with four sets of change-of-direction cones (24 inches, or 61 cm, apart in a vertical line) placed in two vertical columns. Place the first set of cones 5 yards from the start line and the second set of cones 5 yards (4.6 m) to the left on the 10-yard line. Put the third set of cones 5 yards to the right of the second set of cones (the 15-yard line), and place the fourth set of cones on the 20-yard line, 5 yards to the left of the third set of cones. Each team gets in a shuttle formation at each end of the 25-yard area. The first player from team 1 and the first player from team 2 start with a ball at their respective 25-yard start area. Push the ball forward using a short push pass to yourself and then accelerate into a speed dribble to the right side of the first cone. Push the ball to the left between the cones to change direction. Turn your shoulders, head, and hips as you execute a quick stick turn with your right hand. Run outside the cones as the ball travels between the cones as you change direction to your left. Go to the left of the next set of cones and push the ball to the right between the cones. Repeat the speed dribble, going to the right of the third set of cones and back to the left between the cones. Finish with a change of direction between the fourth set of cones and immediately pass to your teammate behind the 25-yard endline. Player 2 receives the 5-yard (4.5 m) pass and repeats the change of direction back through the four sets of cones, then passes the ball to the third player, and so on. Each player goes twice. To win, the ball must be stopped beyond the endline before the other team stops their ball. The winning team gets 1 point for the victory. Play the best of five races.

To Increase Difficulty

- Increase the distance from the starting line to the cones.
- Reduce the distance between the cones.
- Increase the number of attempts.
- Place more sets of cones in the race area.

To Decrease Difficulty

- Increase the distance between the cones.
- Reduce the number of attempts.
- Decrease the distance from starting line to the first cone.

Success Check

- Maintain close control of the ball in your control box.
- Bend your knees and maintain a low center of gravity.
- Maintain your balance on the power points of your feet. Feet remain shoulder-width apart.
- Combine sudden changes of speed with changes of direction.
- Push the ball when dribbling.

Score Your Success

3 points or more = 5 points

2 points = 3 points

1 point = 1 point

0 points = 0 points

Your score ___

Speed Dribble Drill 3. *Vision Dribbling*

Select a partner. Set two cones 25 yards (22.9 m) apart in a line. Your partner stands 5 yards (4.6 m) in front of you and backpedals to the 25-yard cone while keeping her stick head on the ground to point in a direction. The direction that your partner's stick points is the direction you turn the speed dribble. Your partner should do five direction points within the 25-yard area. Keep the ball out in front and use quick turns so that you can see the direction of your partner's stick point. When you complete the 25-yard distance, change roles with your partner. Each player completes five rounds. Earn 1 point for each successful round without a dribbling error.

To Increase Difficulty

- Increase the distance between the cones.
- Increase the frequency of direction points.
- Increase the number of rounds.

To Decrease Difficulty

- Reduce the distance between the cones.
- Reduce the number of rounds.
- Reduce the frequency of stick points.

Success Check

- Maintain ball control in your control box.
- Bend your knees.

- Maintain your balance on the power points of your feet. Feet remain shoulder-width apart.
- Combine sudden changes of speed with changes of direction.
- Push the ball when dribbling.

Score Your Success

4 or 5 points = 5 points

2 or 3 points = 3 points

1 point = 1 point

0 points = 0 points

Your score ____

Power Dribble

When opponents crowd the area of the field where AR1 has the ball or when a one-on-one move is needed to beat a defense role 1 player, AR1 uses the power dribble to create additional space. The power dribble uses forehand and reverse stick positions and allows a change of direction. A talented power dribbler is a coordinated, balanced bundle of ball, stick, and person, efficient in changing direction and speed while the ball remains seemingly glued to the stick.

To execute the power dribble (figure 3.4), push or silently tap the lower half of the ball in unison with your directional footwork. The ball remains in your control box and rarely loses contact with the blade of the stick. Body posture is lower than that required for the speed dribble since intense footwork is needed to maintain possession during the power dribble. The position of the left hand is vital as it must be changed drastically when receiving, pushing, hitting, and speed dribbling. The left hand holds the stick near the top of the handle and does all the work of turning the stick from right to left (counterclockwise) and back. The right hand does not firmly grip the stick; only the fingers and thumb of the right hand encircle and hold the stick in a relaxed position about 5 1/2 to 7 inches (14 to 18 cm) below the left hand. The right hand grips the stick only to support the left hand when moving the ball backhand and forehand. Relax your right hand grip when the left hand rotates the stick over the top of the ball. The V formed by the left thumb and forefinger must be moved toward the back of the handle in order to change the stick's direction and speed effectively.

Misstep

Stick is slow and clumsily handled.

Correction

Allow the stick to freely rotate in your right hand while your left hand turns the stick.

Misstep

Pushing or tapping the upper half of the ball.

Correction

Move the ball 12 to 24 inches (30.5 to 61 cm) from your feet in your control box. Concentrate on touching or pushing the lower half of the ball.

Figure 3.4   Power Dribble

a

b

c

PREPARATION

1. Receive the ball next to your stick
2. Knees are flexed
3. Be in a crouched position with a low center of gravity
4. Lead with your head over the ball
5. Glance up and the look back down at the ball

EXECUTION

1. Use your left hand to turn the stick
2. Allow the stick to rotate in your right hand
3. Stick should be next to the lower half of the ball
4. Use deceptive sidesteps and body swerves, with silent pushes of ball
5. Control the ball with the stick behind the ball
6. Ball remains in your control box
7. Change speed, direction, or both

FOLLOW-THROUGH

1. Keep your stick close to the ball
2. Accelerate away from your opponent
3. Look up and be ready to pass or shoot

Power Dribble Drill 1.   *Faking*

Set up two cones 7 yards (6.4 m) apart along a line on the hockey field. Stand with a ball on one side of the line midway between the cones while a defender faces you with a ball 2 yards (1.8 m) from the opposite side of the line. Your objective is to power dribble the ball laterally to a cone before the defender can get there. The defender tries to react instantly to your every move so that you cannot beat her to a cone with the ball. Use body fakes, deceptive sidesteps, and quick changes of speed and direction to unbalance the defender. Neither player is allowed to cross the centerline between the cones at any time. Earn 1 point each time you dribble and stop the ball at a cone before the defender can establish position there with her ball. Play for two minutes, then switch roles. Play six games, three in each role. The player with the most points wins.

To Increase Difficulty

- Increase the distance between the cones.
- Increase the frequency of turns.
- The partner without a ball becomes a defender who attempts to tackle.

To Decrease Difficulty

- Reduce the distance between the cones.
- Reduce the number of turns.

Success Check

- Maintain ball control in your control box.
- Bend your knees.
- Maintain your balance on the power points of your feet. Feet remain shoulder-width apart.
- Combine sudden changes of speed with changes of direction.
- Push the ball when dribbling.

Score Your Success

Win game = 5 points

Your score ___

Power Dribble Drill 2. *Burst Away From Defender*

Divide into groups of six. Set four cones in a 20-by-20-yard (18.3 by 18.3 m) square. Three or four players are passers, one outside each side of the square. The attacker (AR1) starts inside the square and plays against one defender, who is also inside the square. One of the passers starts with a ball and passes the ball not more than two consecutive times to the other passers outside the square. The ball is passed inside the square to AR1, who receives and controls the ball with a burst of speed away from the defender. AR1 should maintain possession of the ball using the power dribble, creating the time and space to pass the ball to a passer outside the square. The attacker earns 1 point for each ball that is received and controlled and then passed back outside the square. AR1 stays in the square for one minute before becoming a passer. Every player takes two turns as AR1. The highest point total wins.

To Increase Difficulty

- Decrease the size of the square.
- Increase the time.
- Add another defender inside the square.
- Set up a 4-yard-wide (3.5 m) goal 5 yards (4.5 m) outside the endline of the square. The attacker earns 3 points for a goal.

To Decrease Difficulty

- Increase the size of the square.
- Remove the defender.
- Reduce the amount of time.

Success Check

- Maintain ball control in your control box.
- Move away from the nearest defender.
- Maintain balance on the power points of your feet. Feet remain shoulder-width apart.
- Combine sudden changes of speed with changes of direction.
- Push the ball when dribbling.

Score Your Success

5 points or more = 5 points

4 points = 4 points

3 points = 3 points

2 points = 2 points

1 point = 1 point

Your score ___

Indian Dribble

The stick in the reverse position initiates all advanced skills in field hockey. The Indian dribble, or zigzag, is a more advanced technique that uses the reverse stick. The object of the Indian dribble is to get the opponent on the wrong foot by sweeping or zigzagging the ball across and in front of your feet in both directions. Moving the ball from side to side—forehand to backhand and back—combines the elements of successful ball control and good stick work.

To execute the Indian dribble (figure 3.5), use the split grip with the V of left hand near the back of the stick handle. Feet remain shoulder-width apart, knees bent. Body is crouched slightly. The ball is 18 to 24 inches (46 to 61 cm) from your feet as you run with the ball. If slowed or stationary, the ball is 12 inches (30.5 cm) from the feet. Keep the ball out in front of you where you can see it. Head remains still and it leads the upper body forward to the ball. The stick must move faster than the ball when it is turned over the top of the ball because it must reach a position to check the ball's zig or zag movement before the ball arrives. The zigzag ball movement involves coordinating the movements of the stick, ball, and feet. When the ball is in front of the right foot, your weight is on your right leg. The ball is dragged to your left foot and your left foot now bears your body weight.

Your stick strikes the lower half of the ball, which improves the speed of the Indian dribble. Your stick should be no more than 1/2 inch from the ball. Concentrate on using your left foot as the left-side boundary to keep the ball within the bounds of your control box and within the limits of your advancing feet. Sometimes, though, players take the ball beyond the feet, such as to change direction or evade an opponent.

From a stationary position, top players can perform the zigzag more than 90 times in 60 seconds. Using lots of concentration and correct technique, you can perform more than 50 zigzags in one minute. If you are inspired and determined to work hard, the Indian dribble can be a dangerous and glamorous attack technique for you.

Misstep

You lose dribbling speed and overreach for the ball.

Correction

The ball is too far from your feet and outside your control box. Place your stick on the lower half of the ball and keep it close to the ball.

Misstep

You dribble the top half of the ball.

Correction

Do not lift your stick more than 1/2 inch over the ball.

Spin Dribble

The spin dribble (figure 3.6) is used to protect the ball while pivoting or turning away from a defender who is blocking the forward space. As with all dribbling techniques, proper body position in relation to the ball and the opponent is important. Establish a pivot foot and turn sideways. Assume a slightly crouched posture and spin dribble or drag the ball—in a forehand or reverse direction—away from the opponent. The crouched position provides a wide base of support and can create greater distance between the opponent and the ball. In field hockey, the attack role 1 player—the player with the ball—may not stand still and shield the ball; this is an obstruction foul. To avoid the penalty, you must pivot and immediately move with the ball away from the defense role 1 player.

Figure 3.5 Indian Dribble

a

b

c

PREPARATION

1. Receive the ball
2. Feet are shoulder-width apart
3. Knees are bent; body is crouched
4. Head is leading
5. Ball is in your control box
6. Use a split grip

EXECUTION

1. Change the V position of your left hand
2. Glance up and then look back down at the ball
3. Use quick, short, forward strides or sidesteps
4. Stick is close to, or in contact with, the lower half of the ball
5. Work the ball with silent tapping movements
6. Ball is checked within the bounds of your advancing feet
7. Keep correct angle of zigzags

FOLLOW-THROUGH

1. Dribble within the limits of your advancing feet
2. Keep the ball in front of you
3. Follow the ball with ease

Misstep

Weak left-to-right movement.

Correction

On the reverse stick side, check the ball and keep the ball from passing more than a few inches outside the left foot.

Misstep

Your zigzag dribble escapes on your backhand side.

Correction

Turn your stick counterclockwise so that it can touch the lower half of the ball before the ball arrives.

Figure 3.6   **Spin Dribble**

a   *b*   *c*

PREPARATION

1. Keep close control of the ball
2. Position yourself to pivot or turn
3. Be in a crouched posture, with your knees flexed
4. Head is down
5. Eyes glance up to see the opponent or free space and then look back down at the ball

EXECUTION

1. Use body fakes and deceptive sidesteps
2. Control the ball in the direction of your pivot or turn
3. Control the ball with reverse or forehand stickhandling
4. Maintain your base of support during the pivot
5. Look at the ball and then at the opponent
6. Maintain correct ball-from-feet distance

FOLLOW-THROUGH

1. Readjust your body position in response to your opponent
2. Accelerate away from the opponent
3. Maintain close ball control
4. Prepare to pass or shoot

Misstep

You run into the defender.

Correction

Begin to turn sideways to pivot or turn away from the defender a few yards sooner.

Misstep

The ball hits your feet.

Correction

The stick and your hands are too close to your body. Keep your arms extended away from your body with your stick on the ball. The ball remains on the outer edge of your control box.

Lifted Dribble

The lifted dribble (figure 3.7) is sometimes called the *motorcycle* by the Argentineans and the *jink* by the Australians. It is a more advanced dribbling technique that is used to get out of trouble. Defenders who have initially blocked the forward or lateral spaces position their sticks low to the ground in a block-tackle spot. Often defenders use the low block tackle to prevent AR1 from penetrating the circle or from advancing the ball along the endline to the goal. The lifted dribble can be performed with two hands on the left or right side of the body. While running, the dribbler executes a small (12 to 18 inches, or 30.5 to 46 cm), gentle lift of the ball followed by a tap to the right or left while the ball is in the air. To execute the lifted dribble on the forehand side with both hands on the stick, slide your stick under the ball by using the right hand. As the ball is picked up a few inches into the air, use your left hand to turn the stick. Before the ball falls to the ground, tap the ball in the direction you want.

Misstep

You fail to lift the ball from the ground.

Correction

Bend your knees and lower the stick handle with the left hand as you slide the stick under the ball.

The reverse lifted dribble is a bit more difficult because it is performed with only the left hand on the reverse-stick side. This skill is used to dribble the ball wide to the left of your body. The left hand is lower on the stick for added strength and coordination.

Figure 3.7   Lifted Dribble

PREPARATION

1. Run forward with the ball close to your stick
2. Two hands are on the stick (forehand) or lower left hand only (reverse)
3. Maintain your running form
4. Eyes glance up to see the opponent and free space
5. Turn the stick in order to slide the flat side of the stick head under the ball

a

b

c

EXECUTION

1. Lift the ball a couple of inches into the air
2. Turn the stick with your left hand
3. Maintain balance on your power points
4. Shift your attention from the ball to the opponent
5. Maintain correct ball-from-feet distance

FOLLOW-THROUGH

1. Tap the aerial ball either right or left
2. Readjust your body position in response to the opponent
3. Accelerate away from the opponent
4. Maintain close control of the ball
5. Prepare to pass or shoot

Misstep

You kick the ball or overrun the ball while attempting to lift it.

Correction

Keep the ball on the right or left side of your body, slightly outside your control box. Avoid dribbling the ball directly in front of your feet.

Misstep

The umpire calls a dangerous-play penalty on the lifted dribble.

Correction

Lift the ball only a small distance off the ground so that the aerial dribble cannot lead to dangerous play.

Dribble Drill 1. *Right-to-Left and Left-to-Right*

Start in a stationary position with feet shoulder-width apart. Place a ball 12 inches (30.5 cm) in front of your feet and in line with the right foot. Grip the stick with your left hand using the reverse grip so that the V is on the back of the stick. Add your relaxed right hand. Place your stick on the right side of the ball and tap the lower half of the ball to the left and then to the right, keeping the ball in your control box. Push the ball, then turn your stick counterclockwise over the top of the ball, then tap the ball back to the right. Your stick should be only 1 or 2 inches (2.5 to 5 cm) from the ball. Your goal is to increase the speed of your stick movements as you develop control. Count the number of pushes you perform without error in 10 seconds. Errors include tapping the ball too far outside your left or right foot or when your stick is more than 2 inches (5 cm) from the ball. Do 10 rounds of 10 seconds.

To Increase Difficulty

- Move (walk, jog, run) forward and backward.
- Increase the time or distance.
- The partner without the ball becomes a defender who attempts to tackle.

To Decrease Difficulty

- Decrease the amount of time.
- Reduce the number of repetitions.

Success Check

- Use a firm grip with your left hand, loose grip with your right hand.
- Turn the stick close to the ball.
- Controlled pushes on the lower half of the ball.
- Ball remains in your control box.
- Combine sudden changes of speed with changes of direction.

Score Your Success

36 pushes or more in 10 seconds = 5 points

30 to 35 pushes in 10 seconds = 3 points

20 to 29 pushes in 10 seconds = 1 point

Your score ___

Dribble Drill 2. *1 v 1 Dribble*

Set up two cones 10 to 15 yards (9 m to 14 m) apart along a line on a hockey field or in a gymnasium. Stand with a ball 5 yards (4.6 m) on one side of the line midway between the cones while a teammate (DR1) faces you without a ball on the line between the cones. Your objective is to use ball control, fakes, and dribbles to move the ball laterally and forward in order to penetrate toward and behind one of the two cones before the defender can get there and block your dribble. Use body fakes, deceptive sidesteps, quick changes of speed and direction, and Indian, spin, or lifted dribbles to unbalance the defender. Award yourself 1 point each time you dribble and stop the ball behind a cone before the defender (DR1) can establish position to block or tackle. Play for two minutes, then switch roles and play again. Play six games, three as the dribbler (AR1) and three as the defender (DR1). The player with the most points wins the game.

To Increase Difficulty

- Increase the distance between the cones.
- Increase the amount of time or the number of games.

- AR1 receives a passed ball to start the game.
- AR1 penetrates between cones and shoots at a target.

To Decrease Difficulty

- Reduce the distance between the cones.
- Reduce the number of games.

Success Check

- Use a firm grip with your left hand, loose grip with your right hand.
- Turn the stick close to the ball.
- Use controlled pushes on the lower half of the ball.
- Ball remains in your control box.
- Combine sudden changes of speed with changes of direction.

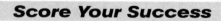

Score Your Success

Win game = 5 points

Your score ___

Dribble Drill 3. *Partner Relay Dribbling*

Partner with a teammate and stand 25 yards apart (23 m) (on the endline and on the 25-yard line). Compete against other pairs. Set a pair of cones 5 yards (4.5 m) apart and 2 yards (1.8 m) outside each line. The cones are perpendicular to the lines. You have the ball on the endline, and your partner is ready to move in front of the 25-yard line to receive your pass. Begin the relay by dribbling as quickly as possible back to the nearest cone (2 yards, or 1.8 m, behind endline) and back to the endline. Change direction and dribble the ball back to the second cone (5 yards, or 4.5 m, from the first cone) and back over the endline. Pass the ball to your partner, who steps in front of the 25-yard line to receive and repeat the sequence of dribbling behind the 25-yard line. The first pair to complete this cycle twice is the winner and is awarded a point. Continue to play until one pair wins 5 points.

To Increase Difficulty

- Increase the dribbling distance between the cones.
- Increase the frequency of cycles.
- Use only small, lifted dribbles over the cones.
- Do a combination of dribbles to each cone (spin dribbles and small, lifted dribbles).

To Decrease Difficulty

- Reduce the distance between the cones.
- Reduce the number of cycles.

Success Check

- Use a firm grip with your left hand, loose grip with your right hand.
- Turn the stick close to the ball.
- Use controlled pushes on the lower half of the ball.
- Ball remains in your control box.
- Combine sudden changes of speed with changes of direction.

Score Your Success

Win game = 5 points

Earn 3 or 4 points = 3 points

Earn 1 or 2 points = 1 point

Your score ___

SUCCESS SUMMARY OF BALL CONTROL AND DRIBBLING

Dribbling is a skill you can practice by yourself. A good hockey player will build up speed as she moves the ball with her stick. You will greatly improve your team's ability to attack and score goals if you practice stick work, which is the essence of ball control and dribbling. Practicing handling the ball with your stick is fun. All you need is a ball, a level spot, and an eagerness to improve. Concentrate on synchronizing the movements of the stick, ball, and feet so that you are effective when you change direction and speed, so that your body and foot movements are deceptive, and so that you are able to keep your stick on the lower half of the ball.

Ball Control Drills

1. North-South Ball Check With Pipe	___ out of 5
2. Lateral Ball Check	___ out of 5
3. Box Exercise for Drop Step	___ out of 5
4. Ball in the Playground	___ out of 5
5. Ball Control and Vision Game	___ out of 5

Speed Dribble Drills

1. Change of Direction	___ out of 5
2. 25-Yard (23 m) Race	___ out of 5
3. Vision Dribbling	___ out of 5

Power Dribble Drills

1. Faking	___ out of 5
2. Burst Away From Defender	___ out of 5

Dribble Drills

1. Right-to-Left and Left-to-Right	___ out of 5
2. 1 v 1 Dribble	___ out of 5
3. Partner Relay Dribbling	___ out of 5
Total	___ *out of 65*

A combined score of 58 points or more suggests that you have satisfactorily mastered ball control and dribbling and that you are prepared to move to step 4. A score in the range of 45 to 57 is considered adequate. You can move on to step 4 after additional practice of the ball control and dribbling skills that you find most difficult. A score of 44 points or fewer implies insufficient control of various movements. Review and practice the techniques discussed in step 3 before progressing to step 4.

Tackling

Championships are won with defense. The ability to stop the opponent with the ball game after game will put your team in a position to win. The heart of the defense is the player nearest to the ball carrier. This defense role 1 player (DR1) leads the effort to regain possession of the ball for her team. How you perform the DR1 skills is critical to your team's defense.

Winning the ball from a talented attack role 1 dribbler requires more than average defense skills. It requires footwork, balance, self-discipline, and a determined attitude. In field hockey, the term *tackling* describes the techniques applied by the defense role 1 player to the ball, not to the dribbler of the ball. A good DR1 player has good timing—she knows when to tackle and when not to tackle. During the transition from defense roles 2 and 3 (see step 9), the DR1 player can avoid having to tackle by intercepting the pass. Three basic defensive techniques—engaging distance (setting up your body to perform a skill), the jab and fake-jab tackles, and the block tackle (attack block and defensive block)—are used in direct encounter and pursuit, both on the forehand and backhand sides of the body. Engaging distance and give enable you to keep the ball in front of you. These are the most crucial techniques to learn because defense requires that you be able to judge distance well, much like passing. You can use a jab tackle and a block tackle to get the ball only if you learn to properly judge distance from the ball while maintaining a balanced, staggered stance, which includes using a lead foot.

The best defense is having the ball. Without the ball, your team cannot score goals. In addition to pass interceptions, tackling to win ball possession is critical. All field players, even the goalkeeper—although techniques differ—must learn to execute tackling techniques, because when a team loses the ball, all players fall back on defense and must get into position to take the ball back. Do not settle for merely spoiling the opponent's attack by poking the ball out of play. Although it is important to break up a play or to knock the ball off the sideline, it is better to gain possession of the ball by executing proper tackling techniques.

Tackling has three objectives:

1. to keep the ball in front of the defensive player so that AR1 is forced to pass a ball that can be intercepted by DR2,
2. to force AR1 to pass the ball so that possession of the ball can be regained; and;
3. to stop AR1's forward progress and ball control by blocking space and by creating a tackling threat.

Of course, a clever dribbler will avoid being tackled most of the time and will choose to pass to another area of the field. A battle of cleverness develops between the tackler and the dribbler, each attempting to outmaneuver the other or to force the other to make an error. A common fault of the DR1 player is to charge a ball carrier who is in full control of the ball or to charge after a loose ball that is closer to the opponent—in other words, mistakenly committing the body and feet to the ball. Other errors include planting the feet and swinging or flailing your stick at the ball.

Understanding the correct approach—engaging distance and give—will help you avoid these unbalanced errors and will eventually prepare you to execute successful jab and block tackles.

DEFENSIVE FOOTWORK

If you stop your feet, you're beat. To perform the defensive footwork necessary for the three defense roles, you must have desire, discipline, anticipation, and superb fitness so that you can keep your feet moving. The key is to be in balance and to move your feet so that you can react to your opponent's attack moves and block the forward space to the goal.

Defensive footwork requires short, quick steps and weight evenly distributed on the power points of the feet. Avoid crossing your feet. Push off the back foot farthest and keep adjusting with the lead foot. The only time you change your lead foot is when AR1 moves by your lead foot. Always execute a drop step, then resquare your hips and shoulders to the ball in order to recover your defensive position.

Feet are staggered shoulder-width apart so that you can instantly move laterally, forward, or backward. Keep your hips low and your head steady. Your head directs your upper body forward. Keep your eyes focused on the ball so that you can judge the distance between your probing stick and the ball. Hold your stick in both hands out in front of your feet. Keep the stick head near the ground and inch it closer to the ball as you decide when to tackle.

The four basic defensive footwork movements are engaging distance and give, slide or shuffle, drop step, and backward run. All defensive footwork movements, except engaging distance and give, were described in step 1 (see page 18).

TACKLING

Whether the ball carrier is moving toward you or whether you are pursuing a dribbler to your left or right, the basic requirements for the tackle are the same. The ball must be within the reach of your stick. To determine your reach, your body must be in a low crouch with your knees and back bent. Balance is essential for quickly adjusting to the dribbler. Learn to control your center of gravity by keeping your body weight down on the power points of your feet, not on your toes, because if your weight is too far forward, you won't be able to recover quickly. Remember the cliché—if you stop your feet, you're beat. A balanced, defensive stance (figure 1.8, page 18) that establishes a lead foot for ready, agile footwork is vital.

For the most part, the stick is held in both hands. Extend your left hand and arm away from your body at the height of your left knee. The jab tackle is a one-handed tackle that is executed with the left hand and arm. The right hand, though, is immediately placed on the stick in the

shake-hands grip once you are ready to steal the ball. The head of the stick slides on the ground because the ball is on the ground, controlled by the dribbler. From here, the defender's stick tracks the ball, and the defender tries to hasten the dribbler's stick movement, perhaps causing the attacker to make an error such as losing ball control or moving the stick too far from the ball. When you use the stick to tackle, it must be done with decisive contact to the lower half of the ball. Your eyes should be focused on the ball and not on any deceptive body, stick, or foot movements that the AR1 dribbler may perform.

A patient and calm DR1 player will avoid committing her body, feet, or stick in a hasty forward or lateral direction. A patient DR1 player will better judge the distance between the ball and her own stick and her opponent's stick. Keep the ball in front of you, and be alert for a sudden change of pace or direction from the dribbler, both of which determine when you should use a jab, or fake jab, and a block tackle. If AR1 beats you, your immediate priority is to deny further penetration. Channel AR1 into areas of the hockey field where space is limited (for example, into a nearby teammate or toward the nearest sideline) or force AR1 to pass the ball so it doesn't penetrate further or move back toward her own goal. If you can delay penetration via the pass or dribble, your teammates will have time to recover to goal-side positions and support you.

Engaging Distance and Give (Push Back)

The basic defensive stance (see figure 1.8, page 18) was introduced in step 1. For defense, it is necessary to combine a defensive stance with engaging distance and give. Defensive footwork and a balanced, defensive stance are impossible to isolate from one another. The concept of engaging your distance to the ball and pushing backward in order to give ground and adjust to the speed of AR1 is so significant to the defensive roles, and especially to one-on-one defense, that a thorough examination is necessary. The responsibility of the defense role 1 player (DR1) is to block the dangerous space leading to the goal by getting in position to halt the ball carrier's forward progress. The key in all one-on-one situations is to keep the ball in front of you and to maintain your playing or reaching distance to the ball.

Engaging distance is also referred to as approach distance, the distance needed to move close to your opponent in order to apply defensive pressure. *Give* or *push back* refers to pushing away from the ball or opponent in order to avoid getting too close before you can reestablish your defensive stance and pressure the ball. The defense role 1 player ultimately wants to take the ball from the attacker by blocking and controlling the forward space to the goal. This is not an easy skill; it requires agile footwork combined with good judgment and balance. The most important aspect of successful defensive footwork is correctly judging distance in order to get close to the ball or opponent. You must be close enough to be a defensive threat without being beaten by the opponent. Engaging distance is equal to about 1 or 1 1/2 stick lengths, depending on the speed of the opponent. You should be able to reach the ball with your stick by taking one short, quick step. Approach the ball at a speed that will allow you to maintain balance and to change direction.

To execute engaging distance (figure 4.1), use short, quick approach steps without crossing your feet, and protect your lead foot by positioning it slightly outside the opponent's body. If your opponent makes a move toward the goal on the side of your back foot, you must give or push back without losing balance. As with your engaging, or approach, steps, use short, quick push-back steps without crossing your feet and losing balance.

| Figure 4.1 | Engaging Distance and Give |

PREPARATION

1. Position yourself between the ball and the goal
2. Shoulders and feet face the ball
3. Run or move toward the ball
4. Judge your distance from the ball
5. Hands are separated on the stick

a

(continued)

(continued)

b

c

EXECUTION

1. Within 7 yards (6.4 m) of the ball, establish your left lead foot with your right shoulder aligned to the ball
2. Engage by pushing off your back foot; give by pushing from the lead foot
3. Use short, quick steps on the power points of your feet
4. Feet are shoulder-width apart
5. Flex your knees in a semicrouched position

FOLLOW-THROUGH

1. Stick head is on the ground in front of your feet
2. Pressure the ball with a quick, tracking stick
3. Use balanced, defensive footwork
4. Patiently judge the distance from the ball or attacker
5. Decide when to tackle

Misstep

You run toward an opponent who has close control of the dribble and are then beaten.

Correction

Establish a lead foot, and push back in order to keep dribbler in front of you.

Engaging distance and push-back techniques basically require the same footwork but in different directions. They both use short, quick steps, with one foot up and the other foot back. Keep your weight evenly distributed on the power points of the feet. Push off the back foot, and step with your lead foot to approach the attacker; push off your front foot and step with your back foot to give. When engaging, never cross your back foot in front of your lead foot. When giving, never cross your lead foot in front of your back foot.

Misstep

AR1 fakes and swerves around you.

Correction

Concentrate only on the lower half of the ball in order to maintain your reach distance.

Remember these guidelines for engaging distance:

- *Keep the ball in front of you.* Position yourself between the dribbler and the goal you are defending. This *goal-side positioning* (see step 9) is important for shutting off the opponent's direct route to the goal.

- *Engage or approach AR1.* Determine the speed of the dribbler as you move to deny time and space to the ball carrier (AR1). As a general rule, the closer AR1 is to your goal, the closer you (DR1) should be to her. If AR1 is within the shooting circle, she must be denied the opportunity to shoot the ball. When engaging AR1, who is about to receive the ball, DR1 must use defensive power steps and align the ball in front of the right shoulder.

- *Give, or push back, by pushing off the lead foot.* To deny penetrating passes, quickly gain your balance. Evenly distribute your weight on the power points of your feet and maintain a low center of gravity. Move in a balanced position if the dribbler suddenly sidesteps or swerves laterally. Maintain ball-to-right-foot-and-shoulder alignment.

- *Evaluate.* The less space you give the opponent, the less time AR1 will have to make decisions and handle the ball. Judge the distance between the ball and the dribbler's stick and your stick. Give AR1 a bit more space if she has great speed or quickness with the ball. This will prevent AR1 from simply pushing the ball forward and outracing you. If AR1 relies on a high degree of skill rather than on quickness, move quickly toward her to within your stick-reach distance. Deny AR1 reasonable time and space to use her skills to beat you.

- *Maintain a lead foot.* A lead foot (primarily the left foot) will help you move laterally or to push back in step with AR1's speed and ball control. Force the dribbler to make a decision by keeping your stick on the ground to track the ball and by keeping the ball aligned with your right shoulder. Be patient and calm while you constantly adjust distance from the ball and maintain your balance. Keep your eyes focused on the lower half of the ball, looking for an opportunity to tackle, or, depending on the situation, to give more ground, to delay the attacker long enough for a teammate to come help, or to force the ball in the right (forehand) direction. Be ready to check the ball with your stick, avoiding overcommitment with a reckless stick swing.

- *Tackle the lower half of the ball.* When the time is best for you and your team, tackle hard to gain possession of the ball. The decision of when to tackle is based on your judgment of when you can effectively reach the ball with your stick while maintaining your balance and of when your stick is closer to the ball than AR1's stick.

Misstep

AR1 has too much dribbling space.

Correction

Engage your distance closer for an effective reach and better tackling threat.

Tackling Footwork Drill 1. *Engage and Pushback*

Select a partner. Your partner stands 7 yards (6.4 m) away with her back to you. Take two sprint strides toward your partner and immediately shorten your strides into a defensive stance with a pronounced left lead foot. Maintain a lead foot and shuffle forward to your partner until you are able to extend your left arm and to place it on your partner's back. Using the coordinated force of your left arm and the power of the push from your left leg, push back and away from your partner approximately 3 yards (2.8 m). Maintain a left lead foot in a low, crouched position as you recover. Keep both hips facing your partner. Award yourself 1 point for each engage and pushback without error. Errors include losing your balance, changing your lead foot, standing up from your low, crouched position, and crossing your feet. Repeat five times with your left foot as the lead and fives times with your right foot as the lead foot.

To Increase Difficulty

- Increase the number of repetitions.
- Increase the distance between the start area and your partner.
- Your partner has a ball. She turns to dribble past you during the pushback.

To Decrease Difficulty

- Decrease the distance.
- Reduce the number of repetitions.

Success Check

- Set your body in a balanced, defensive stance.
- Maintain the same lead foot before the push-back (during the shuffle forward) and after the pushback.

- Bend your knees and maintain a low center of gravity.
- Hands grip the stick after the pushback.
- Maintain your balance on the power points of your feet. Feet remain shoulder-width apart.

Score Your Success

Nine or ten repetitions without error = 5 points

Seven or eight repetitions without error = 3 points

Five or six repetitions without error = 1 point

Four repetitions or fewer without error = 0 points

Your score ___

Jab Tackle

The one-handed jab tackle (figure 4.2) is more popular on artificial surfaces and can be used in a variety of one-on-one defensive situations. Usually the jab tackle, sometimes called the *poke*, is not as strong a tackle as the block tackle. It is used to fake or bluff a dribbler, not to win the ball outright. The purpose of the fake jab is to get AR1 to lower her head and eyes to the ball and to react to your stick, thereby slowing down her dribble and making it more predictable. A successful jab typically forces the dribbler to lose the ball. The pressure defender then goes in to cleanly steal it. You can also use the jab to delay the opponent's attack until more of your teammates are in po-

sitions to help defend. Forwards use this tackle often for tackling while retreating. Generally, you will use this tackle from a position in front of the dribbler, with your lead foot closer the dribbler as you run alongside her. The secret of the jab tackle is the long reach of the left hand and arm and the easy shift into other tackles. The quick poking action of the stick is like a sneak attack, as the objective remains to force the ball beyond the dribbler's stick so that you can steal it. In the shooting circle, where fouls result in penalty corners and penalty strokes, use a two-handed jab or block tackle to better prevent the ball from hitting your feet.

Misstep

AR1 dribbles past your left side and behind you.

Correction

Increase your distance from the ball using push-back footwork, and maintain a left lead foot with your right shoulder aligned with the ball.

Figure 4.2 | Jab Tackle

a

b

c

PREPARATION

1. Engage or push back with breakdown footwork
2. Establish the left lead foot, with your right shoulder aligned with the ball
3. Hands are separated on the stick
4. Feet are shoulder-width apart
5. Have a low center of gravity on the power points of your feet
6. Head of the stick is on the ground, with your left hand below your left knee
7. Eyes are focused on the lower half of the ball

EXECUTION

1. Move the left-hand V grip to the right
2. Sense when to jab or fake jab
3. Transfer your weight with a downward stick jab
4. Strike the lower half of the ball
5. Recoil the stick to both hands
6. Maintain a lead foot and keep the stick head on the ground
7. Adjust your distance in order to keep the right shoulder aligned with the ball

FOLLOW-THROUGH

1. Use a shake-hands grip
2. Control the ball with the stick next to the lower half of the ball
3. Prepare to pass, dribble, or shoot

Misstep

Your jab misses the ball and the ball goes under your stick.

Correction

Keep your stick head on the ground and concentrate on poking under the lower half of the ball.

Misstep

Stick is slow and clumsily handled.

Correction

Change your left-hand V to the front of the stick and jab through the lower half of the ball.

Remember these guidelines when executing the jab tackle:

- *Use the right stick position.* Initially both hands are on the stick, which is held away from your body. Your left hand is away from the body and below the left knee as it grips the top of the stick. The face of the stick is turned slightly to the right so the flat side of the stick is facing up, placing the V of your left hand on the front of the handle. The head of the stick is on the ground or as close to it as possible throughout the entire tracking and poking action.

- *Maintain a balanced body and lead foot.* Knees are bent. Body is balanced and slightly crouched. The ball is aligned with your right shoulder if your left foot is the lead foot. To jab tackle a dribbler who is in front of you and is moving to your right side, maintain your left lead foot and keep the ball from moving outside your right shoulder. Move your right foot forward to tackle a player moving to your left. In this situation, keep your left shoulder aligned with the ball. When running along the dribbler's right side, start with your stick head on the ground and thrust the head of the stick at the lower half of the ball. Running along AR1's left side requires that you overtake the dribbler's run in order to avoid the fouls of body contact and obstruction. Because the dribbler more often will carry the ball on her forehand side, you must outrun the dribbler's run before reaching for the ball with the left-handed jab. To jab tackle while running alongside the ball carrier, transfer much of your weight through to the left leg at the moment you jab with the stick. Whether you are jab tackling alongside or from a front position, avoid transferring all your weight to the lead foot because this commitment makes it difficult to recover on missed attempts.

- *Time the jab or poke under the ball.* Always time your jab downward in a stabbing motion under the ball. Recoil your stick to both hands so that you are ready to jab again, block tackle, or pass the ball. Keeping the ball aligned with the right shoulder will enable you to keep the ball in front of you for tackling.

Misstep

Your reach is restricted.

Correction

Crouch low, leading with your left foot and shoulder. Hold your stick in your left hand and extend your left arm for a jab or fake jab.

Misstep

You are unable to recover from a missed jab tackle or to retreat in time.

Correction

Do not overly commit forward by placing all your body weight on the lead foot. Recoil your stick quickly and maintain your balance.

Tackling Drill 1. *Jab Skill Warm-Up*

Your partner faces you from approximately 5 to 7 yards (4.5 to 6.4m) away. Your partner has a stationary ball in front of her stick, ready for your jab. Engage to the ball with a left lead foot and execute a strong jab tackle. Your partner controls the jabbed ball and attempts to push pass the ball past your left lead foot. As the jab tackler, be sure to jab and recoil your stick as you push back to a balanced, defensive stance. Maintain a left lead foot and a low crouch as you recover. Keep both hips facing your partner. Repeat five times and change roles. Next, execute a fake jab while your partner attempts to pass the ball past your left lead foot. Repeat five times and change roles. Award yourself 1 point for each jab or jab fake without an error. Errors include losing your balance, changing your lead foot, standing up from your low crouch, letting the ball roll by your left foot or letting it hit your feet, and crossing your feet. Repeat the jab tackle and fake jab tackle five times with your right foot as the lead foot.

To Increase Difficulty

- Increase the number of repetitions.
- Increase the distance between the start area and your partner.

To Decrease Difficulty

- Decrease the distance.
- Reduce the number of repetitions.

Success Check

- Set your body in a balanced, defensive stance.
- Keep the stick head on the ground.
- Maintain the same lead foot before the pushback (shuffle forward) and after the pushback.

- Hands grip the stick after the pushback.
- Maintain your balance: knees bent, weight on power points of your feet, feet shoulder-width apart.
- Strike the lower half of the ball.
- Control the ball.

Score Your Success

15 to 20 repetitions without error = 5 points

12 to 14 repetitions without error = 3 points

10 or 11 repetitions without error = 1 point

9 repetitions or fewer without error = 0 points

Your score ___

Block Tackle

The two types of block tackles are the *attack block* and the *defense block*. Use the attack block tackle when an opponent slows down and power dribbles directly at you or after a speed dribbler has been forced into you. Use your stick in the 2 o'clock position as a horizontal barrier in front of your feet or wide to your right on the forehand (figure 4.3). On the reverse or left side, use a horizontal stick in a 10 o'clock position. Take a small forward step toward the ball and push your horizontal stick toward the ball. Keep both hands on your stick, which is out away from your feet. Your knuckles touch the ground.

| Figure 4.3 | Forehand Block Tackle |

PREPARATION

1. Position yourself on the goal side
2. Engage or give distance with breakdown steps
3. Establish a left lead foot and shoulder
4. Align your right foot and shoulder with the ball
5. Use a shake-hands grip, with the head of the stick on the ground
6. Have a low center of gravity on the power points of your feet
7. Eyes are focused on the lower half of the ball

a

(continued)

(continued)

b

c

EXECUTION

1. Time the attack block with a short step toward the ball, or give back with your feet for a defensive block
2. Stay in balance
3. Trap and then strike the lower half of the ball on the stick label

FOLLOW-THROUGH

1. Steer the ball away from the dribbler
2. Keep the stick on the ball
3. Be ready to look up to pass

Misstep

You are slow to move with AR1's sidestep.

Correction

Stay on the power points of your feet and keep one foot in front of the other. Align ball with your right shoulder.

Misstep

You block tackle the ball but lose it immediately.

Correction

Keep your stick still in a 2 o'clock position (forehand) and let the ball come to it. Strike the lower half of the ball and control it with your right hand on the stick. Control the ball away from the dribbler.

Generally the attack block tackle is used when you have successfully forced the AR1 dribbler into a one-on-one situation in which the dribbler has no choice but to try to beat you with the forward dribble. Use the defensive block tackle while pushing back away from a speed dribbler. Allow the ball to come to your stick. Block tackling, the most common method of tackling, requires good balance, good foot positioning, and good timing.

Remember these guidelines when executing the forehand block tackle:

• *Position yourself on the goal side.* While in control and balanced, move between AR1 and the goal you are defending. Your left foot and left shoulder lead as you force the AR1 dribbler into a position for a forehand tackle. Keep the ball in front of you. Imagine a straight line running from the ball to your right shoulder. When forcing the dribbler to your right side and to the outside of the field near the sideline, use a wide forehand block tackle. Always position yourself to play goal side. On the inside, deny the dribbler escape routes to the shooting circle in the center of the field.

• *Align your right foot and shoulder with the ball.* Ignore the dribbler's stick and foot fakes as you align your right foot and right shoulder with the ball. Bend your knees and crouch down in order to lower your center of gravity.

• *Keep your stick head low and use a shakehands grip.* Keep your eyes focused on the lower half of the ball. Hands are apart on your stick, each in a shake-hands grip. Improved timing and strength will allow you to grip the stick and tackle with a left-hand grip only. Sometimes the forehand block tackle is preceded by fake jabs or a show of a block on your left side. In any event, the head of your stick always remains close to the ground, ready to block the ball on the stick-label area as the dribbler takes her stick away from the ball.

• *Remember, timing is key.* Time your tackle for when the ball is well away from the opponent's stick. Allow the ball to come to your stick as you give backward with your feet. Your stick must align in a 2 o'clock position from your feet. Do not move your stick forward or swing at the ball as you will certainly give the ball back to the dribbler. Use the strength of your legs and forearms to trap the ball, and immediately control the ball away from the dribbler.

Reverse Block Tackle

The reverse block tackle is a more difficult tackle to master than the forehand block tackle and it is almost impossible to cleanly execute if the dribbler has won the goal-side position. When the sideline is an ally, however, left-side defenders must be familiar with this tackle. The principles of the reverse block are the same as the forehand block. The only difference is the 10 o'clock horizontal stick position, which is outside the line of your body on your left side but still in front. Good dribblers who cleverly get the ball to their forehand side nearly always attempt to beat left-side defenders on their backhand side. Let the one-on-one battle begin, because a good defense role 1 player will be able to use quick footwork and good balance to force the ball to his or her forehand.

To execute the reverse block tackle (figure 4.4), hold your stick in your left hand using a reverse grip. Get in a low position on the goal side and lead with your right shoulder and foot. Lock your left elbow and point the toe of your stick at the ground. Time your block tackle to trap the ball using a horizontal stick (knuckles of left hand on ground) so that AR1 overruns the ball.

| **Figure 4.4** | **Reverse Block Tackle** |

PREPARATION

1. Position yourself on the goal side
2. Engage or give distance with breakdown footwork
3. Establish a lead foot and shoulder
4. Align your left foot and left shoulder with the ball
5. Eyes are focused on the lower half of the ball

a

(continued)

(continued)

b

c

EXECUTION

1. Use a reverse V grip of your left hand
2. Keep a low center of gravity on the power points of your feet
3. Time the block by lowering the handle of the stick
4. Toe of the stick is on the ground
5. Stay in balance
6. Trap and then strike the lower half of the ball

FOLLOW-THROUGH

1. Steer the ball away from the dribbler
2. Keep the stick on the ball
3. Be ready to look up to pass

Misstep

You hasten your approach and tackle before your teammates are in position to cover inside passing options.

Correction

Delay your approach by holding and giving.

Misstep

AR1 pushes the ball between your feet and behind you.

Correction

Keep the head of your stick on the ground in front of your feet. Keep moving your feet to block space behind you.

Tackling Drill 2. *Block Skill Warm-Up to 1 v 1 Game*

Face a partner who is approximately 5 to 7 yards (4.5 to 6.4 m) away. In a small space of 5 by 5 yards (4.5 by 4.5 m), your partner power dribbles a ball in front of you. Engage to the ball with a left lead foot in order to execute a strong attack block tackle. Keep both hands on your stick and away from your body and keep your stick head on the ground. Be sure to time your attack block with a small step toward the ball. To execute the attack block, maintain a left lead foot in a low, crouched position as you place your stick on the ground in a 2 o'clock horizontal position. Repeat five times and change roles.

Next, your partner dribbles the ball forward. Execute a defensive block tackle while pushing back in a balanced, defensive stance. Repeat five times and change roles.

Play a 1 v 1 game for points in a 5-by-5-yard (4.5 by 4.5 m) square. The objective is to use defensive tackling skills in a small space. Each game consists of five restart balls for AR1 before you change roles. Award the DR1 player 1 point each time he or she touches the ball with the stick and 2 points for a successful block tackle that results in a controlled pass or dribble that hits the cones behind AR1. The AR1 dribbler receives a point if he or she successfully dribbles the ball forward across the 5-yard goal line behind DR1. Play three games and total your score to determine the winner.

To Increase Difficulty

- Increase the number of repetitions or games.
- Increase the length of the goal line.

To Decrease Difficulty

- Reduce the number of repetitions.
- Reduce the length of the goal line.

Success Check

- Set and move your body in a balanced, defensive stance.
- Keep the stick head on the ground with your left hand in front of your body and below the left knee.
- Align your left lead foot and ball with right shoulder.
- Use good block-tackling techniques.
- Strike the lower half of the ball.
- Follow through.

Score Your Success

Win three games = 5 points

Win two games = 3 points

Win one game = 1 point

Your score ___

Recovery Tackle

At some point, every player will be required to tackle while retreating or recovering because sometimes the ball will get into the space behind the player. Tackling while recovering does not differ from direct-approach tackling. You still must concentrate on using engaging distance and jab-and-block techniques—balance and footwork; stick position and grip; stick tracking with timing of the tackle; and patience. The only variation in recovery tackling is that the execution requires the DR1 to run at maximum speed in an attempt to get alongside and parallel to AR1. This approach will enable DR1 to keep AR1 to one side while DR2 gets into position to help stop the forward penetration by AR1.

Your objective when executing a recovery tackle is to keep the ball to one side by running parallel—as if along a railroad track—to the dribbler (figure 4.5). Always sprint at maximum speed in order to overtake the dribbler on the goal-line side. You surely will be beaten if you overcommit and run toward the ball carrier or directly at the ball.

Figure 4.5 | Recovery Tackle

a

b

PREPARATION

1. Run at maximum speed in order to catch up to the ball carrier
2. Run parallel and alongside AR1
3. Put the stick head on the ground, stick in your left hand only
4. Eyes are focused on the lower half of the ball

EXECUTION

1. Jab at the ball when it is loose from AR1's stick
2. Continue running parallel to the attacker if a jab is not possible
3. Strike the lower half of the ball
4. Stay close to attacker

FOLLOW-THROUGH

1. Position yourself on the goal side of AR1
2. Steer the ball away from the dribbler
3. Keep your stick on the ball
4. Look up to pass

Misstep

Your footwork is slow during the recovery run.

Correction

Run at your maximum speed in order to overtake or to get alongside AR1. Run parallel to the attacker.

Misstep

The dribbler beats you again after you have caught up to her.

Correction

Avoid stepping to the ball or committing your stick to the ball. Patiently run parallel to the attacker.

The keys to recovery tackling from the dribbler's forehand side are speed and body posture. You must run faster than the dribbler to overtake her, and when you are ahead of the dribbler, concentrate on timing when or when not to tackle. Never tackle while trailing behind the opponent, which is dangerous to the dribbler and which will certainly cause you to be penalized. Attempting to tackle before you are in position usually results in pushing, tripping, and stick obstruction fouls being called on DR1. When running at maximum speed, your body should be in a more upright position. Lower your center of gravity while running when you are ready to tackle. While your stick head is inches from the ground, lunge your stick toward the lower half of the ball and control the ball away from the attacker.

Speed and patience are required for recovery tackling from the dribbler's backhand side because this tackle is the most difficult of all defensive efforts. Again you must run to overtake and pass the dribbler on the goal side so that your body is even with the ball. You must at least run close and parallel to the left side of AR1 in order to run the ball carrier into an awaiting DR2 teammate, who then executes the defensive block tackle. Your stick is in your left hand only, in a reverse V grip. As soon as you run even with the ball, lower your body for a possible tackle. If the dribbler keeps the ball next to his stick, keep tracking your stick and time your jab, or block to the lower half of the ball when the ball is no longer on AR1's stick. In addition to your goal-side positioning and speed of recovery, a high level of patience will help you decide when or when not to tackle.

Tackling Drill 3. *Tackling Build-Up*

Organize into groups of five players. For step 1, set two cones 7 yards (6.4 m) apart. Each player takes a turn as DR1, who stays in this position until four back-to-back repetitions are completed. The first AR1 player dribbles the ball laterally back and forth from cone to cone. DR1 maintains a left lead foot and keeps her right shoulder in line with the ball in order to set up for a jab tackle or an attack block tackle. DR1 earns 1 point if she successfully tackles the ball before AR1 dribbles through the cones with the ball. Total DR1's points.

For step 2, use four cones to set up a rectangle area 7 yards (6.4 m) wide and 5 yards (4.5 m) long. Designate two passers, one on the outside left and one on the outside right at the top of the rectangle. Each passer has a stack of balls. DR1 starts at the left back cone while AR1 positions herself outside the square at the top of the rectangle, approximately 6 yards (5.5 m) from DR1. As soon as a ball is passed to AR1, DR1 may close down space and push back, ready to use her defensive tackling skills. DR1 takes four turns (two from the left back cone and two from the right back cone). DR1 maintains a left lead foot and keeps the ball in front. DR1 earns 1 point for each successful tackle. All players take four turns as the DR1 player. Total DR1's points.

For step 3, add two more cones 5 yards (4.5 m) from the top two cones from the step 2 area.

The play area is now 7 yards (6.4 m) wide and 10 yards (9 m) long. Passers are positioned on each side, near the 10-yard cones. Repeat the same procedure as step 2 from a 10-yard distance. Total DR1's points.

To Increase Difficulty

- Increase the number of repetitions.
- Increase the length of the goal line.
- Increase the distance to 15 yards (14 m).

To Decrease Difficulty

- Reduce the number of repetitions.
- Reduce the length of the goal line.

Success Check

- Set your body in a balanced, defensive stance.
- Keep the stick head on the ground.
- Align your left lead foot and ball with your right shoulder.
- Use tackling techniques.
- Keep the ball in front of you.
- Strike the lower half of the ball.
- Follow through.

Score Your Success

3 or 4 points out of four repetitions = 5 points

2 points out of four repetitions = 3 points

1 point out of four repetitions = 1 point

Total points for steps 1, 2, and 3 ___

Your score ___

Tackling Drill 4. *Railroad Tackles*

Organize into groups of four to six players. Use four cones to set up an area 20 yards (18.5 m) long and 10 yards (9 m) wide. AR1 starts 2 yards (1.8 m) inside the play area. DR1 has her back to the play area and starts 2 yards (1.8 m) behind AR1. A passer gets in position on the outside of the area, level with DR1. Another defender is on the goal line, 20 yards (18.5 m) from DR1. DR1 may turn and recover when the ball is passed to AR1. DR1 runs to catch up and run parallel with AR1. DR1 maintains patience by not going for the ball unless it comes loose from AR1's stick. If the ball comes off AR1's stick, DR1 uses a jab tackle. If the ball remains close to AR1's stick, DR1 continues to railroad run with her stick head on the ground so that AR1 is herded to the defender (DR2) on the goal line, 20 yards (18.5 m) from the start area. DR2 remains aligned with ball and uses a block tackle to assist DR1. Take five turns from the DR1 recovery position. Award yourself a point when you or your teammate successfully executes a railroad tackle before AR1 penetrates the goal line.

To Increase Difficulty

- Increase the number of repetitions.
- Increase the length of the goal line.

To Decrease Difficulty

- Reduce the number of repetitions.
- Reduce the length of the goal line.
- Play without DR2.

Success Check

- Run at controlled, maximum speed, parallel to the attacker.
- Grip the stick with the left hand only.
- Keep the stick head inches from the ground.
- Time a jab tackle if the ball is loose.
- If the ball remains close to AR1's stick, patiently railroad run AR1 into a teammate's block tackle.
- Strike the lower half of the ball.
- Follow through.

Score Your Success

4 or 5 points = 5 points

3 points = 3 points

1 or 2 points = 1 point

Your score ___

Tackling Drill 5. *2 v 2 Game to Goal*

Organize into teams of four to six players. Set a goal cage on the 25-yard line facing the shooting-circle goal cage. A goalkeeper in each goal cage is optional. Use four cones to mark a field that is 25 yards (23 m) long and 40 yards (36.5 m) wide. Each team starts with two players on the field and a passer on each sideline. The passers are mobile, moving up and down the 25-yard sideline in order to combine with the attack team. Play for six minutes, and award a point for each goal scored. When a team scores on one goal, they go in the other direction to attempt to score on the other goal. The team with the most goals at the end of six minutes wins the game.

To Increase Difficulty

- Play longer.
- Increase the size of the field.
- After a score, the team that scored keeps possession of the ball at the restart of the game.

To Decrease Difficulty

- Reduce the time.
- Reduce the size of the field.
- Play without goalkeepers.

Success Check

- Keep AR1 in front of you.
- Engage and push back in order to get your body in a balanced, defensive stance.

- Keep the stick head on the ground.
- Align your left lead foot and ball with your right shoulder.
- Use tackling techniques to steal the dribble.
- Strike the lower half of the ball.
- Follow through and transition pass to your teammate or sideline passers.

Score Your Success

Win game = 5 points

Lose game = 0 points

Your score ____

Tackling Drill 6. *Coach Pass 1 v 1 Game*

Divide into two equal teams. Set up a 10-by-10-yard (9 by 9 m) square. One player from each team starts outside of the square, behind their respective goal lines. The coach is centered outside the sideline. The coach rolls a ball into play and both players at each end go for the ball. The player who wins the ball is AR1 and the other player becomes DR1. Award a point to the player who successfully dribbles the ball over the opponent's goal line. After a score or after the ball goes out of play, repeat with two new players. Each player on each team takes two turns competing for the ball. Total your team points to determine the game winner.

To Increase Difficulty

- Increase the number of turns for each player.
- Increase the size of the playing area.
- Add a goal on the endline to shoot through.
- Add more players.
- Require players to enter the area from the opposite corners of the square.

To Decrease Difficulty

- Reduce the number of repetitions.
- Reduce the size of the square.

Success Check

- Keep AR1 in front of you.
- Engage and push back in order to get your body in a balanced, defensive stance.
- Keep the stick head on the ground.
- Align your left lead foot and ball with your right shoulder.
- Use tackling techniques to steal the ball.
- Strike the lower half of the ball.
- Follow through and hit the ball over the opponent's goal line.

Score Your Success

Win game (team with highest score) = 5 points

Lose game = 0 points

Your score ____

SUCCESS SUMMARY OF TACKLING

Defense role 1 tackling techniques must be practiced as much as attack role 1 techniques. Although dribbling or shooting skills may be more fun to practice, you will not get a chance to use those skills in game situations unless you first gain possession of the ball. Most tackling errors result from poor judgment of distance, bad timing of the tackle, lack of body control, or improper technique. Maintain a low center of gravity, get close to the ball, and then time your tackle using proper technique and determination. Winning the ball cleanly while tackling provides a team with a good opportunity to counterattack. During a counterattack, the opponent is often out of position. Tackling requires as much concentration, understanding, footwork, balance, and self-discipline as any other hockey skill. When contesting for possession of the ball, the player who has the better balance and ability to keep the ball in front of her will probably win the ball. Tackling techniques are competitive and fun to practice with a teammate because ball control and dribbling are also practiced.

Ask a coach, parent, or teammate to observe your execution of the defense role 1 tackling techniques and to evaluate your overall performance.

Tackling Footwork Drill

1. Engage and Pushback   ___ out of 5

Tackling Drills

1. Jab Skill Warm-Up   ___ out of 5

2. Block Skill Warm-Up to 1 v 1 Game   ___ out of 5

3. Tackling Build-Up   ___ out of 15

4. Railroad Tackles   ___ out of 5

5. 2 v 2 Game to Goal   ___ out of 5

6. Coach Pass 1 v 1 Game   ___ out of 5

Total   ___ *out of 45*

A combined score of 36 points or greater suggests that you have satisfactorily mastered tackling skills and that you are prepared to move to step 5. A score in the range of 29 to 35 is considered adequate. You can move on to step 5 after additional practice of the tackling skills that you find most difficult. A score of 28 points or less implies insufficient control of various tackling skills. Review and practice the techniques discussed in step 4 before progressing to step 5.

Shooting

Although scoring a goal is most often the result of a team effort, field hockey players who can finish a successful attack are noteworthy. Experienced players and coaches know that goal-scoring players increase the confidence of their teams. Each hockey position requires specialization and a sound tactical understanding of the sport, which includes being familiar with the roles of attack and defense. The skills of stick work, ball control, and passing, however are common to all good shooters. Attack role 1 techniques and tactics deal with similar requirements for shooting, which is merely the act of passing the ball behind the defense and toward the opponent's goal. A good shooter needs to understand which techniques to use.

Shooting is a specialized skill that requires daily practice. Success as a goal scorer depends on several ingredients: basic athletic instincts, including aggression and creativity; field position and awareness; and integration of team play. A goal scorer must be able to move the ball to get into position for an angled shot so that the opposing goaltender cannot block the shot. The ability to shoot early and accurately and to follow the shot for rebounds is essential. Because the opposing defenders are expected to possess stick work and mobility equivalent to attack role 1 players, scorers must be proficient in all skills. Quick footwork and balance will help you develop the ability to use all types of shots.

During a game, you will have little time to look at your target before shooting, so developing a visual image of the goal cage will allow you to shoot without looking up. Remain in a low position, with your stick head down, as you use skill and imagination to dribble and pass. To take advantage of scoring opportunities, use swift and early passing at maximum speed in order to get into scoring position in the shooting circle. You also must know when to one-touch or two-touch a ball.

Moving into position without the ball—attack roles 2 and 3 (see step 8)—creates a dangerous attacking unit and develops team combination play that results in scoring chances. No matter how gifted a scorer you may be, remember to regard yourself as a member of the team. A team that plays together scores together.

The aim of every attack is to score a goal, and all players enjoy scoring goals. Players who often play in the attacking third of the field are expected to penetrate and shoot. It is here that attack players are charged with the most difficult task of all—scoring goals. Top scorers can shoot from all angles, no matter where the ball is in relation to their feet and stick. To score consistently, a player must be able to shoot under actual game pressures (e.g., restricted space, limited time, physical exhaustion, and aggressive opponents). The keys to good shooting are the release speed of the shot, the surprise or deception of the shot, and the placement of the shot. The following general principles will help you develop into an effective scorer:

- Take your defensive role seriously. If you lose possession, recover quickly within the first 10 yards (9 m). You can make a huge difference by winning the space and getting the ball back, which can result in a quality scoring chance.

- Sprint to the wideout areas (touch endline) when the ball is behind you and inside the 25-yard line. Win this position before you make any other cuts.

- Draw a penalty corner when suitable such as when you can not get a quality shot or when you cannot pass to a teammate who is in better position to score.

- Get behind defenders and receive the ball wide of the defenders' stick reach. Beat them 1 v 1 when you have an opportunity in the attack third of the field.

- Practice receptions and one-touches every day.

- In the shooting circle, maintain a low-body and stick-head position.

- In the shooting circle, always be alert and aggressive, but controlled.

- In the shooting circle, make short, angled cuts.

- In the shooting circle, look for deflection shots or move into effective positions with and without the ball.

- Study the opposing goalkeeper for strengths and weaknesses. For example, check to see whether a goalkeeper who lacks quick footwork and agility can be beaten by a shooter's stick skills.

A goal scorer learns how and where to shoot on goal. Learn to create space for your shot by changing speed and direction in order to force the defender or goalkeeper to commit. For a shooter who doesn't yet have the ball, timing is vital. To become a shooter in this situation, your move into the shooting space should coincide with the arrival of the ball. The defenders will try to force you to shoot from a bad position—i.e., from the circle's edge, which is the greatest distance to the goal, from narrow angles—and at a hurried pace. A successful shooter learns both forehand and backhand hits, as well as the sweep hit, drag flick, push, chip, and scoop. She also learns to tip or deflect the ball in the direction of the goal regardless of body position. The shooter must concentrate on her objective while coping with restricted time and space and while being marked or unmarked. Most important, an accomplished shooter learns when a shot is impossible and when to pass to a teammate who is in a better scoring position (figure 5.1).

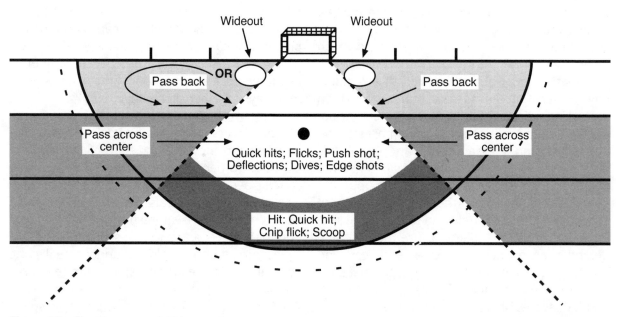

Figure 5.1 Shooting areas of circle.

The higher the level of play, the less time you have to execute an accurate shot on goal. A good shooter can get the ball to the goal quickly using the one- or two-touch method. A shooter values accuracy because even shots on goal that are saved by the goalkeeper may provide another opportunity to score. Because goalkeepers may not catch, hold, or cover up the ball, an accurate shot can produce a rebound and even a goal.

Because many goals are scored off rebounds, learn rebound positioning and follow up your shots. First position your body outside the shooting lane so that you do not get hit by the initial shot. Anticipate where the ball will rebound and get in position to collect the rebound by moving toward the goalkeeper and into the clearing or passing lane. With your hands apart on the stick and ready to touch the ball, move into a ready position before the ball rebounds. Goalkeepers wear foam kickers and leg guards, so your ready distance from the goalkeeper is at least 5 yards (4.5 m) due to the rebound speed. In addition to winning rebounds for extra scoring chances, a high level of concentration and anticipation will enable you to press the opposing defenders in their defense zone to make receiving and passing errors.

Experienced shooters develop a sense of where the opponent's goal is without looking up before shooting. Learn to vary your shots depending on whether the ball is rolling or bouncing by developing your footwork and by shortening or eliminating your backswing in order to shoot the ball from either the forehand or reverse. Practice and repeat shooting until you can shoot accurately with your body weight over either foot. In addition to the passing techniques described in step 2, basic shooting skills include the quick hit, redirection or deflection, dive, backhand, chip shot, drag flick, and the scoop.

To shoot, move to the ball and receive it in a ready position with your hands on the stick in a shake-hands grip. To receive a pass from your right, point your left shoulder to the target; for a pass from your left, point your right shoulder to the target. Keep the head of your stick on the ground. Legs are shoulder-width apart, and your center of gravity is low and evenly balanced. Keep your eyes focused on the lower half of the ball. Be ready to use any shooting technique. Keep your head down and steady and have an image of the goal cage in your mind throughout the shooting action. Finish by transferring your body weight.

QUICK HIT

Defenders rarely give you time to prepare to hit the ball. Because of the lack of time for making a takeaway swing and a downswing, push shots and flicks are frequently used. But when faced with limited time, goal scorers need a more powerful shot than the push or flick. The quick hit (figure 5.2) or short-grip technique produces a fast hit rather than a hard hit, one in which your hands come together at about the bottom of the grip on the stick handle. The quick, short backswing enables you to instantly strike the ball with pace.

Misstep
You undercut or slice the ball when attempting a quick hit.
Correction
Keep your feet shoulder-width apart and position the ball 9 inches (23 cm) away from but in line with your front foot. Face of the stick must be flat at the moment of impact.

To execute the quick hit, get in position to hit the ball by pointing your left shoulder to the goal. Your left foot is in line with the ball, and your knees are bent for balance. Keep your feet 12 inches (30.5 cm) apart to keep your balance.

Speed up your backswing by using the clip grip to slide your left hand down to your right hand. In the clip grip, both hands are together in a hit grip but lower on the stick. Sliding your left hand 12 inches (30.5 cm) down the stick to meet your right hand promotes a quick ball strike. Gripping your stick slightly lower will develop a shorter backswing. Forearms accelerate the wrists and the head of the stick through the lower half of the ball. Transfer your body weight to the front leg to help generate stick speed. Keep your head steady and your eyes on the lower half of the ball. Do not look up until you see your stick strike the lower half of the ball. Finish with your arms and stick in line with your target, and return quickly in order to move toward the goal in a ready position.

Figure 5.2   Quick Hit

PREPARATION

1. Be aware of the goal and the opponent
2. Use short steps and quick footwork
3. Lead shoulder is pointed toward the target in the goal
4. Front foot is in line with the ball
5. Stay balanced, with your knees flexed
6. Head is down and over the ball
7. Eyes are focused on the ball
8. Weight is transferred on the backswing
9. Make a short, quick backswing using your forearms and wrists

a

EXECUTION

1. Use a clip grip
2. Head remains over the ball
3. Weight transfers to the front leg on the downswing
4. Align your hands with your wrists before striking the lower half of the ball

b

FOLLOW-THROUGH

1. Keep your head down and watch the ball leave the stick
2. Momentum moves forward through the front leg
3. Knees remain relaxed and bent
4. Arms and stick finish in line with the target
5. Return to a ready position

c

Misstep

The quick hit is choppy.

Correction

Position the ball in your control box near the front foot instead of near the back foot. Follow through after impact.

Misstep

The quick hit has little power or accuracy.

Correction

Check your grip and make sure your hands are together, not split. Use and coordinate the forearms' and wrists' motion on the downswing and during the weight transfer.

Shooting Drill 1. *Quick Hit and Continue Forward*

Divide into two groups of five players. In the shooting circle, place a cone 3 yards (2.8 m) to the right and another cone 3 yards to the left of the penalty stroke spot. A pass server prepares a stack of balls on the right side between the 5-meter circle and shooting circle, approximately 14 yards (13 m) from the backline. One group forms shooting line A, 3 yards (2.8 m) outside the shooting circle, opposite the right post. The other group forms shooting line B, 3 yards outside the shooting circle, opposite the left post. The drill begins when the first player in line A cuts into the shooting circle on an angle and receives a pass from the server. The shooter quick hits the ball to goal, continues to run forward past the cone, and sprints back to the end of the shooting line. The server passes next to the first shooter in line B. The pass server alternates passing to lines A and B. Shooters have to quick hit and then run past the cone before the next shot. Award your group 1 point for each goal. The first team to score 10 goals is the winner. Change lines and play again. Repeat the shooting drill on the left side of the circle. The pass server stands on the left outside area, approximately 14 yards (13 m) from the backline.

To Increase Difficulty

- Increase the number of required goals.
- Use a goalkeeper.
- Use a reverse quick hit when receiving a pass from your left.

To Decrease Difficulty

- Decrease the number of required goals.
- Reduce the pass distance.

Success Check

- Move or cut into the line of the passed ball.
- Keep your knees bent and maintain a low center of gravity.
- Change your grip to a clip grip.
- Maintain your balance on the power points of your feet. Feet remain shoulder-width apart.
- Ball is in line with your front foot when hit.
- Follow the shot forward.

Score Your Success

Win three or four games = 5 points

Win two games = 3 points

Win one game = 1 point

Your score ___

DEFLECTION SHOT

With a deflection shot, the path of the passed ball is altered without the shooter actually stopping or trapping the ball. The shooter's objective is to merely touch the ball. Often attack players inside the shooting circle are closely marked by defenders. This means that shooters need to position themselves wide in order to expand the cage and execute one-touch shots to deflect the ball into the opponent's goal. Sometimes referred to as the redirection shot or tip, the deflection is effective on hard, fast surfaces. It is used to redirect centering passes, free hits into the circle, and wide shots to the wideout areas in the shooting circle (see figure 5.1, page 96). Learning to execute the deflection shot will promote confidence in many goal-scoring situations.

To execute the deflection shot or tip (figure 5.3), firmly grip your stick using the shake-hands grip, left hand below the left knee. Artificial turf is a smooth playing surface that allows you to angle your stick or to lay it horizontally to deflect passes toward the goal. The horizontal stick dropped to the ground offers the largest possible surface area to touch the ball. The deflection shot can also be executed using a more vertical stick. Use the head of your stick to jab firmly into the line of the approaching ball. Whether using a horizontal or vertical stick, keep your head in line with your stick and the ball. The critical element of this challenging shot is to correctly angle the left side of the stick so that when the lower half of the ball hits your stick, the ball takes a new path to the opponent's goal. To execute a successful deflection shot, place your stick inside the shooting angles to the goalposts. Do not swing your stick. Always firmly grip your stick and guide the ball by establishing the correct stick angle with the stick face. Aim for the near post because your deflection shot has less distance to travel.

Misstep

Ball hits your feet when you try to redirect the ball.

Correction

Your stick and hands are too close to your feet. Extend your arms to place the stick in front of your feet. Keep your eyes focused on the lower half of the ball to better judge the speed and distance of the rolling ball. Keep the left hand below the left knee.

Figure 5.3 — Deflection Shot

1. Be aware of the goal and the opponent
2. Use a short steps and quick footwork
3. Lead foot and shoulder point toward the target
4. Use a firm shake-hands grip
5. Stick is moving to a horizontal position
6. Angle the stick face toward the target and the approaching ball
7. Block the ball's path
8. Body is balanced

Misstep

The height of the deflection shot is too low.

Correction

Strike the lower half of the ball with face of open stick, which will deflect the ball upward.

Misstep

You have poor accuracy with your deflection shot.

Correction

Front shoulder and foot point toward the target and your stick is placed at an angle to the target.

Much practice is needed to execute accurate deflections on both the forehand and reverse. The deflection is a scoring weapon that requires excellent timing and a great deal of hand-eye coordination, but it is an effective way to score.

DIVE SHOT

The sight of a shooter diving fully extended in order to shoot the ball is one of the most exciting and acrobatic scenes in field hockey. Although shooting while on your feet is more desirable because you are better prepared for rebounds, diving is useful to get to balls that are wide and out of your reach. The dive shot is always a surprise move to a goalkeeper or to a closely marking defender because it provides only a fraction of a second to react. Players who play regularly on watered artificial surfaces enjoy performing an advanced form of a deflection called the *dive* or slide shot (figure 5.4). Most players find the dive shot more difficult to execute than any other shot because it requires precise timing as well as correct technique. Sliding your body in a horizontal position—leading with your head—along a watered surface will give you a greater reach to the ball. The watered artificial surface protects your body from injury. Dive shots can be executed on the forehand or reverse stick and are primarily used by a player positioned near the goalposts. Goal-post positioning is also called wideout play. The tactic is to widen the goal by taking a position outside the posts so that you can deflect or tip a wide shot.

The diving mechanics are similar to those used by a base runner in baseball who sprints and dives to reach the base with his hands. The primary difference in hockey is that you reach for the ball with your stick face correctly angled to deflect the ball toward the goal. The initial diving movement begins with short, quick running strides or from a ready position with eyes focused on the rolling ball. Focus on the lower half of the ball to judge the distance and speed of the ball. As with the deflection shot, hold your stick firmly in a shake-hands or receiving grip. Judging the ball speed and distance from your stick's reach will help you decide when to begin the dive. Coordinate the movement of your legs and upper body to vault toward the space when you can intercept the approaching ball with your stick. Move the foot nearest the ball in the direction you will dive. Push off that foot to begin the dive; for example, push off your right foot when diving to your right. Your opposite leg follows and generates additional momentum. Extend your arms and correctly angle your stick toward the ball, maintaining your hands, stick, eye, and head position to the ball. Slide on your side along the ground. To deflect the ball to the goal, angle your stick toward the target and keep your wrists firm.

Figure 5.4   Dive or Slide Shot

PREPARATION

1. Be aware of the goal and the opponent
2. Use short running steps and quick foot-work
3. Square your shoulders to the oncoming ball
4. Lead foot and shoulder point toward the target
5. Use a firm shake-hands grip on the stick
6. Angle the stick's face toward the target and the approaching ball
7. Watch the lower half of the rolling ball
8. Assume a slightly crouched position, with your weight balanced and centered
9. Decide where to start your dive and intercept the ball

a

EXECUTION

1. Step sideways with the foot nearest the ball
2. Dive toward space to intercept the ball
3. Thrust your opposite leg in the dive direction, with the side of your body parallel to ground
4. With firm wrists, extend your arms and horizontal stick toward the goal
5. Watch the lower half of the ball and watch the ball deflect from stick
6. Slide on your side along the ground

b

FOLLOW-THROUGH

1. Momentum moves forward with contact
2. Jump to your feet
3. Return to a ready position in case of a rebound

c

Misstep

Your dive shot lacks power and accuracy.

Correction

You mistimed your dive and failed to keep your stick firm as the ball struck your stick. Strike the ball with the flat surface of your stick.

Misstep

You get the wind knocked out of you as you hit the ground after diving for the ball.

Correction

You may be so intent on diving to the space to deflect the ball that you forget to cushion your fall to the ground. Extend your stick and arms forward and downward as you slide on your side along the ground. This stick and arm movement not only adds momentum to your dive but it also enables you to cushion the side of your body.

When diving with a reverse stick on the left side, use the same mechanics, but change your grip. To reach as far as possible, grip with only your left hand in a firm reverse grip. To deflect the ball upward and forward to the goal, always strike the lower half of the ball with a slightly open stick.

BACKHAND SHOT

Good shooters learn to execute shots despite the restrictions of time and space. Sometimes the shooter must find a way to strike a ball when a defender has a close marking position between her and the goal. The backhand or low reverse shot enables the AR1 shooter to turn either way with her back to the defender. For the backhand shot, the player strikes the ball on the reverse side using the left-facing side or edge of the horizontal stick (figure 5.5). To use the edge, the stick must be positioned horizontally on the ground with the flat side facing the sky. For a successful backhand shot that travels accurately along the ground, lower your left hand to place the handle of your stick on the ground in order to expose a large surface edge to the ball.

Misstep

Your backhand shot lacks power and is unexpectedly lifted.

Correction

Reach for the ball. Strike the ball approximately 26 inches (66 cm) out in front of your right foot and about 4 inches (10 cm) above the hook of your stick.

To execute the backhand shot, square your shoulders to the ball and maintain a low, crouched position with your weight on the power points of your feet. Your lead or front right shoulder points toward your target. To allow for a quicker and more controlled shot, bring your hands together halfway down your stick in order to coordinate the backswing and the downswing. Keep your eyes focused on the lower half of the ball as you position your horizontal stick along the ground. Using a short backswing, with the flat side of your stick facing up and parallel to the ground, strike the lower half of the ball. Keep the edge of your stick shaft approximately 3 to 4 inches (7.5 to 10 cm) from the hook of the stick. Return to a ready position for rebounds. When first learning to execute the backhand shot, start by striking stationary balls while balanced on your left knee.

Misstep

You chop down on the ball and fail to make contact.

Correction

Swing on a gradual angle if you are unable to slide your stick along the ground. Avoid moving your stick on a sharp angle down toward the ball.

Figure 5.5   Backhand Shot

PREPARATION

1. Be aware of the goal and the opponent
2. Use short, quick footwork
3. Square your shoulders to the ball, which is rolling away
4. Front shoulder points toward the target
5. Use a shake-hands grip
6. Assume a crouched position
7. Weight is on the power points of your feet
8. Eyes are focused on the lower half of the ball

a

EXECUTION

1. Turn the stick so that the round side faces the ground and so that the hook points toward the target
2. Position your right foot about 26 inches (66 cm) behind the ball
3. Bend your knees so that you are in a low position, with your right quad parallel to ground
4. Slide your hands together
5. Use a short, low backswing
6. Align your right shoulder with the target
7. Strike the ball 4 inches (10 cm) from the stick's hook
8. Keep your head down at impact

b

FOLLOW-THROUGH

1. Transfer your weight through your right leg
2. Knees remain relaxed and bent
3. Keep your head down and watch the ball leave the stick
4. Arms and stick finish low, in line with the target
5. Return to a ready position

c

CHIP SHOT

Experienced shooters realize that the hit and the quick hit are prerequisites to the powerful aerial hit—the chip shot. The chip shot (figure 5.6) is an advanced shooting technique used to beat a low-sliding goalkeeper or to raise the ball toward the upper part of the goal. By hitting the ball with a partially opened stick head from either the forehand or reverse side, you can loft the ball off the ground to various heights and distances. A chip shot should be used only after you learn to control it. Remember, if the ball misses the goal high and wide, there are no follow-up chances to score.

Chip shot execution is similar to the quick hit, except that the backswing is shorter and the stick face is slightly open at contact. The ball is con-trolled a little farther in front of the lead foot. To hit with an open stick face, turn your stick head slightly clockwise to no more than a 2 o'clock position, or to the desired elevation of the intended shot. Slide your hands together on your stick as you begin the backswing. Transfer your weight to the back leg. Keep your eyes focused on the lower half of the ball. Lower your right shoulder and transfer your weight to your front leg and hip on the downswing. While your hands remain behind the ball at impact, see your open stick strike the lower half of the ball. The follow-through of your stick will determine the accuracy of your shot. To hit a chip shot that has maximum backspin for greater distance and elevation, strike the ball and the ground behind the ball.

Figure 5.6 **Chip Shot**

PREPARATION

1. Prepare the ball beyond your front foot
2. Head is down and over the ball
3. Knees are bent, with a crouched body
4. Your lead shoulder points toward the target
5. Begin the backswing with your hands together

a

(continued)

(continued)

b

c

EXECUTION

1. Open the stick face
2. Begin the downswing with your left arm nearly straight and your right elbow tucked
3. Transfer your weight to your front leg and hip on the downswing
4. Hands are behind the ball at impact
5. Strike the lower half of the ball with an open stick

FOLLOW-THROUGH

1. Fluidly transfer your weight through your front foot
2. Knees remain relaxed and bent
3. Keep your head down and watch the ball leave the stick
4. Arms and stick finish in line with the target

Misstep

Chip shot is wild and uncontrolled.

Correction

A complete follow-through is necessary for the chip shot. Always finish in line to your target. Open the stick face before starting the backswing and swing your arms freely and in unison away from your body. Avoid wrist movement.

Misstep

Your chip shot goes high over the goal.

Correction

Your stick face is open too much. Keep the left facing of the stick in a 1 o'clock position at impact.

CHOP OR SQUEEZE SHOT

Another shot that takes repeated practice to correctly perform is the chop or squeeze shot (figure 5.7). Sometimes a passed ball or a goalkeeper rebound will roll behind your body and control box. Finding a way to get the shot on goal quickly to surprise the defender is your prime objective. The squeeze shot is also a raised shot but one that is deceptive because it resembles a quick hit at the start. The act of squeezing the ball into the turf with your stick to produce a raised ball can be very challenging. However, the squeeze shot is a quick and illusory means of scoring. Like all raised shots, learn to control the accuracy before you achieve power. In order to develop a comfortable feel for the proper chop or squeeze shot technique, start with a stationary ball. Progress to a walk and then a jog so that you eventually shoot at goal with force and precision. Play the ball approximately 24 inches (61 cm) behind the back foot while your body weight is on the back foot. Use a clip grip and perform a short backswing. While remaining on your back foot, begin the downswing by chopping down on the upper back of the ball. The ball is literally squeezed into the turf. Because your hands are well ahead of the ball at impact, there is little if any follow-through with the stick.

Figure 5.7 Chop or Squeeze Shot

PREPARATION

1. Lead shoulder points toward the target
2. Prepare the ball behind your back foot (right foot with forehand chop shot)
3. Knees are bent, your body crouched, and your weight on your back foot

a

EXECUTION

1. Slide your hands together and down on the stick (quick-hit grip)
2. Use a short backswing
3. Start the downswing with a closed stick face
4. Keep your body weight on your back foot
5. Hands should be beyond the ball at impact
6. Strike the upper back of the ball in order to squeeze it into ground

b

FOLLOW-THROUGH

1. Keep your head down and watch the ball leave the stick
2. Arms and stick finish in a short, abrupt line toward the target
3. Transfer your weight to your front leg

c

Misstep

Chop shot does not go into air.

Correction

Swing from above and slightly behind the ball. Your stick head must be closed when you strike the upper back of the ball and squeeze it into the ground.

Misstep

The ball is raised too low.

Correction

Position ball behind back foot with body weight on back foot at impact.

DRAG FLICK SHOT

The drag flick is a powerful push shot lifted into the air. On artificial turf, it is possible to step beyond the ball and to drag the ball a small distance before executing the drag flick. This can produce extra pace for shooting at goal. The drag flick is an advanced shot that is most often used as a shot on goal when taking a penalty corner shot. Because of the speed at which the ball is thrown from the stick, the drag flick requires coordinated footwork and exceptional timing with the stick and ball.

The differences between the drag flick (figure 5.8) and the regular flick (see step 2, figure 2.8, page 50) are that, with the drag flick, the ball starts near the back foot and remains on the stick longer; the cross-behind step is used to generate momentum in limited space; and the whip action created by pulling the left hand back accelerates the stick head forward just before the ball release. Use a separated shake-hands grip and position yourself in front of or parallel to the line of the ball. The parallel position is better for weight transfer during the approach, which is required in order to drag the ball from your back foot so that you can whip or throw it powerfully through the air. With your knees bent, drop your right shoulder and push the lower part of your stick face (12 inches, or 30.5 cm, above the hook) under the lower half of the ball. Prepare to carry the ball down the stick face as you throw the ball into the air. The ball literally rolls down the left face of the stick toward the hook. Begin lifting the stick and release the ball the moment the ball reaches the end of the stick label. The ball remains on the stick as you generate momentum with your cross-behind footwork and hip rotation in order to forcefully whip your stick from behind your right foot to your left hip. Both arms exert power (left hand pulls back and right hand pushes forward) as you transfer body weight from your right leg to your left leg.

Misstep

Drag flick shot is too low.

Correction

With bent knees before the release point, slightly open the stick face when the ball rolls to the end of the label area. Whip the stick and lift the ball upward. The follow-through is high.

Figure 5.8 | **Drag Flick Shot**

PREPARATION

1. Know where the target is without looking
2. Knees are bent in a balanced stance with your right foot forward
3. Use a separated shake-hands grip
4. Ball should be 2 to 3 yards (1.8 to 2.8 m) out in front, but parallel to, the body
5. Focus on the lower half of the ball

a

EXECUTION

1. Take a short step forward with your left foot
2. Drop your right shoulder and transfer your weight forward
3. Take a short cross-behind step with your right foot
4. Place the stick label next to the bottom half of ball
5. Bend your knees, and take a short step on your left foot
6. Rotate your hips as your left hand pulls the stick forward and the ball rolls down along stick label
7. Time the lift through the lower half of the ball when the ball rolls to end of label
8. Adjust the stick angle for the ball's height off the ground
9. Use both of your arms to whip the stick
10. Left hand pulls the stick back while your right hand moves the stick forward to throw the ball

b

FOLLOW-THROUGH

1. Generate momentum through the ball with your hips and shoulders
2. Transfer your weight through your front leg
3. Finish with the stick's toe up and your arms extended to target
4. Return to a ready position

c

Misstep

Drop flick shot is inaccurate.

Correction

Point the left shoulder (forehand) to the target, and follow the line of the ball toward the target with your stick toe.

Misstep

Your shot is too short and lacks power.

Correction

Keep your head over the ball as you generate the lifting action with very bent knees. A coordinated hip rotation (right to left hip) that is timed with the throw will generate speed.

Keep your body low until the ball leaves your stick. On the follow-through, the right hand controls direction. The speed of the drag flick is produced by hip rotation and by throwing or whipping the ball with an open stick blade to left stick-blade rotation. This whiplike action imparts rapid side topspin to the ball. If you want the ball to travel at knee height, keep your hips low during the rotation and close the stick label at the release. Follow through with the right hand in a knee-high position. If a high drag flick is desired, slightly open the stick face at the moment of release and the path of the stick will determine the trajectory of the ball.

SCOOP OR LOB SHOT

To lift the ball high over relatively short distances, the scoop or lob shot is an effective skill. A scoop shot is used to get by a goalkeeper who has moved out of the net and toward the top of the circle. The ball is lobbed over the goalkeeper's head and dropped into the space behind him. Although this type of shot can be difficult to execute, it can greatly increase your team's chance of scoring.

To execute the scoop shot (figure 5.9), face your target with your right foot and right shoulder forward. Your hands are apart on the stick. Your right foot is alongside and just behind the line of the ball. The right hand grips the stick so that the stick can be lifted through the ball. Get your head over the ball and dip your left hand so that the stick handle drops as you move the stick under the ball to lift it.

Figure 5.9   Scoop or Lob Shot

PREPARATION

1. Select the target without looking at it
2. Right shoulder and foot are forward
3. Use a separated shake-hands grip
4. Place your right foot alongside and behind the ball's line
5. Head is over the ball
6. Adjust your grip so that your right hand is lower on the stick

a

b   *c*

EXECUTION

1. Place the stick head under the lower half of the ball
2. Dip your left hand to lower the stick handle
3. Use your left leg to drive your body weight forward
4. Use your right hand to lift the ball toward the goal

FOLLOW-THROUGH

1. Eyes stay focused on the lower half of the ball
2. Arms swing forward and upward to create a high trajectory
3. Finish with the stick face toward the target
4. Return to a ready position

Misstep

Scoop shot is too low.

Correction

Dip your left hand and scoop with your right hand to lob the ball.

Misstep

The scoop shot does not elevate the ball early enough to beat the goalkeeper.

Correction

Position the ball in front of you. Lower the stick handle with your left hand and use your right hand to lift the stick and ball upward.

Shooting Drill 2. *Banana Cuts and Shooting*

Place three passers outside the shooting circle at the following areas: passer 1 is in the center of the field, 35 yards (32 m) from the goal; passer 2 is 15 yards (14 m) to passer 1's right; passer 3 is outside the 5-meter circle on the right, nearly 16 yards (14.5 m) from the backline. Set two cones opposite the 5-yard (4.5 m) defense marks, approximately 1 yard (0.9 m) outside the top of the shooting circle. A shooter in the center of the 5-meter circle makes a banana cut (her running path curves like the shape of a banana) away from the ball and around the cone on the left, toward the penalty stroke spot, to receive a pass from passer 3. Passer 1 starts with the ball and passes to passer 2, who passes to passer 3. The shooter begins her cut while the ball is traveling to passer 3. Award the shooter 1 point for each accurate shot. Deduct a point from the shooter for each shot that goes wide of the goal cage. Complete a round of 10 balls before rotating positions.

To Increase Difficulty

- Increase the number of repetitions.
- Use a goalkeeper or reduce the size of the goal.
- Add a defender.
- Make a banana cut to the right and the inside to left.

To Decrease Difficulty

- Increase the size of the goal.
- Permit three-touch shooting.

Success Check

- Your lead shoulder points toward the target.
- Use short, quick steps on the power points of your feet.

- Stick remains still, with your left hand below your knee.
- Keep your head in line with the ball's path.
- Watch the ball come to the stick when performing one- or two-touch shooting.
- Get ready for the rebound.

Score Your Success

8 to 10 points = 5 points

6 or 7 points = 3 points

4 or 5 points = 1 point

Fewer than 4 points = 0 points

Your score ___

Shooting Drill 3. *Shooting Game*

Divide into teams of four. Use the entire half of the field. Set boards 5 yards (4.5 m) outside the 5-meter circles on both sides of the field, approximately 16 yards (14.5 m) from the backline. Place a cone 5 yards from the sideline at the 16-yard marks on both sides of the field. Place additional cones 5 yards (4.5 m) from the sideline, at the 40-yard areas on the left and right sides of the field. In the center of the field at the 40-yard area, place a cone opposite the left defense mark and a cone opposite the right defense mark. One player (the shooter) from each team starts in the shooting circle. Team A passes on the left side of the field and team B passes on the right side. This is a passing race to determine which team will become the attack team which will then run toward the goal and score. Player 1 from each team takes a ball and gets in position at the board on his or her side of the field. Player 2 from each team takes position at the 40-yard sideline cone. Player 3 sets up at the 40-yard cone in the center. Player 1 passes off the boards, receives the ball, and moves past the first cone to pass to player 2. Player 2 receives the ball and passes it to player 3. The first player 3 to receive

the ball moves to the goal as part of the attacking team. The other player 3 becomes the defender. The shooter on the defending team drops out of play. The attacking team has a 2 v 1 if movement and passes are quick. Rotate after each scoring attempt so that each player gets a turn in the circle—the shooter becomes player 1, player 1 becomes player 2, player 2 becomes player 3, and player 3 becomes the shooter. The team that scores the most goals in five minutes wins the game. Teams change sides of the field and play another game.

To Increase Difficulty

- Use a goalkeeper or reduce the size of the goal.
- Place two players from each team in the circle.
- Permit only one- or two-touch shooting.
- Increase the amount of playing time.

To Decrease Difficulty

- Permit three-touch shooting.

Success Check

- Receive the ball with one touch.
- Lead shoulder points toward the target.
- Use short, quick steps on the power points of your feet.
- Select the appropriate shooting technique.
- Shoot accurately with a quick release.
- Get ready for the rebound.

Score Your Success

Two wins = 5 points

One win = 3 points

Zero wins = 0 points

Your score ____

Shooting Drill 4. *4 v 2 Shooting Game*

Divide into teams of at least four players. Use the shooting circle and the entire width of the field to the nearest 25-yard line. Use cones to create two 5-yard (4.5 m) goals near each sideline. The coach stands in the center of the 25-yard line with a stack of balls. Four attack players position themselves in the circle at the wideout areas, at the top of the circle, and at different depth and width levels from one another. Two players are designated defenders in the shooting circle. The coach puts the ball into play by passing to one of the attack players. The attack team receives 1 point for each score. The defense receives 2 points for hitting the ball through the 5-yard targets at the 25-yard line. Play six minutes and then change teams. Total the team's score after two six-minute periods. The highest score wins the game.

To Increase Difficulty

- Use a goalkeeper or reduce the size of the goal.
- Place three defenders in the circle.
- Permit only one- or two-touch shooting.
- Do not permit excessive dribbling.
- Play 5 v 3, 6 v 4, etc.

To Decrease Difficulty

- Permit three-touch shooting.
- Reduce the number of players to 3 v 1.
- Do not allow defenders to tackle. They can only intercept passed balls.

Success Check

- Move away from the defender by using short, quick steps on the power points of your feet.
- Maintain 7 yards (6.5 m) spacing from teammates.
- Receive the ball with one touch.
- Your lead shoulder points toward the target.
- Select an appropriate shooting technique.
- Shoot accurately with a quick release.
- Get ready for the rebound.

Score Your Success

Win the game = 5 points

Lose the game = 0 points

Your score ____

Shooting Drill 5. *4 v 2 to Goal With Replay Balls*

Divide into two teams of at least seven players each. Use the shooting circle and the field area to the 40-yard line. Use cones to set two 5-yard (4.5 m) goals near each sideline. Determine which team will defend first and then designate two defenders to take positions in the shooting circle with the goalkeeper. From the attack team, select three passers and four attack players. With a stack of balls, passer 1 stands in the center, outside the 25-yard line. The replay balls come from passer 2, who takes a position at the long hit mark on the right side, and passer 3, who is at the long hit mark on the left. Four attack players take positions anywhere inside the 25-yard line to the goal. Passer 1 starts play by passing to one of the four attack players. The four attack players create a scoring opportunity with the first ball. When the attack team scores, loses possession, or fouls, passer 2 sends in a replay ball. When the second ball is finished, a replay ball comes from passer 3. Award 2 points for a goal. If the defense fouls in the circle, award the attack team 1 point for drawing a penalty corner. If the defense fouls outside the shooting circle, award a free hit to the attack team at the spot of the foul. The starting attack team stays in the drill for two rounds of replay balls before substitutions. Play for six minutes on attack and then switch to defense for the next six-minute period. The team with the most attack points wins the game.

To Increase Difficulty

- Place three defenders in the circle.
- Permit only one- or two-touch shooting.
- Play 5 v 3, 6 v 4, etc.

To Decrease Difficulty

- Play without a goalkeeper.
- Permit three-touch shooting.

Success Check

- Move away from the defender by using short, quick steps on the power points of your feet.
- Receive the ball with one touch.
- Your lead shoulder points toward the target.
- A pass from a player A teammate in the circle should result in an immediate shot on goal.
- Select an appropriate shooting technique.
- Shoot accurately with a quick release.
- Get ready for the rebound.

Score Your Success

Win the game = 5 points
Lose the game = 0 points
Your score ___

Shooting Drill 6. *Three-Goal Shooting*

Divide into two equal teams of at least six players each. Set three goal cages and goalkeepers in the shooting circle in the following areas: one cage behind the regular goal line; one cage on the outer edge of the 5-meter circle on the left side, opposite the penalty corner line; one cage on the outer edge of the 5-meter circle on the right side, opposite the penalty corner line. Each team puts three players inside the shooting circle. The remaining players from each team separate and line up behind the backline, at each of the penalty corner lines, team A on the left and team B on the right, with a stack of balls. Players may shoot at any goal cage except at the cage they are initially defending. Once the attack takes the ball away from this cage, though, players may shoot to score. Team A puts the first ball in play while team B defends. If team A scores, team A gets another ball. The 5-meter circle is out of bounds. When the ball travels out of play, team B puts a ball into play from the team B line. The attack players use all types of shots from various positions. Play the best of three five-minute periods to determine the winner.

To Increase Difficulty

- Play longer or for more periods.
- Permit only one- or two-touch passing and shooting.
- Play 4 v 4.

To Decrease Difficulty

- Play without goalkeepers.
- Play for less time or for fewer periods.
- Play 2 v 2.

Success Check

- Move away from the defender by using short, quick steps on the power points of your feet.
- Receive the ball with one touch.
- Be prepared to shoot or to make a pass that leads to a shot.
- Your lead shoulder points toward the target.
- Select an appropriate shooting technique.

- Shoot accurately with a quick release.
- Make a complete follow-through.
- Get ready for the rebound.

Score Your Success

Win two five-minute periods = 5 points

Lose two five-minute periods = 0 points

Your score ___

Shooting Drill 7. 3 v 2 Shooting at Either Goal

Divide into two equal teams of at least five players plus a goalkeeper for each team. Use the entire shooting circle to the 25-yard line (25 yards long by 35 yards wide, or 23 m by 32 m). Center another goal cage behind the 25-yard line opposite the shooting-circle cage. Use the width of the shooting circle as the sideline boundaries. Three players from team A form the attack team against two defenders from team B. Designate two passers at each backline, 10 yards (9 m) to the right of the goal cage. Passes always go to the attack team. The three attack players may shoot at either goal. Start the 3 v 2 game at one end with a pass from the backline passer to an attack team player. When this ball is finished—when the ball goes out of bounds, the shot goes wide, or the attack team fouls—the attack team goes to the other backline to receive a pass. Play a five-minute period and switch roles for the next five-minute period. Attack players use all types of shots from various positions. A goal scored by the attack team who has more players than the defense is worth 1 point. A goal scored by the defense team that has fewer players than the offense is worth 2 points. After two five-minute periods, total your score. The team with the most points wins.

To Increase Difficulty

- Player longer or for more periods.
- Permit only one- or two-touch passing and shooting.
- Do not permit dribbling.
- Increase the size of the field and play 4 v 3.

To Decrease Difficulty

- Play without goalkeepers.
- Play for less time or for fewer periods.
- Play 2 v 1.
- Do not allow defenders to tackle. Defenders may only intercept passed balls.

Success Check

- Create space and move away from defenders by using angled cuts.
- Use short, quick steps on the power points of your feet.
- Receive the ball with one touch.
- Prepare to shoot after the first touch or to make a pass that leads to a shot.
- Your lead shoulder points toward the target.
- Select an appropriate shooting technique.
- Shoot accurately with a quick release.
- Make a complete follow-through
- Get ready for the rebound.

Score Your Success

Win two five-minute periods = 5 points

Lose two five-minute periods = 0 points

Your score ___

SUCCESS SUMMARY OF SHOOTING

The ultimate goal of every field hockey team is to play as a unit in order to score more goals than the opposition. To achieve this goal, each team member must have solid shooting skills. In every game, a player will have a chance to win a game. For this reason alone, every player, regardless of her playing position, should be able to finish an attack by scoring. Beginners should start by shooting without the pressures of restricted time, opponents, or space limitations, which will allow them to better concentrate on executing the correct skill. Develop your ability to shoot first with accuracy and then with power. As your technical skills improve, progress to more game-related training by adding the pressures of time and opponents, and begin to restrict space. Eventually you will be able to execute shooting skills in a full-sided game.

Your objective when executing shooting techniques from either side of your body is to shoot with accuracy and with a quick release. If you can't, you probably will not score many goals. Remember that shots must be accurate so that the goalkeeper has to play the ball. More than 80 percent of all scores result from rebounds off the goalkeeper who was forced to block an accurate shot.

Place the highest value on receiving the ball well (step 2) because you cannot shoot what you do not have. The initial trap of the ball, with quality footwork and balance, will place the ball in the best position for your next skill. Stay alert and get in the best position to create scoring chances.

Shooting Drills

1. Quick Hit and Continue Forward	___ out of 5
2. Banana Cuts and Shooting	___ out of 5
3. Shooting Game	___ out of 5
4. 4 v 2 Shooting Game	___ out of 5
5. 4 v 2 to Goal With Replay Balls	___ out of 5
6. Three-Goal Shooting	___ out of 5
7. 3 v 2 Shooting at Either Goal	___ out of 5
Total	___ *out of 35*

A combined score of 28 points or more indicates that you have sufficiently mastered shooting skills and that you are prepared to move on to step 6. A score in the range of 21 to 27 is considered adequate. Move on to step 6 after you have reviewed and practiced the shooting techniques one more time. If you scored fewer than 21 points, you need to rehearse shooting skills. Review all the material in step 5 and practice each drill at least one more time in order to improve your overall score before moving on to step 6.

Goalkeeping

The goalkeeper needs as much mental, physical, technical, and tactical preparation as the field player. A goalkeeper must be able to block or save all types of shots, shots that can travel at speeds in excess of 90 miles per hour. At times the goalkeeper has to dive through the air or on the ground. She may even have to stop a one-on-one breakaway. To save a shot is only half the job. The goalkeeper must also clear the ball safely and skillfully. Teammates must know that if a deep pass penetrates the defense, the goalkeeper will clear or control the ball with coordination and purpose.

Goalkeeping requires a special type of athlete. The goalkeeper uses protective, lightweight equipment similar to gear worn by ice hockey goaltenders. A goalkeeper in full gear is the only player allowed to use her hands, feet, and body to play the ball, and she may do so only within her team's own shooting circle. Comfortable protective equipment prevents injuries and instills confidence. Goalkeepers who rely on tremendous reflexes, outstanding agility, and an enormous desire to perform must also be totally protected. Because goalkeeping equipment can be expensive, a goalkeeper should take good care of it.

The goalkeeper who has excellent physical and mental qualities inspires confidence in her team. Physically, she should develop the ability to use either foot, her hands, or the stick to block and clear the ball. This requires a high degree of coordination. Strength, flexibility, and stamina promote good balance, solid footwork, and quick reflexes. Mentally a goalkeeper should have courage and be reliable and determined. It is a primary require-

ment for the goalkeeper to remain aggressively calm and to make decisions so that she can play the ball well while under pressure.

Goalkeeping requires a player to completely understand defensive roles. Within the defense, the goalkeeper plays a special position with the foremost responsibility of protecting the goal. A good goalkeeper must develop the ability to read the game because she is in the best position to view the entire defensive plan. She must combine defense role 1's engage-and-give technique with sliding stack tackles in order to handle the one-on-one breakaway. Understanding defensive roles will help her lead her team and protect the goal.

As the last player who can prevent the ball from going into the goal, the goalkeeper must use skills that are different from those used by the field players. Players younger than 12 years old should not specialize in the goalkeeper position but instead should spend time both in the goal and in the field. Although a team usually designates one or two players specifically as goalkeepers, all players should understand goalkeeping skills. Goalkeeping techniques include the basic stance (ready position), blocks or saves of ground and aerial shots (which are shot directly at or to the sides of the goalkeeper), and clearing methods. To clear the ball, the goalkeeper may use kicking techniques, a stick pass, or her glove. (The glove clear is a recent rule interpretation. While on the ground, the goalkeeper may use her glove to clear a ball if she is under pressure from a nearby opponent.)

The aim of every defense is to prevent a goal. Good positioning and timing are essential. Players who often play in the defending third of the field are expected to execute defensive roles in order to prevent attackers from penetrating. It is here that defensive players and the goalkeeper work together to block the space to the goal.

The keys of goalkeeping include the following: understanding the roles of defense, positioning in the space between the ball and the center of the goal line, having good balance and footwork, using good save-clear-recovery techniques, and maintaining a determined concentration in order to execute goalkeeping skills confidently and correctly. Understanding the roles of defense will allow you to control situations and influence the way AR1 shoots. The goalkeeper works with her teammates to force AR1 to shoot from as far away from the goal as possible and from as narrow an angle as possible. Forcing the opponent to make mistakes by hurrying her shot allows the goalkeeper to handle a weaker shot. The goalkeeper who can direct his teammates to force a delayed shot will gain more time to position himself properly, narrow the shooting angle, and make the save. A successful goalkeeper will learn to anticipate where shots are going to be made and get in position to save them.

A good goalkeeper uses many specialized goalkeeping techniques. The technique used by the goalkeeper depends on three factors: the speed of the shot, the position of the opponent, and the playing surface. The goalkeeper must choose between the block and clear (a two-touch save) and the one-time clear that is often used on artificial surfaces at higher levels of play. The one-time clear, or redirection clear, is a save-and-clear-all-in-one-touch movement. Since more goals are scored from rebounds off the goalkeeper than from direct shots, it is essential that the goalkeeper control and clear the rebound using one-time techniques that are accurate and powerful. Goalkeeping techniques that require mobility, quick reflexes, and balance are for higher skill levels and can only be achieved with top physical conditioning and proper technical training. Technique development determines success in goaltending.

GOALKEEPER STANCE

When an opponent has the ball within shooting distance, assume the balanced goalkeeper stance, or ready position (figure 6.1). From the ready position, you will be able to move quickly in any direction by getting in front of the ball. Balance is crucial. All skills start from the classic position of readiness, with a return to the ready position after the clear. Align the head with the shot in order to establish balance. Subsequently control your head position, whether set or moving.

To get in the ready position, square your shoulders to the ball with your feet approximately shoulder-width apart. The closer the ball, the less space there should be between the leg guards. Keep your head and upper body forward and steady in front of the ball. Center your weight forward on the power points of your feet, heels slightly off the ground. Knees remain bent, back slightly crouched. Remain relaxed, yet alert. Keep your chin slightly forward of your knees and your knees forward of your toes. Both arms are alongside the body, hands forward of your knees. The palm of the left hand is open and the pinkie finger touches the outside of the left knee. Your right hand holds your stick midway down the shaft, making it an extension of your right arm. Keep your head steady and your eyes focused on the lower half of the ball.

Figure 6.1 Goalkeeper's ready position.

COVERING THE ANGLES

Although defense of the circle area is a group responsibility, goalkeepers often are beaten because they are out of position. The circle is the goalkeeper's boundary and base. The goalkeeper is a vital part of a cover system. She is the last line of defense. To play the goalkeeper position successfully, you must know where to be in ready position to save a direct shot at goal. Shots at goal come from a variety of angles and distances, from zero to 16 yards (14.5 m), from 90 degrees at the top of the shooting circle to zero degrees along the backline. The aim of the goalkeeper is to give AR1 the smallest possible view of the goal. The correct positioning of the goalkeeper to cover these shots is referred to as "covering the angles."

Draw an imaginary line from the ball through the goalkeeper's legs and to the center of the goal line (figure 6.2). The goalkeeper must narrow the scoring angle available to AR1. As AR1 approaches the attack area, move using quick, short steps to maintain a ready position between the ball and the center of the goal. When the ball is passed, take a new position relative to the ball and the center of the goal.

Positioning is essential to good goalkeeping. Always know where you are in relation to the goal so that you can discriminate between simple and difficult shots. Experienced goalkeepers who are familiar with the angles do not have to make spectacular saves because they know where to get in position. The well-positioned goalkeeper will also know whether a shot is on goal or wide without having to look around and behind herself. Referring to the zones of the circle (figure 6.3) will assist in positioning yourself to cover angles to the goal. Generally, when the ball is in the circle, the goalkeeper positions herself in the space inside the goalposts in either the arc (U-space) or the V-space. If the ball is upfield, the goalkeeper organizes her defensive back players from the stroke spot or higher. Reference points to use when repositioning include the penalty-stroke spot, the opposite goal cage, the flat line at the top of the circle, the goalposts, and the 25-yard line to the sideline. When the ball is near the backline in zone 3 (4 yards, or 3.5 m, from the backline), keep your eyes on the ball and search for the goalpost with your stick on the right side and your glove on the left. Take a position against the goalpost nearest the ball and make sure there is no gap between your legs and between your body and the post. Because of the narrow angle, no shot from this zone should be successful. When the ball moves into zone 2, use quick shuffle steps to stay in line with the ball and the center of the goal. The shooting angle is greater than in zone 3, so you must move forward from the goal line to cover more of the goal. In zone 1, AR1 has maximum view of the goal. To defend this angle, position yourself at the extremity of the arc, from one goalpost to the other. To cover the angles, develop speed of movement around a 3- or 4-yard (2.8 or 3.5 m) arc in front of the goal and between the posts.

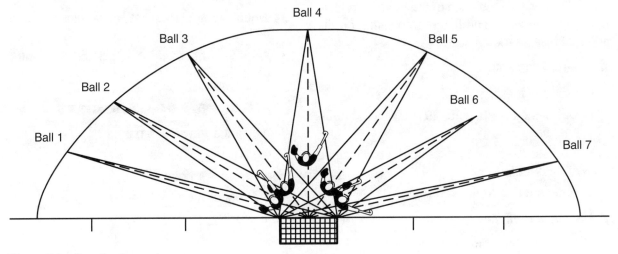

Figure 6.2 Covering the angles.

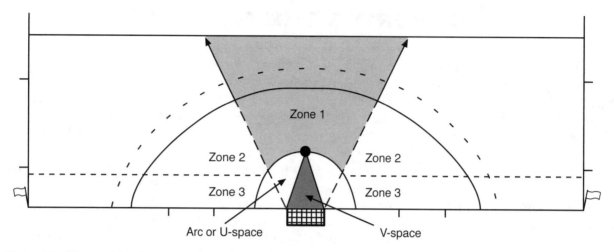

Figure 6.3 Zones of the circle.

When advancing to play the ball, do so with a shouted directive such as "Mine!" In addition to reading play, the goalkeeper must be able to organize play by communicating with teammates. Correct and consistent communication can prevent shots as well as force shot attempts from narrow angles such as zone 3. Always call the name of your teammate first and then give clear and decisive directions. Never interfere if a teammate is tackling or harassing an opponent. Wait in ready position for the play to develop, then save the shot or move to a new position.

Goalkeeping Positioning Drill 1. *Covering the Angles*

A teammate dribbles the ball along the edge of the shooting circle, starting from the backline (zone 3). Take a position next to the post. As the angle widens to zone 2 and zone 1, change your position relative to the ball to prepare for a possible shot. The angle narrows as the ball is dribbled toward the backline. When the ball is dribbled around the circle and back, one cycle is completed. You must cover the angles without an error on two complete cycles. Errors include poor balance of the head, hands, or feet; wide footwork; and failure to position on the line that bisects the angle.

To Increase Difficulty

- Increase the number of repetitions.
- Dribbler starts 10 yards (9 m) from the goalkeeper.
- Increase the pace by passing the ball instead of by dribbling.
- Add shooting from each zone.

To Decrease Difficulty

- Decrease the number of repetitions.
- Have the dribbler walk with the ball.

Success Check

- Maintain a ready position while moving your feet.
- Use short, quick steps on power points of feet.
- Get set in a ready position before the ball is shot.
- When the angle narrows, move closer to the goal posts.
- When the angle widens, move closer to the ball.
- Align your head with the ball and the center of the goal line.

Score Your Success

Two errors or fewer = 5 points

Three errors = 3 points

Four errors = 1 point

Five errors or more = 0 points

Your score ___

Goalkeeping Positioning Drill 2. *Protect the Goal*

Put four to six teammates (you may use other goal-keepers) in a circle formation with a radius of 10 yards (9 m). Use two cones to set a 5-yard-wide (4.5 m) goal in the center of the circle. Take a position inside the circle to protect the goal, which is open to attack from both sides. The players around the circle attempt to pass the ball to each other through the goal. Your goal is to cut off as many passes as possible by using proper positional play. Award yourself 1 point for each pass you intercept. The attacking team earns 1 point for each ball that travels through the 5-yard goal. The first to score 5 points wins the round. Play the best of five rounds.

To Increase Difficulty

- Increase the number of rounds.
- Increase the circle radius.
- Use more players.
- Increase the size of the goal.

To Decrease Difficulty

- Decrease the number of rounds.
- Decrease the circle radius.
- Use fewer players.
- Reduce the size of the goal.

Success Check

- Maintain a ready position while moving feet.
- Use short, strides on the power points of your feet.
- Keep your body weight centered between your feet.
- When the angle narrows, move closer to the goal posts.
- When the angle widens, move closer to the ball.

Score Your Success

Win three rounds = 5 points

Win two rounds = 3 points

Win one round = 1 point

Winless = 0 points

Your score ___

BLOCKING GROUND BALLS

The goalkeeper's technique for blocking ground balls is the same for grass and artificial surfaces. Because of the faster pace and higher standard of play on artificial turf, the goalkeeper will more often use her entire body to block the ball. Making routine saves consistently is just as important as making an occasional spectacular play. If teammates play defense well, most saves will be routine; shots at the goal will roll along the ground. Depending on the nature of the shot, you will use either the upright or the horizontal position to stop or block the ball. Remember, every ball stopped by the goalkeeper should be cleared away from the goal quickly and safely.

The goalkeeper must either stop and control the shot or redirect (one-time) the rebound. On artificial surfaces and with higher levels of play, the experienced goalkeeper will almost always save and clear the ball in one action. Performance of the one-time, or save-clear, technique requires good head positioning and good timing. To play a ball that is rolling directly at the goalkeeper requires not only a balanced, ready stance, but also a blocking position, which is the most basic precursor for all other goalkeeping skills.

Controlling the rebound is critical when stopping a ball that is hit directly at you. Always move your head and body in front of the ball and let the ball come to you. A novice goalkeeper learns to block or stop the ball with both her legs together and her body weight forward on the power points of the feet. Both knees are slightly bent in order to confine the rebound to the control box. The block save can also be executed with a single-leg stop against shots that are coming hard at leg guard height. The double-leg stop is also used for shots that are bouncing, or are slightly lofted, on hard, uneven grass surfaces.

121

To execute the block save (figure 6.4), position your head and body in front of the ball. From the ready position, be prepared to give with the shot in the same way that the stick absorbs the impact of the ball when trapping or receiving. Keep your leg guards together and watch the ball come to you. When the ball strikes the pads, bend your knees over your toes; keep your head over the ball and your chin over your knees. Hold the stick in your right hand and open the left hand with the palm facing the ball. Maintain a low center of gravity so that you can move quickly.

Figure 6.4   Block Save

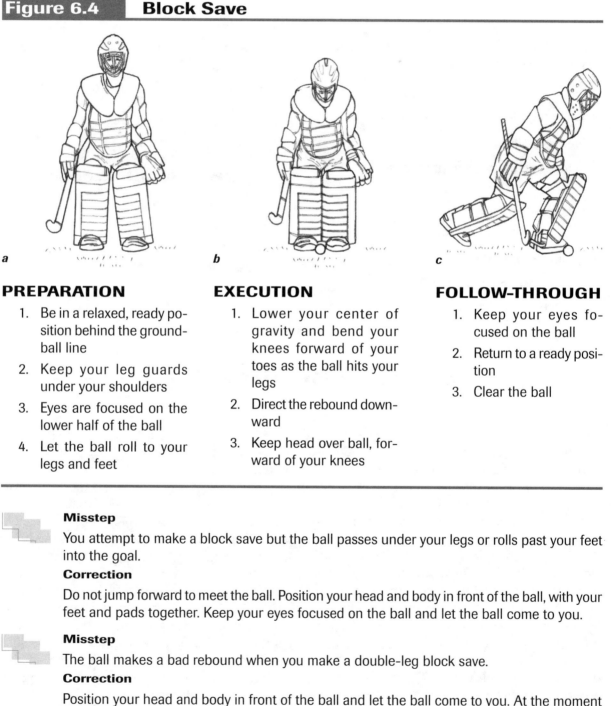

a   b   c

PREPARATION

1. Be in a relaxed, ready position behind the ground-ball line
2. Keep your leg guards under your shoulders
3. Eyes are focused on the lower half of the ball
4. Let the ball roll to your legs and feet

EXECUTION

1. Lower your center of gravity and bend your knees forward of your toes as the ball hits your legs
2. Direct the rebound downward
3. Keep head over ball, forward of your knees

FOLLOW-THROUGH

1. Keep your eyes focused on the ball
2. Return to a ready position
3. Clear the ball

Misstep

You attempt to make a block save but the ball passes under your legs or rolls past your feet into the goal.

Correction

Do not jump forward to meet the ball. Position your head and body in front of the ball, with your feet and pads together. Keep your eyes focused on the ball and let the ball come to you.

Misstep

The ball makes a bad rebound when you make a double-leg block save.

Correction

Position your head and body in front of the ball and let the ball come to you. At the moment the ball strikes your pads, bend both your knees forward, slightly beyond your toes, to control the rebound.

Block Save Drill 1. *Peek-a-Boo Tennis*

Stand 5 yards (4.5 m) in front of your goal cage inside the shooting circle. Select another goalkeeper to stand 5 yards (4.5 m) in front of you to purposely obstruct your view of the tennis balls being shot along the ground from the top of the circle in zone 1. The obstructing goalkeeper provides distraction with each shot. For example, she may jump away at the last second or fake to block the shot. The coach or a teammate rapidly shoots five rounds of 10 tennis balls. After each round, change positions with the obstructing goalkeeper. Award yourself 1 point for each ball you block. Deduct a point for each ball that goes into the goal.

To Increase Difficulty

- Increase the number of repetitions.
- Reduce the distance from the shooter.
- Increase the velocity of the shot.

To Decrease Difficulty

- Use only shots from zones 2 and 3.

- Remove the obstructing goalkeeper.
- Server reduces the velocity of the shot.

Success Check

- Cover the shooting angle to the center of the goal.
- Maintain a ready position while moving your feet.
- Use short strides on the power points of your feet.
- Keep your body weight centered between your feet.
- Keep your head steady.

Score Your Success

43 points or more = 5 points

38 to 42 points = 3 points

30 to 37 points = 1 point

29 points or fewer = 0 points

Your score ___

Block Save Drill 2. *Rapid Fire From 12 Yards (11 m)*

Set up 10 balls, 1 yard (0.9 m) apart. Select a player to hit the balls at goal in rapid succession. The shots are hit along the ground from a distance of 12 yards away (11 m). Award yourself 1 point for each ball you block. Deduct 1 point for each ball that goes into the goal. Complete five rounds of 10 balls and total your points.

To Increase Difficulty

- Increase the number of rounds.
- Reduce the distance from shooter.
- Increase the velocity of the shot.

To Decrease Difficulty

- Use only shots from zones 2 and 3.
- Reduce the number of rounds or repetitions.
- Server reduces the velocity of hit.
- Increase the distance from the shooter or between the set balls.

Success Check

- Cover the shooting angle to the center of the goal.
- Maintain a ready position while moving feet.
- Use short strides on the power points of your feet.
- Keep your body weight centered between your feet.
- Get set in a balanced stance to block the shot.
- Keep your head steady.

Score Your Success

43 points or more = 5 points

38 to 42 points = 3 points

30 to 37 points = 1 point

29 points or fewer = 0 points

Your score ___

CLEARING GROUND BALLS

Every shot stopped by the goalkeeper must be redirected or cleared away safely. The two goalkeeping methods of clearing the ball from the circle area are kick clears and stick clears. Controlling the stick with the right hand only, in order to make an occasional push or hit pass, can be a quick and safe way to clear the ball under pressure when the goalkeeper is in either an upright or grounded position. The hit is seldom used by the goalkeeper except in situations in which the goalkeeper loses her kicking privileges as a result of intercepting outside the shooting circle. From here, the goalkeeper uses the hit to clear the ball over the sideline and away from the opponent. The most frequently used method is clearing the ball with the feet in order to direct the ball wide or to pass to teammates. To execute a successful clear following a rebound off the glove or stick, body, and pads, remain calm and control your weight transfer before kicking. Although you may use your feet as well as your stick to clear the ball away, you must be conscious of safety. You may not clear a ball in any manner that is dangerous or that can lead to dangerous play. At higher levels of play, shots can travel up to 100 miles per hour largely because of the fast artificial turf, stiffer sticks, and quality shooting. This situation presents an opportunity for the goalkeeper to redirect or one-time touch the ball, especially if using modern goalkeeping equipment, which is made of lightweight, high-density foam that produces a quick and powerful rebound.

Once you understand proper body positioning and movement for making block saves, you are well prepared to execute various kicking techniques—jab, crossover jab, lunge, split save, and punch clear—without first stopping the ball. While under pressure, the goalkeeper kicks the ball in order to distribute it to space, to a narrow shooting angle parallel to the backline, or to the nearest sideline so that the ball is put out of play. Kicking techniques are also used to distribute a controlled pass to a teammate. The complete goalkeeper must be able to kick with the right and left feet equally well and with accuracy and power. Favoring one kicking foot will lead to miskicking across the line of the body and to poor balance, resulting in weak skill performance. Always kick through the line of the body in order to strike the ball with as much of your foot as possible. Proper positioning with a balanced stance will help the goalkeeper kick a rolling ball in one fluid movement.

The drop kick and punt kick are used to kick an aerial ball from the glove or one that is bouncing off the turf; these will be covered in the section on aerial balls.

Often in field hockey, the ball comes toward the goal at a pace that does not give the goalkeeper time to move her whole body in front of the ball to execute a block save. With any shot that is rolling to the goalkeeper's side, the goalkeeper must move her leg, with her head also moving in sideways, to stop the ball.

Jab Kick

On artificial surfaces or on hard, fast ground, it is necessary to save the ball and clear it all in one movement. The jab kick is a redirected rebound or save-clear that is used by the goalkeeper to accurately pass the ball to a target after a ground shot. It requires no backswing of the foot, so the goalkeeper can make contact with a hard shot and, with proper timing, be assured that the ball will quickly travel 20 to 40 yards (18 to 36.5 m) away. The foot is aligned with the oncoming ball, and the ball is cleared to the nearest sideline. Using a one-touch jab action, with the inside of the foot thrust only inches in front of the body, requires good head positioning and good timing. Correct positioning will enable you to turn and angle your foot so that you can rebound the rolling ball with the inside wall of your kicker and then swiftly di-

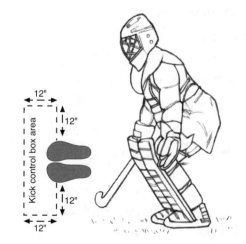

Figure 6.5 Goalkeeper's control box.

rect the ball away. Like a field player receiving and controlling a ball in his control box, the goalkeeper also has a kicking control box (figure 6.5). Proper balance and contact are promoted when the jab clear is executed in the kick box area.

To successfully perform the jab kick (figure 6.6), get between the ball and the center of the goal. Assume a ready position with your weight balanced and your eyes focused on the ball. As the ball approaches, keep your head in line with the ball and kick with the foot that is directly in line

with the ball. Turn or angle your shoulders, hips, and the inside of your kicker to the target. Keep your head over your knees and your knees over your toes as you firmly kick the ball. Transfer your body weight through the power point of the jab foot. To maintain your balance, face your palms forward with the pinkie fingers on the outer sides of the knees. Generate momentum through the ball with your head well forward. Follow the ball from your foot with your eyes, and then bring your legs back together to a ready position.

Figure 6.6 **Jab Kick**

a   b   c

PREPARATION

1. Assume a ready position between the ball and the center of the goal line
2. Arms are along your sides for balance
3. Left palm faces the ball, slightly forward of the left knee
4. Head is steady, in the path of the ball
5. Determine the ball's direction and target
6. Eyes are focused on the ball

EXECUTION

1. Body over ball
2. Turn the inside wall of your contact foot toward the oncoming ball
3. Push your contact foot forward a few inches
4. Keep your jab foot firm
5. Shoulders, hips, and contact foot face the target
6. Meet the ball in front of your body
7. Strike the lower half of the ball with the inside surface of your foot

FOLLOW-THROUGH

1. Transfer your body weight onto your jab foot
2. Head and chest are forward of your knees, and your knees are forward of your toes
3. Face palms forward, pinkies next to knees
4. Generate momentum through the ball
5. Eyes follow the ball
6. Bring your legs together
7. Return to a ready position

Misstep

You have poor rebound power and control when jab clearing.

Correction

Strike the ball in front of the body in the kick control box.

Misstep

The ball rises up dangerously when you attempt a jab kick.

Correction

You are reaching your contact foot outside the kick control box, causing you to lean backward. Let the ball roll into the kick control box and transfer body weight onto the jab foot. Keep your head forward and both hands near the saving knee.

Crossover Jab Kick

When the shot is hit hard, directly at the goalkeeper's feet, the crossover jab kick (figure 6.7) enables the goalkeeper to save-clear the ball parallel to the backline and toward the sideline. The jab action of the crossover is to the side and across the path of the ball. The mechanics are the same as the jab kick except for the placement of the foot at the contact point. Push the ankle and toes of the contact foot 45 degrees forward, out in front and alongside the back foot's big toe. Squeeze your knees together and keep your head directly over the ball. At contact, watch the ball hit the inside of the foot and then move off the foot. Move through the kick and return to ready position. The crossover jab foot placement consists of no backswing, only a firm jabbing action through the ball. The timing of the contact foot is crucial for a proper rebound that runs parallel to the backline.

Figure 6.7   Crossover Jab Kick

a *b* *c*

PREPARATION

1. Position yourself between the ball and the center of the goal line
2. Assume a ready position
3. Head is steady, aligned with the ball
4. Determine the ball direction and target
5. Eyes focused on the ball
6. Let the ball roll into the kick box area

EXECUTION

1. Body is set over the ball
2. Push your contact foot and ankle forward 45 degrees in front of your nonkicking foot
3. Squeeze your knees together and keep your crossover jab foot firm
4. Keep the toes of your contact foot forward
5. Meet the ball in front of your body
6. Strike the lower half of the ball with the inside surface of your foot

FOLLOW-THROUGH

1. Transfer your body weight onto your jab foot
2. Head is steady forward of your knees, and your knee is forward of your toes
3. Face your palms forward, pinkies next to your knees
4. Generate momentum through the ball
5. Eyes follow the ball away from your contact foot
6. Return to a ready position

Misstep

The ball passes between your leg guards.

Correction

Squeeze your knees together as you push the jab foot 45 degrees in front of the noncontact foot.

Misstep

The ball hits the back foot instead of the intended forward foot.

Correction

Focus on the ball so that you push the contact foot forward early enough to redirect the ball parallel to the backline. Meet the ball in front of the body at a point across the ball's flight line.

Clearing Ground Balls Drill 1. *Jab Kick to Low Target*

Use cones to set two targets 2 yards (1.8 m) wide inside the shooting circle. Place cones on the backline, 12 yards (11 m) from the right goal post and on the 2-yard line to make the zone 3 target. Near the zone 2 area of the zone 3 cones, stack 10 balls on the 4-yard (3.5 m) line to use for zone 3 jab clears. Set the second target in zone 2 on the 5- and 7-yard (4.5 to 6.4 m) areas, approximately 12 yards (11 m) from the goal. Again stack 10 balls near the zone 1 and zone 2 boundaries, approximately 9 yards (8.3 m) from the backline. Select a teammate to serve hard push shots along the ground for you to jab clear to the low target. A shot from zone 3 is jab cleared to the target in zone 3 using the foot that is farthest from the post. A shot from zone 2 is cleared with either foot through the low target in zone 2. A shot from zone 1 is cleared through zone 2 on either the left or right side of the shooting circle. Award yourself 1 point for each successful jab clear—a clear that is accurate through the target and is well paced. Perform two rounds with 10 balls from zones 2 and 3 on both sides of the circle. Next, complete one round of 10 balls from zone 1. Total your points.

To Increase Difficulty

- Increase the number of repetitions.
- Shooter quick hits all shots.
- Reduce the distance from the shooter.

- Increase the velocity of served shots.
- Reduce the size of target or increase the distance from the target.

To Decrease Difficulty

- Increase the distance from shooter.
- Reduce the velocity of your shots.
- Increase the size of the target.

Success Check

- Cover the angle while in ready position.
- Turn the inside wall of kicker to ball.
- Head and hands are above the ball.
- Shoulders, hips, palms, and foot wall face target.
- Strike the ball in front of your body.
- Watch the ball leave your firm foot.
- Follow through to a ready position.

Score Your Success

72 to 90 points = 5 points

63 to 71 points = 3 points

54 to 62 points = 1 point

53 points or fewer = 0 points

Your score ____

Lunge Save

If a shot travels toward the goal but wide of the jab kicking box, the goalkeeper must stretch to make the save. The lunge save (figure 6.8) is a reflex save. The goalkeeper saves the ball from entering the goal by stretching out her leg and foot. The inside of the lunge foot is placed on a direct line with the ball and your head must be over your lunge knee. To execute the lunge save, the goalkeeper must first identify the direction of the shot and then time the save. From the ready position, open the hips, bring both arms in front of the leg that is in the ball's path to goal, and have your knee over the ball at contact. Transfer your body weight onto the saving leg. Both hands and arms are in front of your lunge leg. The correct hand and arm position ensures that your head and chest are forward and near the inside of your lunge knee. The ball strikes the inside of the saving foot slightly in front of the body. The more you stretch to make a lunge save, the more your hips turn toward the side of the field. Coordinated hip and shoulder rotation is necessary for clearing the ball wide so that you maintain your balance in the direction of the clear. Complete the lunge by continuing to move your weight forward. Return to a ready position.

Figure 6.8   Lunge Save

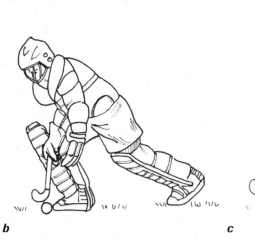

a

b

c

PREPARATION

1. Assume a ready position between the ball and the goal
2. Identify a wide ball direction
3. Eyes are focused on the lower half of the rolling ball

EXECUTION

1. Open your hips and turn your shoulders to the ball's direction
2. Both hands and arms are in front of your lunge knee
3. Lunge leg and foot are in line with ball
4. Transfer your body weight to your saving leg
5. Head is over your lunge knee and ball
6. Strike the ball with the inside of your lunge foot
7. Continue moving your body weight forward

FOLLOW-THROUGH

1. Watch the ball come off your lunge foot
2. Return to a ready position

Misstep

You attempt to lunge to your right side to save a shot, but the ball glances off your kicker and into the goal.

Correction

Bring both hands to the inside of your right leg as you transfer your weight onto the power point of your right foot, which is in line with the ball. Keep your right knee forward of your toes and your head and chest over your right knee.

Misstep

The ball passes your left lunge leg only inches from your foot.

Correction

While on the power points of your feet, open your hips to the left and push from your right leg to your left. Land on the power point of your left foot, with both hands to the inside of your left leg. If you are unable to judge the speed of the ball in time to save it with a lunge, use a split save to the left.

Split Save

When a fast shot along the ground is too wide for the lunge save, the goalkeeper must use a reflex technique—the split save—to save the shot. Before practicing the split save, thoroughly stretch the groin and hamstring muscles. To execute the split save (figure 6.9), keep your eyes on the ball while in your set, ready position. From the ready position, judge the direction and width of the shot so that you can make the correct decision to lunge or split. Get your head as close to the path of the ball as possible. Push from the leg that is further from the ball and fall into a hurdle-seat position with the leg closer to the path of the ball outstretched. The trail leg is tucked behind you in support. At contact with the ground, the hands remain on the ground, close to either side of the extended knee while the saving foot points to the sky. The back of the calf muscle of the extended leg is on the ground. After hitting the ground, stretch the corresponding hand of the extended leg behind and beyond the knee while bringing your head and opposite arm in front of your saving knee.

On a right-side split, the right hand and stick are placed behind the right leg in order to extend the reach of the right foot. On the left side, the glove-hand extension on the ground from the knee to the foot increases the length of the left leg and the height of the pad. Strike the ball with the inside of the ankle, with your toes turned to the sky. Keep your opposite hand and arm extended to the inside of the split leg. Recover to a ready position in one motion. Use both hands and arms to push off the ground. Place the corresponding hand of the extended leg behind your hip and the other hand in front of your hip. Continue moving your weight forward while pulling the extended leg and while pushing up with the tucked leg. Snap your legs together as you return to a ready position to play the rebound.

Figure 6.9 | Split Save

PREPARATION

1. Assume a ready position between the ball and the goal
2. Identify the wide ball's direction
3. Eyes are focused on the lower half of the rolling ball

EXECUTION

1. Open your hips and turn your shoulders to the ball
2. Push from your left leg and hip in order to split to the right side
3. Slide to right side with the stick behind the right split leg

4. Left arm is extended along the inside of the split leg and toward the ball
5. Keep your head and chest forward of your hips
6. Put the stick to the ground
7. Extend the stick wide along the ground with the split leg movement
8. Strike the ball with the inside of your right ankle, toes skyward, or with an extended stick

FOLLOW-THROUGH

1. Continue moving your body weight forward
2. Watch the ball come off your forward foot
3. Use both hands and arms to push your hips up and forward
4. Snap your legs together into a balanced, ready position

Misstep

The ball hits the calf of your extended leg.

Correction

The ball is too close to your body for a split save. Keep your eyes focused on the ball and instantly judge the direction and width of the shot. Use a stand-up skill such as the lunge save if the ball is too close for a split save.

Misstep

Your recovery to your feet is slow.

Correction

Continue moving your body weight forward as both arms push hips up and forward. Snap your legs together as you jump to your feet.

Stick Dive

Balls that are out of reach and wide of the goalkeeper's split distance can be intercepted with a lateral stick dive. Although the goalkeeper's first choice is to remain on her feet as much as possible—this provides mobility for playing second shots and for delivering powerful clears—in some situations a dive is the goalkeeper's only choice

for redirecting the shot away from the goal. The stick is used like a racquet, an extension of the goalkeeper's right arm, for blocking and saving wide balls. Situations that may require a stick dive to the right or a reverse stick dive to the left include accurate shots that are wide of your split reach, interceptions or breakups of centering passes through the shooting circle in order to prevent shots on goal, or tackles in a one-on-one situation in order to prevent AR1 from dribbling around you.

To execute the stick dive (figure 6.10), start from a ready position and focus on the ball. Coordinate the movement of your legs, head, and upper body to vault toward a spot where you can intercept the ball with your extended stick. The feet and knees face forward and the arms remain at your sides as you take a short step with the foot nearer the ball in the direction you intend to dive. Transfer your body weight to the leg nearer the ball, which is fully flexed, and push off both feet to begin the dive. To generate additional momentum, let your opposite leg and arm follow. Extend your stick, right arm, head, and shoulders into the ball's path.

Figure 6.10 | Stick Dive

PREPARATION

1. Assume a ready position between the ball and the goal
2. Judge the direction and width of the shot beyond split distance
3. Eyes are focused on the ball
4. Prepare a right-hand stick grip
5. Use a short step with your near foot into the ball's flight path
6. Transfer your weight onto the flexed leg that is nearer the ball

a

EXECUTION

1. Push off both feet from the power points and extend your legs
2. Vault toward the spot to intercept ball
3. The side of your body is parallel to the ground
4. Extend your stick, arm, head, and shoulders into the ball's path
5. Land on the ground on your outer thigh, hip, ribs, and shoulder
6. Head is between your arms
7. Maintain a firm right wrist
8. Block or redirect the ball with an angled stick

b

FOLLOW-THROUGH

1. Eyes are focused on the lower half of the ball
2. Momentum is forward throughout contact with the ball
3. Pull your knees to your chest and jump to your feet
4. Return to a ready position

c

Misstep

You slide on your chest when attempting a stick save. You fail to reach the ball with your stick and you watch it roll into the goal.

Correction

Vault toward the spot where you can intercept the ball with your extended stick. Transfer your body weight onto the leg that is closer to the ball. Contact the ground on your side, with your feet, pads, and chest protector all turned to the ball.

Misstep

You are slow to recover to a ready position after a stick save.

Correction

Maintain forward momentum throughout contact with the ball. Lead with your head as you pull your knees to your chest and then push off your hands and feet. Jump to your feet and return to a ready position.

When diving to your left, extend both arms to the ball, right hand holding the stick with a reverse-stick grip. With the reverse-stick dive, keep your left glove hand behind your stick and block the ball with the stick in your right hand or in the palm of your left glove.

When possible, place your head behind the ball with the left palm facing the ball. Contact the ground with your side, not with your chest. Keep your right wrist firm and angle your stick to block or deflect the ball away from the goal. Do not swing the stick. When landing, your outer thigh hits the ground first, followed by the hip, rib cage, and finally the shoulders. Your head remains between the arms, eyes focused on the lower half of the ball as you watch the ball meet your stick. Immediately move your head and upper body behind the ball and pull both knees to your chest to recover to an upright position.

Punch Clear

A powerful and useful technique that goalkeepers at all levels must master is the punch clear. The punch clear is used for tackling the ball away from the ball carrier and for sliding to clear a loose ball out of the shooting circle. The sliding action is similar to a baseball slide into a base or a slide tackle in soccer that is initiated foot first on the side of the body. Use of the punch clear is based on correctly judging distance from the ball. Because you leave your feet to challenge for the ball, you are briefly in a poor position to recover should you miss the punch. While sliding into a punch clear, the lower leg and sole of the punch foot thrust toward the ball and, at contact, clear it powerfully. Especially on watered, artificial surfaces, the punch clear is an effective way to intercept or win an unsecured ball.

To execute the punch clear (figure 6.11), judge the speed of the rolling ball and advance quickly toward the ball in a pretackle position. Slide the moment the ball comes loose and is less than a body length away. When you are 1 or 2 yards (0.9 to 1.8 m) from the ball, fall to the ground on the side of the punch leg. If your advance to the ball requires a hard run, shorten your running strides when you are 5 yards (4.5 m) from the ball so that you can regain your balance for the upcoming punch. When beginning the slide into the punch clear, bend the punch leg at the knee. The knee of the rear leg is also bent slightly. The force is absorbed by the arm on the side that is nearer to the ground and by the punch leg. With the outside ankle of your punch foot turned to the ground, strike the ball with the sole of the punch foot. Rotate in the direction of the punch leg and forward to the ball during the slide. During the rotation, the outer part of the shin of the punch leg touches the ground first, followed by the hip and the side of the trunk, which slide along the turf. For balance, bring the arm opposite the punch leg up and forward to the ball. The sliding action of the punch clear should be continuous and gradual. Keep your eyes focused on the ball as it leaves the sole of your foot. After punching the ball, continue moving your weight forward, keeping your head in line with the cleared ball. Immediately recover to a ready position by using the hand and arm on the punch leg side to push your hip up from the ground.

Figure 6.11 Punch Clear

a

b

c

PREPARATION

1. Approach between the ball and the center of the goal line
2. Judge the speed and distance of the ball
3. Assume a crouched position with short steps as you near the ball
4. Head is in the path of the ball
5. Maintain balance and body control
6. Eyes are focused on the loose ball

EXECUTION

1. Leave feet
2. Slide on the side of the punch leg with both legs flexed at the knee
3. Rotate your body to the punch leg side
4. Catch your fall with the arm that is nearer to the ground
5. Reach the arm that is opposite the punch leg forward to the ball
6. Extend your punch leg to the ball
7. Flex your opposite leg at the knee
8. Snap the punching leg and foot into the ball
9. Strike the ball with the sole of your foot

FOLLOW-THROUGH

1. Generate momentum through the ball
2. Keep the outside of your punch foot on the ground
3. Place the arm that is opposite your punch leg out in front of your punch knee
4. Head is well forward, in line with the ball
5. Eyes follow the ball away from the foot
6. Push from the ground with the hand and arm of the punch side
7. Jump to your feet into a ready position

Misstep

You land hard on your buttocks when attempting a punch clear.

Correction

Rotate your body to the side of the punching leg. Bring the arm opposite the punch leg to the ball and slide to the ground with both knees flexed. Catch your drop with the arm nearer the ground.

Misstep

Your punch leg slides over the ball.

Correction

Judge the speed of the ball to time your slide and advance 1 or 2 yards (0.9 to 1.8 m) from the ball. Keep your eyes focused on the ball and strike the ball with the sole of your foot.

Clearing Ground Balls Drill 2.
Five Ball Clear and Reposition

Select five teammates to take shots inside the circle. Position a server with a bucket of balls at the penalty corner mark to the left of the goalpost. The aim of the drill is for the goalkeeper to strongly and accurately clear the ball outside the circle into a low zone 2 or zone 3. All attack players can pressure or follow the rebound of each of the five balls in play. Player A is in zone 2 to the server's left; player B is in zone 1 at the top of the circle; player C is in zone 2 to the server's right; and player D is at the wideout near the right post. To start the drill, the goalkeeper stands next to the left post as the server hits the first ball parallel to the backline and to goal. The goalkeeper uses her right foot to clear back to the server. The server passes the second ball to player A, who receives and shoots. The goalkeeper clears to the server, who passes the third ball to player B. While the ball is traveling to player B in zone 1, the goalkeeper repositions herself in order to bisect the angle and save the shot from player B. The goalkeeper attempts to clear zone 1 shots to a low zone. The fourth ball is served to player C, followed by the fifth ball to player D. The goalkeeper earns 1 point for each clear (jab, lunge, split, stick dive, or punch) that passes the attack player and rolls outside the circle to a low target area. Complete six rounds of five balls. Total your score.

To Increase Difficulty

- Increase the number of rounds.
- Add a defender. The goalkeeper must communicate with the defender and organize the defense.
- Decrease the distance of shooters from the goal.

To Decrease Difficulty

- Increase the distance from shooters.
- Reduce the number of rounds or balls per round.

Success Check

- Get set in a ready position before clearing.
- Use short, quick steps on the power points of your feet.
- Reposition on correct angles.
- Apply appropriate skills.
- Clear the ball through a low zone 2 or zone 3.

Score Your Success

22 to 30 successful clears = 5 points

18 to 21 successful clears = 3 points

15 to 17 successful clears = 1 point

14 or fewer successful clears = 0 points

Your score ___

BLOCKING AND CLEARING AERIAL BALLS

The goalkeeper must also be able to block balls that move through the air. For shots above leg-guard height, use the glove or stick to block the ball. Never swing your stick or arms at a speeding ball. Using both hands equally well—for powerful chip shots, fast-spinning or high-lofted flicks, and aerial deflections—requires excellent hand–eye coordination. Field hockey rules permit only the goalkeeper (in her respective shooting circle) to stop, kick, or redirect the ball using the body and hands. But the goalkeeper is not allowed to catch or hold the ball or to propel it forward dangerously. The rules also permit the goalkeeper to stop the ball above the shoulders with the stick. By using your body, arms, hands, and stick, you can successfully save aerial shots of various heights, direction, and speed.

The key to blocking aerial balls is to position your hands, eyes, head, and chest in line with the ball as it moves toward you. Follow the flight of the ball into your body, hands, or stick. When you make an aerial save, play the ball out of the danger area. Redirect the ball out of play over the crossbar or wide of the goalposts beyond the backline. If time permits, absorb the shot's power and redirect or guide the ball downward for a controlled kick or stick clear. The harder the shot, the more give or cushion you must provide in order to keep the ball from rebounding away from you. Remember, to successfully defend against aerial shots of various heights, direction, and speed, position your head and body in the ball's flight path and execute a solid blocking technique or safely redirect the ball to a teammate.

To execute aerial saves, get in a ready position with your left glove hand alongside your body and slightly forward, fingertips up. The right hand holds the stick midway down the shaft and remains close to the right hip, above knee level. Eyes remain focused on the ball to determine direction, width, height, and speed of the shot. It is crucial that your head remain as close as possible to the path of the ball. Your objective is to concentrate on coordination and control, which will enable you to block (and, ideally, guide the ball down to your kick control box) or redirect the aerial ball to clear space in one smooth motion.

Whatever the height and direction of the aerial shot, it is vital to watch the ball come to and then bounce off your glove, stick, or body.

As you control the aerial shot, use your peripheral vision to decide where to clear the ball after the save. Proper positioning of the hand and head will allow you to easily play a ball away from an approaching opponent. Some aerial shots are lofted over the goalkeeper's head, dropping down dangerously near the goal. When this occurs, use quick, short footwork to recover to the goal line. Execute a drop step with the leg closer to the path of the ball. As you move back to the goal line, keep your opposite shoulder turned to the oncoming ball. The hand closest to the ball's flight path should block or deflect the ball.

Aerial Glove Save

When saving an aerial shot that is coming directly at you or close to your body on either side, the left glove hand plays the ball by guiding the ball downward or by redirecting it into a safe area. For aerial shots above your waist and chest, point your left glove fingers up and block the ball. Position the left hand so that your fingers point down for aerial shots below waist height. To save an aerial shot that is above your head or wide and high to your left, stretch or lunge and redirect or block the ball downward with your left glove hand. Depending on the height and speed of the shot, you can also redirect the ball around the goalpost or over the crossbar. Against a wide, high aerial shot to your left, bring your stick hand to the midline of your body with the toe of the stick pointed down in a reverse-stick position. Save the ball with your left glove hand by redirecting the ball over the crossbar or wide of the goal or, if time permits, block and clear the ball safely to the outside of the field. Play any aerial ball close to your right side with your left glove, which is moved across the front of the body and above the stick. The thumbs of both hands come together. In this position, keep the left palm turned to the ball and make contact with the ball on your glove, with your head and chest as close to the path of the ball as possible.

Misstep

When you attempt to block an aerial shot above the waist, the ball bounces off your chest protector and out of your kick control box.

Correction

Round your shoulders and jump back a few inches as the ball arrives in order to absorb its impact.

To execute the aerial glove save (figure 6.12), position yourself in line with the ball in the ready position. Hold your stick about waist high, with the right hand halfway down the stick. Keep your eyes focused on the ball and determine the direction, speed, height, and width of the aerial shot. With elbows slightly flexed, extend your head and chest in unison, then extend the left hand to the ball. Block the ball using the palm of the glove or redirect the ball using the heel of the glove. Watch the ball come off the glove. From the kick control box, clear the ball and return to a ready position.

Figure 6.12 | Aerial Glove Save

a   b   c

PREPARATION

1. Position yourself in the path of the ball
2. Assume a ready position, elbows flexed, with the left palm of the blocker glove forward
3. Eyes are focused on the ball
4. Determine the direction, height, and speed of the shot

EXECUTION

1. Move chest and head in front of the ball and extend left hand
2. Palm facing ball
3. Keep your head close to the ball's path and watch ball hit left blocker glove
4. Block the ball with the glove palm or redirect it with the heel of the glove

FOLLOW-THROUGH

1. Watch the ball come off your glove
2. Maintain your balance
3. Kick clear any blocked aerial shots that drop into the goalkeeper's control box
4. Return to a ready position

Misstep

When you attempt to block a high-lofted ball, the ball goes over your head and into the goal.

Correction

Face the ball and judge its flight path. Move toward the oncoming ball or drop step back toward the goal line as you prepare to jump. Wait until the last possible moment, then leap up and block or redirect the ball while at the highest point of your jump.

Misstep

The aerial shot tips off the fingers of the glove hand and flies into the goal.

Correction

Keep your eyes focused on the ball and watch it onto the upper palm area of the glove. Guide the ball down to your kick control box and then clear it.

Aerial Stick Save

Against aerial shots that are high and away from the right side of the body, the stick alone has to be used to block the ball. A high shot (penalty stroke) in this direction often requires a reflex response using the goalkeeper's stick. For the aerial stick save (figure 6.13), hold the stick with the toe pointing up. If time allows, bring the left arm above the stick with the palm turned to the ball. In ready position, face the oncoming ball. Keep your head steady and focus on the ball to determine its flight and direction. Lower your center of gravity by flexing both knees. Keep your chest protector turned to the shot and turn your chest toward the ball. As you push from both feet, extend your stick toward the ball and extend your left leg. Pull your right leg up toward the ball. Keep the front of your body turned to the oncoming ball and strike the ball using the flat face of the stick. Position your head in the flight path of the ball and watch the ball hit your stick. When vaulting or diving through the air, prepare for a safe landing at the moment the ball hits the stick. While in the air, pull both knees to your chest to create a tucked, ball-shaped body. Land on the outside of your right thigh and hip and on the back of your right shoulder while watching the ball. The momentum of the landing sometimes causes the goalkeeper to roll from her shoulder to her back. Pull your knees to your chest, place your hands near your hips, and push off the ground. Jump to your feet and clear the ball if it has not rebounded away from you. Return to a ready position.

Figure 6.13	Aerial Stick Save

PREPARATION

1. Face the oncoming ball
2. Assume a ready position, elbows flexed, with your left palm forward
3. Keep your head steady and focus on the ball to determine the ball's direction
4. Lower your center of gravity by flexing both knees
5. Keep your chest protector square to the ball

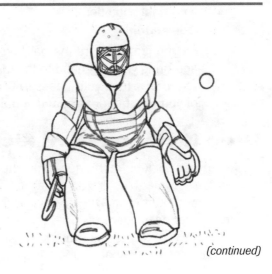

a

(continued)

137

(continued)

b

c

EXECUTION

1. Push from both feet and thrust your chest into the ball's path
2. Extend your left leg
3. Extend your stick toward the ball and keep the left glove at your chest
4. Pull your right leg up toward the ball
5. Watch the ball strike the stick face
6. Extend your left glove hand toward your right hand

FOLLOW-THROUGH

1. Pull your knees to your chest
2. Keep your eyes focused on the ball
3. Land on your right back side of your tucked body
4. Remain tucked and roll from your back
5. Place your hands on the ground to push up
6. Jump to your feet
7. Return to a ready position

Misstep

The ball slips past your stick and glove hand when you attempt to save a shot at medium height close to your right side.

Correction

Put your glove and stick hands close together behind the ball, thumbs and forefingers almost touching, and save the ball with the palm of your glove hand. Keep your eyes focused on the ball. Watch the ball into your glove and then out of your glove.

Misstep

You land on the front of your chest protector and fail to save the high aerial shot outside your right shoulder.

Correction

As you jump toward the ball, keep the front of your chest perpendicular to the ball's path and bring your left hand to the middle of your chest. As you extend your right arm and stick to the ball, tuck your knees to your chest so that you can rotate and land on the back side of your right thigh, hip, and shoulder blade.

Drop Kick and Punt Kick

Two common kicking techniques that the goalkeeper can use after blocking an aerial ball are the drop kick and punt kick. The kicking mechanics are nearly identical, but rarely does the goalkeeper have time to execute the more difficult punt, which requires more space to safely volley the ball directly out of the air. The drop kick, or half volley, is a useful alternative to the punt because it requires less space and time to execute. Although less accurate than a jab kick, the drop kick can result in a powerful clear along the ground or through the air. The goalkeeper kicks the ball just as it hits the ground.

To execute the drop kick, stand erect and face your target. Block the aerial ball with your hand or stick and anticipate where the ball will drop in your kick control box. Move to that spot and step forward with the nonkicking foot. Keep your head steady. Draw back your flexed kicking leg. The instant the ball hits the ground, fully extend your kicking leg to strike the ball below knee height with the instep (shoe laces) of your kicking foot.

For a low clear, strike the lower half of the ball with the ankle between knee and waist height. For a high clear (figure 6.14), lean back and use the instep of the kicking foot to strike the bottom of the ball. With your hips and shoulders square to the target, use a complete follow-through motion of the kicking leg. The high clear must be kicked high over the heads of all players in order to eliminate the possibility of danger.

Figure 6.14   Drop Kick With High Clearance

1. Maintain your balance and face the target
2. Extend the arm that is opposite the kicking foot
3. Lean forward and guide the ball down to your kick control-box area
4. Take a short step toward the target with your nonkicking foot
5. Strike the ball's center with your instep at the instant ball hits the ground
6. Keep your kicking foot extended and firm
7. Square your hips and shoulders to the target
8. Bring your momentum forward and maintain your balance on the power point of your nonkicking foot
9. Follow through with your kicking leg to waist height or higher
10. Return to a ready position

Misstep

Your drop kick is inaccurate.

Correction

Step toward the target with your nonkicking foot. Square your shoulders and hips to the target. Strike the ball with the full instep of your kicking foot.

To execute the punt kick (figure 6.15), face your target and guide the dropped ball from the palm of your glove that is opposite your kicking foot. Extend your glove hand forward so that the ball is approximately at waist level. Keep your head steady and watch the ball. Step forward with your nonkicking foot (left foot if you are punting with your right foot) as you drop the ball, then punt the ball high into the air and follow through. Keep your shoulders and hips square to the target and strike the lower half of the ball with the instep of your punting foot. Your punt foot must be firmly extended at the moment of contact with the ball. Proper foot and knee position are essential for controlling the height of the punt.

Figure 6.15   Punt Kick

1. Maintain your balance and face the target
2. Extend the arm that is opposite the kicking foot
3. Lean forward and with your glove or stick; guide the ball down to waist level
4. Take a short step toward the target with your nonkicking foot
5. At knee level, strike the lower half of the ball with your instep
6. Keep your kicking foot extended and firm
7. Square your hips and shoulders to the target
8. Bring your momentum forward and maintain your balance on the power points of your nonkicking foot
9. Follow through with your kicking leg to waist height or higher
10. Return to a ready position

Misstep

Your punt kick lacks height and distance.

Correction

Lack of height and distance are usually due to insufficient follow-through of the kicking motion. Keep your foot firmly positioned and kick through the point of contact with the ball. Your kicking foot should swing upward to waist level or higher.

Misstep

Your kick clears generally lack power.

Correction

Complete your follow-through, and keep your head over the ball, foot, and knee.

GOALKEEPING SPECIALTIES

Although it can be learned only through experience, the ability to read the game is one of the most important aspects of the goalkeeper's development. The goalkeeper is in the defensive spotlight in three special situations: one-on-one breakaways, penalty strokes, and penalty corners. Performing well in these situations is critical if the team is going to win.

One-on-One Breakaway

Because talented attackers now often play on fast, artificial turf surfaces, the one-on-one breakaway against the goalkeeper is a frequent occurrence in today's game. If AR1 breaks away from other field players and moves dangerously toward the shooting circle, the goalkeeper has no choice but to confront the ball carrier. As the last line of defense, your one-on-one mission is to either delay play until help arrives or to block or tackle the ball to prevent an easy score. To be successful, it is crucial to master the engage and give before using stick dives to tackle the ball or before attempting a more advanced one-on-one goalkeeping block tackle—the double-leg stack.

The double-leg stack is an advanced skill in which the goalkeeper decides whether to remain on her feet to block space and delay play or to slide and smother the ball to prevent a shot. The aim of the double-leg stack is to tackle the AR1 player by using the pads to block shots at goal. In one-on-one encounters with AR1, the basic standing goalkeeper block save (figure 6.4, page 122) is a not an effective way to stop or prevent a shot. When the goalkeeper is the nearest defender to AR1 and AR1 is about to enter the shooting circle in zone 1, the goalkeeper gets in position to tackle the ball in the confrontation area in order to prevent a scoring opportunity.

When playing one-on-one defense, the goalkeeper quickly advances from the 7-yard (6.4 m) area to the confrontation area (11 to 16 yards, or 10 to 14.5 m, from the goal line), moving confidently with determination to take the ball off the attacker. If the goalkeeper is caught standing still when AR1 enters the circle, the goalkeeper must pounce on the ball the instant AR1 attempts to move the ball laterally. Although AR1 players are more mobile on artificial surfaces, it is essential to close down space by keeping your body between the center of the goal line and the ball. The goalkeeper should pay attention to the ball's line and not to AR1's body. Close down space by running fast to establish the goalkeeper's pressure distance. A goalkeeper who charges out of control or who is uncertain is easily beaten. There is no room in a one-on-one situation for hesitation!

Move toward AR1 so that you reach the top of the circle at the same moment as the ball. You must engage and push back to establish a pressure distance of 4 yards (3.5 m) or less in the confrontation area in zone 1. Never push or give back into the V-space area because you will give AR1 a high-percentage shot. During the fast, engaging run into breakdown footwork, move a little to your left to allow AR1 to drag the ball to your stick side. As you force AR1 to move to

your preferred right side, the attacker's reverse stick side, your judgment is crucial in timing your tackle from your DR1 position. Refuse to allow the ball to get around you as you maintain a playing distance that will allow you to block a shot or tackle a loose ball. Let AR1 make the mistakes, such as poor dribbling, rather than committing to an early slide or dive. Stay on your feet as AR1 starts to dodge or pull the ball beyond the line of your head and shoulders.

If you have engaged using short, quick footwork within the proper playing distance, you are in a position to time a dive tackle with your stick when AR1 loses control of a ball pulled to your right side. Always slide on your right side with your stick thrust toward the ball. If the attacker insists on dragging the ball to your left, stay on your feet and maintain your playing distance in order to prevent AR1 from going around you. By keeping the ball in line with your right shoulder and by maintaining a pressure distance from the ball, you are in a good position to time a reverse-stick tackle of a loose dribble or to time a double-leg stack (figure 6.16) on a shot attempt. When using stick dives to tackle or a double-leg stack to block, try to slide through the ball and through AR1's stick in order to tackle and clear the ball at the same time. If you allow AR1 to get around you, you will lose the one-on-one confrontation. If you can force AR1 wide and into zone 2 or 3 while maintaining a position between the ball and the center of the goal line, you will delay the opponent's attack. You can be satisfied with a job well done.

To execute the double-leg stack slide (figure 6.16), you must be close enough to the ball to slide into it before the shooter can shoot at the goal. A goalkeeping tackle such as the stack should be executed from 4 yards (3.5 m) or closer, depending on your ability to establish a playing distance to pressure the ball. Move toward AR1 within the confrontation area and arrive at the top of the circle at the same time as the ball. Do not hesitate moving toward the ball. Step forward during the shooter's takeaway swing and initiate the stack slide when the shooter begins his downswing. Position yourself so that you can time your slide into the ball with your pads stacked on top of each other, creating a wall. The center of the pads face the attacker's stick and the ball as your head and chest remain in line with the ball in a 12 o'clock position—chin on top of your left knee. During the slide, the outside of your slightly bent right leg hits the ground first. The bent left leg, with the pad also turned to the ball, falls on top of the right leg. The right arm and stick are behind the upper body and they push up through the slide at the moment of contact. The glove hand guards the space above the left leg at the moment of contact. Eyes remain focused on the lower half of the ball. During the recovery to a ready position, bring your head and left hand to the front of your body or to your leg guards, toward the ball, and push up to your feet.

Figure 6.16   Double-Leg Stack Slide

PREPARATION

1. Engage and give from 7 yards (6.4 m) to the confrontation area
2. Stay between the ball and the center of the goal line
3. Establish a pressure distance of 4 yards (3.5 m) or less from the ball
4. Maintain a ready position while moving your feet
5. Hold your head steady, in line with the ball

EXECUTION

1. Take a short step forward to the ball on AR1's backswing
2. Start your slide on the downswing
3. Bend your right leg and place your stick hand on the ground near your right hip
4. Slide on the right outer thigh and buttocks
5. Keep your left hand at left knee
6. Place your bent left leg on top of your right leg
7. Head and chest are forward at 12 o'clock
8. Make contact with the ball on the center of the pads

FOLLOW-THROUGH

1. Keep your eyes focused on the ball
2. Head is forward, with your left hand placed in front of the pads
3. Push up from the ground with your stick hand
4. Return to a ready position

Misstep

AR1 drags the ball around you as you attempt a double-leg stack slide.

Correction

You are going down into a double-leg stack too early. Focus on the ball and get in position 4 yards (3.5 m) or less from the ball. Step forward to the ball during the shooter's backswing. Time your downward slide with the downswing of the shooter's stick.

Misstep

You attempt a double-leg stack tackle and miss the ball, instead sliding into AR1. The umpire awards a penalty corner to your opponent.

Correction

Move toward AR1 and reach the top of the circle when the ball does. Position yourself as DR1 in order to tackle the ball and prevent a shot. Keep your pads turned to the ball and keep your head in line with the ball. Time your slide into the ball for the moment when the ball is being hit.

One-on-One Drill. *1 v GK to Goal*

The goalkeeper gets in position in the shooting circle on the penalty-stroke spot. Five or more players form a line of attackers in the center of the field at the 25-yard line. A recovery defender starts on the ground with her back to her goal in a push-up position. A server starts the drill by pushing a loose ball toward the 5-meter circle. An attack player starts on the 25-yard line and runs toward the served ball, challenging the goalkeeper. When the attacker initially moves, the recovery defender may push up and sprint back. The goalkeeper stays in for three balls and alternates with another goalkeeper. Each successful 1 v 1 tackle or stack slide by the goalkeeper counts as a point. Each goalkeeper does three rounds of three balls. Total your score.

To Increase Difficulty

- Increase the number of repetitions.
- Set a target for a goalkeeper clear.
- Place a time restriction for clearing each ball.

To Decrease Difficulty

- Reduce the number of repetitions.
- Take one-on-ones in zones 2 and 3.

Success Check

- Read play to engage and give.
- Use short, quick steps on power points of feet.

Score Your Success

7 to 9 points = 5 points

5 or 6 points = 3 points

Fewer than 5 points = 1 point

Your score ___

Penalty Stroke

The goalkeeper is the only defender who can defend against an awarded penalty stroke. When the defending team commits an unintentional or intentional foul in the circle that prevents the probable scoring of a goal, the umpire will whistle for a penalty stroke. Also, the umpire will award a penalty stroke for any continuous early running off the backline by the defenders positioned at penalty corners. Many tournament structures provide for a penalty-stroke competition to determine a winner if overtime play does not determine a winner. As the goalkeeper, be prepared for a one-on-one push or flick from 7 yards (6.4 m) out. It is crucial to watch the ball in order to determine the ball's direction and then to commit yourself 100 percent to making the save.

To defend against the penalty stroke, stand on the center of the goal line in ready position. A lower center of gravity will allow easier and swifter movement up than the downward movement with a higher center of gravity does. The rules do not permit you to leave the line or to move your feet until the ball has been played. With your heels over the front portion of the goal line, move your body weight forward. Learn to react to the direction of the ball while keeping your eyes focused on the ball. Though your legs are longer than your arms, your arms and hands are quicker than your legs. Whether the penalty shot is rolled along the ground or is shot into the air to your left or right side, be prepared to vault or dive in order to put your head and chest into the ball's path so that you can save the shot with your hands. Remain relaxed and confident; the attacker feels more pressure to complete the score than you do to stop the shot. To practice saving penalty strokes, use a gymnastic crash pad to absorb your landing. Train to save shots in front of the goal. With focus and self-discipline, you will stop a high percentage of shots in the goalkeeper save area and, on occasion, stop the quality stroke outside your save area.

Penalty Corner

The goalkeeper's role in the defense of a penalty corner is perhaps the most important. The success of your team's five-player penalty corner squad depends on your ability to defend the first shot on goal. Decide early which of the three styles will be successful: the stand-up set position, the lie-down position, or the pressure, or fly, position. The stand-up ready position (figure 6.4, page 122) is used at all levels of play because of the mobility it provides if the point of attack changes or if the goalkeeper needs to reposition herself after a rebound. At higher levels of play—in which shooters are very skilled and can strike hard, accurate shots at the 18-inch backboard—a down position is used to stop direct hits from the top of the circle. If you are a fast and agile goalkeeper, use the pressure position to run at a shooter who favors a flick shot or to surprise the attacker by running at her and stack sliding (figure 6.16, page 142) into the shot. The two methods of lying down include the body drop and the knee slide on watered artificial surfaces. They differ only in the preparation phase. Both methods are simple to execute; remember, however, that your subsequent mobility is limited. With any method, the goalkeeper must read the attack play and only use the down technique if the hitter is committed to the shot.

To execute the body drop, start behind the goal line with your left foot forward. Step out on the field with your right foot, followed by your left. Between the 2- and 3-yard lines, center your body weight as you place your right leg slightly behind your left. You are now prepared to drop to your right side.

The knee slide uses the same footwork preparation from the goal line—i.e., right-left-slide on your right knee. You must watch to see whether the hitter is truly committed to the shot. Quickly position yourself on both feet in a stand-up ready position if the ball is passed or lifted.

SUCCESS SUMMARY OF GOALKEEPING

The ultimate defensive goal of every field hockey team is to play as a unit to prevent the opposition from scoring. To achieve this goal, a team must have a dependable goalkeeper. Mastering goalkeeping skills requires a great deal of time and effort. Field and match-related goalkeeping requires the cooperation of three or more field players. Beginners should start by positioning themselves to block shots without the pressures of restricted time, opponents, or limited clearing space. Focus on the basic techniques and gradually increase the speed of the movements until you are confident, which will allow you to better concentrate on the correct skill. Eventually, you will progress to more challenging game situations.

Each of the drills described in step 6 can be modified for practicing aerial saves as well as for saving and clearing ground balls. Use the point values assigned for each drill to help chart your progress. Total your points to assess your goalkeeping development.

Goalkeeping Positioning Drills

1. Covering the Angles   ___ out of 5

2. Protect the Goal   ___ out of 5

Block Save Drills

1. Peek-a-Boo Tennis   ___ out of 5

2. Rapid Fire From 12 Yards (11 m)   ___ out of 5

Clearing Ground Balls Drills

1. Jab Kick to Low Target   ___ out of 5

2. Five Ball Clear and Reposition   ___ out of 5

One-on-One Drills

1. 1 v GK to Goal   ___ out of 5

Total   ___ **out of 35**

A combined score of 28 points or more indicates that you are competently performing fundamental goalkeeping skills and that you are prepared to move on to step 7. A total score of 21 to 27 is considered adequate. Move on to step 7 after you review and practice each of the goalkeeping techniques one more time. If you scored fewer than 21 points, practice the goalkeeping skills several more times before moving on to step 7.

Leading the Attack and Defense

Field hockey is a fast and exciting team game that requires players to solve problems. Attacking players work to create and use space, and defending players work to block and control space. Although hockey is a team sport, every game includes a series of one-against-one battles in which players try to either maintain possession of the ball or gain it. To win these one-against-one encounters, you must understand and execute attack and defense role 1 tactics. These tactics are your decisions or plans to win confrontations. Players with a thorough understanding of role 1 responsibilities, who can also execute those responsibilities well, create a team that thinks and plays together.

Because each player will spend nearly a third of a 70-minute game in one-on-one confrontations near the ball, the player's ability to make good decisions and to use the correct technique at the right moment is primary. The attack or defense role 1 player is responsible for making good decisions at the start of her team's attack or her team's defense.

All players must be able to both defend and attack. In field hockey, the player with the ball is the attack role 1 player (AR1). The opponent nearest that attacker is the defense role 1 player (DR1). Your success in the first roles of attack and defense depends in part on your ability to choose the best option for solving game situations. As the leader of the attack and defense, the role 1 player must make good decisions. Good decisions are based on useful guidelines and responsibilities and lead to better skill performance. Attention to the location of the ball and to the positions of teammates and opponents helps a player make decisions with or without the ball.

ATTACK ROLE 1 TACTICS

When you have the ball, you are the leader of the attack team. You must execute the attack strategy while taking care of the ball. AR1's assignment is to pass the ball and to initiate team attack play. The player with the ball must decide how, where, and when to pass it. A pass is used to achieve one of three basic goals: to penetrate into the opponent's space behind and in front of the goal; to establish an advantage by gaining ground on the opponent; or to secure possession of the ball by using a safe, or possession, pass. A good AR1 player will look first to deliver the killer pass, which penetrates through and behind the opponent. If the killer pass is unavailable or too risky, then AR1 looks to gain ground by using an advantage pass. An advantage pass is sent toward the goal but not necessarily behind the defense. If the advantage pass is too risky, AR1 should maintain possession by not approaching the defender too closely. Because she maintains a greater distance from the defender than when she moves toward the goal and because of a lack of immediate pressure from the defender, the attacker can use back space to change the point of attack.

Maintain Ball Possession

Although AR1 is primarily a passer, he or she must maintain possession of the ball (refer to step 3) as she looks up to pass. You must value your team's ball possession and work hard not to lose it. If you cannot complete a penetrating pass or an advantage pass, maintain possession of the ball so that you can change the point of attack. Change the point of attack by using a possession pass to pass the ball back to a support teammate who has more time and space to pass the ball to the other side of the field.

Misstep

You lose the ball when attempting to change the point of attack.

Correction

Use sudden change of direction or a drop step to create space between you and DR1. Avoid changing the point of attack without first creating space from which you can pass.

Cut the Ball Into Free Space

You become a better field hockey player simply by creating space for yourself and for your teammates. The more space there is between the AR1 player and the DR1 opponent, the more time AR1 will have to pass and to lead the team's attack. Quickly cut or diagonal dribble the ball away from the nearest opponent and into free space. This action will create space and time. Cutting the ball on short angles will change the point of attack and usually will make the opponent move laterally after the ball, opening up through spaces to the opponent's goal.

Misstep

DR1 steals the ball away from you.

Correction

Keep the ball next to your stick as you look to pass. When pressured (DR1 within 5 yards, or 4.5 m), immediately cut the ball to free space or change your speed in order to separate from DR1.

Go One-on-One With the Role 1 Defender

Forcing DR1 to either commit to tackling the ball or to holding or withdrawing to delay penetration is commonly referred to as "going one-on-one," or as "taking on a defender." Your objective is to keep possession of the ball as you attempt to move DR1 and to get the ball behind her. If you force DR1 to make a poor decision, you will have created a dangerous attack penetration or a numbers-up situation (more attack players than defenders), which may lead to a scoring opportunity. Attempt to make the opponent commit by cutting the ball forward and diagonally, outside of DR1's stick reach. To mislead or unbalance DR1, be creative when using body fakes and change-of-pace movements with the ball.

Go one-on-one only in areas in which the potential to create a scoring opportunity far outweighs the risk of losing the ball, which would provide the opponent an immediate scoring chance. The best area to use your dribbling skills to take on DR1 is in the attacking third of the field. In this area, AR1 uses the dribble to break down defenses outside the circle in zones 1 and 3 (figure 6.3, page 120) and inside the circle in zone 3. Losing possession in this area is not as critical as losing possession in your defensive half of the field. Think of safety first in your defensive half of the field, and avoid dribbling to take on your opponent.

When cornered or outnumbered by the opponent in a tight space, keep possession of the ball by drawing a foul, which will then produce a free hit. A free hit will allow you more time and space to examine your options. A free hit taken quickly can also catch your opponent unorganized, giving your team an advantage.

Misstep

You hesitate when going one-on-one against DR1.

Correction

Be decisive in forcing a commitment from the nearest defender. Diagonally dribble the ball with speed and control away from DR1's stick reach.

Penetrate Using the Shortest Line to Goal

Once you have successfully beaten a defender in the dangerous space (space behind DR1), keep him on your backside and penetrate using the shortest line to the goal. You should never have to beat the same defender twice on your path to the goal.

Misstep

The defender you just beat has recovered to the goal side to again block the dangerous space to goal.

Correction

After beating a defender, run at maximum speed and take the shortest route to the goal. Keep the defender behind you by positioning the ball and your body to keep the forward space.

Attack Role 1 Drill 1.
Change Direction Away From DR1

Create an imaginary DR1 player by using cones to set up a 5-by-5-yard (4.5 by 4.5 m) area. This area represents the position of the nearest defender. Select a teammate to serve passes to you as you cut from area 2 (space alongside DR1) to area 1 (space in front of DR1). Changing direction and speed with your first touch of the ball, move away from DR1's position. Score a point each time you maintain possession using a change of direction away from DR1's space. Complete 10 turns and total your points.

To Increase Difficulty

- Increase the number of repetitions.
- Use an active defender.
- Reduce the size of the playing area in order to limit the attacking space.

- Allow only one second to change direction away from DR1.

To Decrease Difficulty

- Reduce the number of turns.

Success Check

- Move or cut into the line of the passed ball.
- Change direction on the first receiving touch of the ball.
- Create space between yourself and DR1.

Score Your Success

8 to 10 points = 5 points

6 or 7 points = 3 points

0 to 5 points = 1 point

Your score ____

Attack Role 1 Drill 2. *Cut Back and Turn on DR1*

Set up the same-size playing area as in the previous drill. Start in area 1 and cut back for the ball, which is passed in from the server. Turn, or change direction and speed, with your first touch of the ball, 5 to 7 yards (4.5 to 6.4 m) away from DR1. Score a point each time you maintain possession using a turn or change of direction at the proper distance of 5 to 7 yards from DR1's position. Complete 10 turns and total your points.

To Increase Difficulty

- Increase the number of repetitions.
- Use an active defender.
- Reduce the size of playing area in order to limit the attacking space.
- Allow only one second to turn and change direction away from DR1.

To Decrease Difficulty

- Reduce the number of repetitions.

Success Check

- Move or cut into the line of the passed ball.
- Turn and change direction at the first touch of the ball.
- Create 5 to 7 yards (4.5 to 6.4 m) of space between yourself and DR1.

Score Your Success

8 to 10 points = 5 points

6 or 7 points = 3 points

0 to 5 points = 1 point

Your score ____

Attack Role 1 Drill 3. *Penetrate Behind Nearest Defender*

Set up the same-size playing area as in the previous drill. Start in area 2 to receive a ball from the server. At your first touch of the ball, immediately accelerate on a diagonal line to penetrate into the dangerous space to goal. Score a point each time you maintain possession using a change of speed while penetrating into the dangerous space. Complete 10 turns receiving from area 2 and 10 turns receiving from area 3 (space behind DR1's stick reach). Total your points from both areas.

To Increase Difficulty

- Increase the number of repetitions.
- Use an active defender.
- Reduce the width of playing area in order to limit the penetration space.
- Allow only one second to select the shortest possible line to goal and then accelerate along that line.

To Decrease Difficulty

- Reduce the number of repetitions.
- Widen the playing space.

Success Check

- Move or cut into the line of the passed ball.
- Use sudden changes of speed when you first receive the ball.
- Accelerate past the defender.

Score Your Success

15 to 20 points = 5 points

10 to 14 points = 3 points

0 to 9 points = 1 point

Your score ____

Attack Role 1 Drill 4. *Make It, Take It*

Play one-on-one within a 10-by-20-yard (9 by 18 m) area. Designate the goal lines of the playing area. Begin by receiving a ball from a server on either sideline of the playing area. Try to keep the ball away from your opponent by closely controlling the ball and by using sudden changes of speed and direction. Score a point by maintaining possession of the ball while penetrating the opponent's goal line. If you score a point, turn and penetrate the opposite goal line—make it, take it. Continue to play for two minutes and total your score. The player with the most points wins.

To Increase Difficulty

- Increase the length of the playing period.
- Play more periods.
- Use two defenders in the playing area.
- Reduce the size of playing area in order to limit the attacking space.

To Decrease Difficulty

- Increase the size of the playing area.
- Reduce the amount of playing time.

Success Check

- Use sudden changes of speed and direction.
- Use deceptive body and stick fakes.
- Keep the ball next to your stick.
- Create space between yourself and DR1.

Score Your Success

Win the game = 5 points
Lose the game = 3 points
Your score ___

DEFENSE ROLE 1 TACTICS

The defender's goal is to keep the ball in front of her in order to prevent the attacker from penetrating forward with a pass or dribble to the goal. The moment you become the defender nearest to the ball, you are the leader of your team's defense. Playing defense role 1 (DR1) puts you in charge of the defense strategy of your team using one-on-one tackling techniques.

Once you recognize that you are DR1, decide how to immediately block or slow AR1's penetrating attack, or force AR1 to pass toward your teammate, who can intercept. This action is referred to as "pressuring the ball." Use the following list of responsibilities to guide your decisions and actions when defending in a one-on-one confrontation.

Block Dangerous Space

Taking the best position in relation to the opponent, ball, and goal is the most basic defensive tactic. Placing immediate pressure on the ball gives your teammates time to drop back and organize defensive help. Always position yourself goal side in order to block the dangerous space to goal. Goal side is the position between AR1 and the goal you are defending. The dangerous space is the space between the ball and the goal you are defending. From this position, keep the ball and the opponent in your view at all times and deny a penetration dribble as well as any diagonal through pass.

It is to your team's advantage to shut off AR1's direct route to goal. To execute this maneuver effectively, accurately determine your distance from the ball and engage your approach to the ball.

Engage Distance to the Ball

As soon as you see that AR1 is about to receive the ball, quickly move to the ball (figure 4.1, page 79). Close the space to the ball as the ball is in flight. Typically you should arrive at any spot on the field at the same time the ball does. Slow your approach as you near AR1 by using breakdown and push-back footwork to maintain balance and body control. The less space you permit AR1 to receive and control the ball, the less time she will have to make attack decisions and to play the ball. As a general rule, when AR1 is controlling the ball on her stick, DR1 must control her own engaging movement, defensive stance, and playing distance.

Misstep

AR1 passes a killer pass into the dangerous space behind you.

Correction

Engage to a closer distance from the ball to deny through and diagonal forward passes. Apply immediate pressure on the ball in order to force the attacker to pass square or back to a supporting teammate.

Take a Defensive Stance

For the defensive stance, partly crouch with flexed knees and keep a low center of gravity (figure 1.8, page 18). Feet are staggered, with the lead foot slightly forward. Feet are a comfortable distance apart. Balance on the power points of your feet. Both hands grip your stick, with the left hand away from your body and left knee. The head of your stick is low or on the ground to prevent the ball from hitting your feet or from going through to the goal you are defending. From this position you can instantly change direction in response to AR1's movements.

Determine Playing Distance

DR1's playing distance is the distance from which purposeful pressure can be applied to the ball. At what distance should you begin to pressure the AR1 player? Base your decision on these factors:

- AR1's ability. Evaluate AR1's speed and ability to control the ball. Give more space if AR1 has great speed and quickness. This will prevent AR1 from merely pushing the ball forward and outracing you to the ball.

Move to within stick reach of the ball if AR1 relies on a high degree of ball-control skill rather than on speed and quickness. Position yourself to deny AR1 adequate time and space to use her ball-control skills to beat you.

- Area of the field. The closer the ball is to your goal, the closer you must be to defend. An opponent within scoring range of your goal must be denied the opportunity to shoot, dribble, or pass the ball forward.

- Position of the opponent in relation to the ball. Be aware of the position of your opponents as you engage playing distance from the ball. If AR1 has unmarked teammates in the immediate area who can support the attack, keep those players in front of you and maintain more playing space from the ball until your team has enough defenders to mark up each of their attackers.

- Position of your teammates in relation to the ball. Be aware of the positions of your nearest teammates (DR2) as you engage your playing distance from the ball. Pressuring the ball, while getting help from your teammates to win back the ball is the essence of team defense.

Misstep

AR1 successfully passes the ball forward into free space.

Correction

Check your playing distance and position yourself closer to AR1 in order to deny AR1 space to dribble forward.

Maintain Control and Balance

AR1 will use deceptive body and stick movements to unbalance you or to draw a commitment. Strive to maintain your playing distance with good balance and stick control. Keep your weight centered over the power points of your feet. Attempt to break up the play or steal the ball in a controlled manner. Do not swing or flail your stick or commit yourself or crash in after the ball and risk being beaten. If the ball is passed before you are able to set up effective pressure, do not chase the pass; instead drop step to a ball-side and goal-side position and reorganize in your new defensive role.

Force or Channel the Attacker

DR1's priority is to deny penetration. Force or channel (railroad run) the opponent to areas of the field where space is limited, such as the sideline or into a nearby teammate (DR2), or force AR1 to pass the ball square (laterally across the field) or back toward her goal. When the ball is in the center of the field or on the field's right side, pressure the ball by forcing or channeling it to your forehand side. When AR1 is 10 yards (9 m) or less from the left sideline, force the ball toward the sideline.

If you can delay penetration, forcing AR1 to back pass or dribble, your teammates will have time to recover to positions on the goal side of the ball in order to support you on defense.

Misstep

You overcommit in an effort to tackle the ball and are beaten on the dribble.

Correction

In a one-on-one confrontation, your first priority is to prevent penetration. Gaining possession is your second priority. Force or railroad the ball toward limited space or toward a teammate. Challenge for the ball when a teammate is covering the space immediately behind you or when you are sure that you can execute a successful tackle.

Tackle the Ball

With patience and control, watch until AR1's head goes down to the ball and she allows the ball to move outside her range of control. Time the execution of a hard block or jab tackle and gain possession of the ball. Another situation in which a tackle should be applied is when you slow AR1 or when AR1 attempts to move the ball laterally. Tackle the ball before AR1 moves the ball outside your shoulders. Finish your tackle by controlling the ball, and then deliver a strong, accurate attack pass.

Misstep

AR1 pushes the ball forward and outraces you to the ball.

Correction

Give more space if AR1 has great speed and quickness.

Defense Role 1 Drill 1. *1 v 1 to Goal*

Play in a 20-by-20-yard (18 by 18 m) square with a 3-yard (2.8 m) extended area on each sideline. Place a 4-yard-wide (3.5 m) goal 7 yards (6.4 m) behind both backlines. One defender and one attacker start in the center of the playing area. A passer is outside each sideline of the 3-yard (2.8 m) extended area. Passers must stay 3 yards away from the 20-by-20-yard playing area, and only the attacker may use the passer to combine. The defender may be in the 3-yard extended area, but not the attacker. A passer starts with the ball and serves it to AR1. DR1 defends and plays 1 v 1. The attacker earns 5 points for crossing the line and scoring a goal. The defender earns 1 point every time AR1 uses the passers. Play for three minutes and total your score. The player with the highest point total wins.

To Increase Difficulty

- Increase the amount of playing time.
- Add another player to each team.
- Increase the size of the playing area.

To Decrease Difficulty

- Reduce the amount of playing time.
- Decrease the size of the playing area.

Success Check

- Position yourself between the ball and the goal.
- Establish a playing distance from the ball.
- Maintain stick control and body balance.
- Use appropriate tackles.
- Use speed in role transition.

Score Your Success

Win game = 5 points

Lose game = 1 point

Your score ___

Defense Role 1 Drill 2. *1 v 1 Passer Joins*

Play in a 20-by-20-yard (18 by 18 m) square with a 3-yard (2.8 m) extended area on each sideline. One defender and one attacker start in the center of the playing area. Place a 4-yard-wide (3.5 m) goal 7 yards (6.4 m) behind the defender's backline. One passer is outside each sideline of the 3-yard extended area. A passer may join AR1 in order to play more players against DR1. Make a line in the square; the passer may enter the playing area above the line to join AR1. As in the previous drill, the defender may be in the 3-yard extended area, but the attacker may not be. A passer starts with the ball and serves it to AR1. DR1 defends and plays 1 v 1. DR1 earns 1 point for a successful tackle or interception that is finished by passing over the sideline. DR1 earns 3 points for regaining possession by using an interception or a tackle and then passing accurately to the remaining passer on the sideline. DR1 is awarded 5 points for a possession win that results in a clearing pass that accurately hits either of the boundary cones located at the corners of AR1's backline. Play for two minutes and switch roles. Total your defensive score. The player with the most defensive points wins.

To Increase Difficulty

- Increase the amount of playing time.
- Passer can enter anywhere in the square.
- Increase the size of the playing area.

To Decrease Difficulty

- Reduce the amount of playing time.
- Decrease the size of the playing area.

Success Check

- Position yourself between the ball and the goal.
- Keep both attack players in front of you.
- Establish playing distance and angle from the ball.
- Maintain stick control and body balance.
- Read and anticipate in order to drop and delay or to intercept or tackle.
- Use speed in role transition.

Score Your Success

Win game = 5 points

Lose game = 2 points

Your score ___

Defense Role 1 Drill 3.   *Individual Defense Marking*

Use four cones to set up a 10-by-10-yard (9 by 9 m) square. One defender and one attacker start in the center of the playing area. Position an attack player (passers) on each sideline. The two players must remain more than 5 yards (4.5 m) from DR1's goal line and outside the sideline boundaries. While the attack players outside the playing area pass the ball to each other, DR1 marks AR1 by positioning herself closer to the ball and between the goal line and AR1. DR1 defends and plays 1 v 1 to prevent AR1 from receiving the ball while moving forward or to deny AR1, who has the ball on her stick, penetration across the 10-yard goal line. DR1 earns 1 point for a successful tackle or interception that is finished by passing to the sideline passers. DR1 earns 3 points for a winning possession that results in a clearing pass that hits either one of the boundary cones located at the corners of AR1's backline. Play for two minutes and switch roles. Total your defensive score. After each player has played DR1 twice for two two-minute periods, total your score. The player with the most defensive points wins.

To Increase Difficulty

- Increase the amount of playing time.

- Add another attacker and defender inside the playing area.
- Increase the size of the playing area.

To Decrease Difficulty

- Reduce the amount of playing time.
- Narrow the width of the playing area.

Success Check

- Position yourself between the ball and the goal.
- Maintain stick control and body balance.
- Establish ball-side playing distance with the proper lead foot.
- Apply immediate pressure on AR1.
- Deny penetration.

Score Your Success

Highest score = 5 points

Second highest score = 3 points

Third highest score = 1 point

Your score ____

Defense Role 1 Drill 4.
1 v 1 Marking-in-the-Circle Game

Use two cones to set up a 5-yard (4.5 m) defense target on the 25-yard line, approximately 4 yards (3.5 m) from the sideline. Place a stack of balls off the field at the long hit mark and at the 16-yard mark. One attacker starts at the 16-yard mark and two attackers start in the shooting circle on the opposite side of the goal. One defender starts on the edge of the shooting circle near the stack of balls. Two other defenders start inside the shooting circle. The coach serves the first ball from the 16-yard mark to the nearest attack player who receives the ball and runs with it toward the goal. The defender on the circle's edge becomes DR1 and defends AR1. The second ball is served from the long hit mark after the first ball either rolls outside the boundary, or after a goal is scored, or after a penalty corner foul is committed. The defense scores 1 point for a successful hit through the

5-yard target and 2 points for a controlled dribble through the target. The attack team receives 3 points for a goal, 2 points for a penalty corner draw, and 1 point for a shot on goal. Play for five minutes and then move to the other side to repeat the drill. Total the scores from both sides. The highest point total wins the game.

To Increase Difficulty

- Increase the amount of playing time.
- Add another attacker and defender inside the playing area.
- Increase the distance of the defense target.

To Decrease Difficulty

- Reduce the amount of playing time.
- Add a goalkeeper.

Success Check

- Position yourself between the ball and the goal.
- Maintain stick control and body balance with a lead foot.
- DR1 establishes pressure distance to keep AR1 near the sideline area.

- Deny penetration and shot.
- Transition from defense to attack quickly.

Score Your Success

Win game = 5 points

Lose game = 3 points

Your score ____

SUCCESS SUMMARY OF LEADING THE ATTACK AND DEFENSE

The purpose of a field hockey game is to create time and space in the opposition's area in order to score goals. You must do this more times than your opponent, who has the same objective, does. Role 1 tactics deal with the creation and denial of time and space, which is directly related to your skill level. Playing one-on-one is very competitive, physically demanding, and fun to practice because individual battles test your ability to perform skills that require quick decisions under game conditions.

Making the correct decision of what to do and when to do it in a one-on-one situation spearheads your team's attack and defense. Successfully leading her team's effort to think and play together makes the role 1 player the catalyst of a winning team.

To help evaluate and gauge your performance and progress, the drills provided in step 7 have been given a point value. Record and chart your total points in order to get an idea of your skill level in the first role of attack and defense.

Attack Role 1 Drills

1. Change Direction Away From DR1	___ out of 5
2. Cut Back and Turn on DR1	___ out of 5
3. Penetrate Behind Nearest Defender	___ out of 5
4. Make It, Take It	___ out of 5

Defense Role 1 Drills

1. 1 v 1 to Goal	___ out of 5
2. 1 v 1 Passer Joins	___ out of 5
3. Individual Defense Marking	___ out of 5
4. 1 v 1 Marking-in-the-Circle Game	___ out of 5
Total	___ *out of 40*

A combined score of 34 points or more indicates that you have sufficiently mastered the tactics of attack role 1 and defense role 1. A total score in the range of 28 to 33 is considered adequate. Review and practice AR1 and DR1 once again before moving on to step 8. If you scored fewer than 28 points, you have work to do before moving on to the next step. Review all the material and perform all the drills at least one more time. The additional practice will boost your confidence and performance, preparing you for steps 8 and 9, support of the lead attacker and lead defender.

Supporting the Lead Attacker

Although each player must be able to execute the role 1 techniques and tactics discussed in step 7, the team will not be successful unless all players are thinking and working together to achieve the same objective. Field hockey demands a high level of technical and tactical interaction among players. During a 70-minute game, each player will be without the ball for about 65 minutes. Most of this time is devoted to supporting the role 1 player. About 33 minutes of this time is used in support of the lead attacker—AR1. A team that has a thorough understanding of attack-support responsibilities—attack role 2 and attack role 3—and that can execute those responsibilities well will be a team that thinks and attacks together.

To effectively play without the ball requires that attacking players react intelligently in transitional play to find space. Immediately running into open spaces allows passes, dribbles, and finishing techniques to be used in a potent team attack. Because attack role 2 (AR2) players, or helpers, are within 15 yards (13.8 m) of AR1 (considered one pass away), their primary responsibility is to support the leader of the attack by using movement and combination play. The assistant helpers of the attack are the attack role 3 (AR3) players who are two or more passes, or more than 30 yards (27.5 m), away from the ball. The responsibility of AR3 is to create and use spaces of greater width and

depth from the ball than AR2 creates and uses and to support AR2 and the ball. Proper support movement from AR2 and AR3 will unbalance the opponent's defense and will allow your team to create passing combinations to maintain possession of the ball, to penetrate the defense, and to score goals.

The attack players who do not have the ball are responsible for making decisions that will allow their team to continue attacking. To be a successful problem solver, you must know where the ball is, where your teammates are, and the where the opponent is. Understanding attack roles 2 and 3 will give you a greater opportunity for increased contact with the ball and for involved decision making with teammates—a formula for successful team play.

All field players must be able to attack when they have the ball. Team attack tactics create time and space, provide attacking players with an assortment of possibilities, trigger an advantage in numbers during attack situations, and, of course, increase the number of scoring opportunities. Understanding the relationship of time and space on the hockey field is crucial to executing a team's attack. The more space available to you, the more time you will have to receive, control, pass, or shoot the ball. For a team to be successful, the ball must move from player to player.

Attack roles 2 and 3 provide the tactical means for the ball to move from player to player during a team attack.

The tactical responsibilities of attack roles 2 and 3 are to move to create space and then to use this space to support the player with the ball. AR2 and AR3 must create and use three types of space—possession space, advantage space, and dangerous space. Possession space is alongside and behind the ball, where ball possession is more easily maintained. Advantage space is forward space between the ball and the opponent who is trying to block penetration to goal. Dangerous space is behind the opponent, between her and the goal line. Dangerous space is the best area for attack tactics because of the penetration and scoring opportunities it holds. AR2 and AR3 players must move to create a path for the ball or for other teammates into one of these three spaces.

ATTACK ROLE 2 TACTICS

AR1 must have several passing options both in possession-style offenses and, especially, in fast-break (counterattack) attack play. The moment your team wins possession of the ball, transition into team attack by making rapid counterattacks into the space behind the defense.

Attack role 2 players use two basic attacks to create nearby passing options: support in attack and combination play. AR2 must decide, communicate, and execute runs into the immediate spaces around the ball to create passing lanes for the ball.

AR2 Support Movement

To effectively support the ball, you must create spaces or passing lanes where AR1 can pass to you. The creation of passing lanes is a primary responsibility of AR2. The passing lane is the space through which the ball can travel safely to you from AR1. The basic passing lanes include behind the ball, alongside the ball, and in front of the ball. To create passing lanes, you must move toward the ball, away from the ball, back behind the ball, and, if you are already in front of the ball, diagonally forward. Deceptively change direction and speed and be ready to receive the ball. Proper support enables your team to consistently have more players than the opponent near the ball. A lack of support for AR1 leaves your leader isolated and increases the chances that she will lose possession.

Organizing capable support for AR1 depends on several factors, including the number of AR2 players near the ball, the angle of support, the distance of support, and communication of support.

The number of AR2 helpers near the ball is critical. Having too few players will limit AR1's choices. Too many AR2 players near the ball can also be a disadvantage because they attract additional opponents to the congested area, restricting open space. As a guideline, three AR2 teammates should support AR1. Two AR2 players should be diagonally in front of and on each side of AR1, working the dangerous spaces to establish passing lanes ahead of the ball. The third AR2 player should work the space behind the lateral line of the ball. AR2 players should only hold space for a second and then immediately move 5 to 10 yards (4.5 to 9 m) into a new open space.

As a general rule, AR2 players should position themselves away from AR1, the opponent, and other AR2 players in order to form angles that allow passes to be made and received with relative ease. The angle of the AR2 player varies according to the position of the opposition and teammates. The wider the angle of support, the more difficult it is for the DR1 player to challenge the ball. Narrow support angles allow the DR1 player to pressure the ball and to cover the passing lanes. There is no offensive advantage to positioning directly behind AR1 because the range of passing possibilities is severely reduced—AR1 has restricted vision of where you are providing support and you have limited vision of the field. A position directly alongside AR1 also limits the effectiveness of a team's attack because of the lack of depth between AR2 and the ball. A pass has a greater chance of being intercepted by a covering opponent. Also, AR2 has little chance of covering the opponent's AR1 player if the opponent gains possession. Too much ground would have to be covered in a limited time to effectively move from attack role 2 to defense role 1.

When moving into a support angle in front of the ball, always try to win a space into which the ball can be passed to your stick and away from the defender's stick reach. When providing angles of support in space behind the ball, position yourself on the goal side of AR1 in case AR1 loses the ball. This positioning is especially important when you are close to your own defensive goal because a safety pass is assured, defense can be used quickly if required, more passing possibilities are available, and AR2's vision of the field is improved because she has more time and space.

Generally AR2 helpers are one pass away from the ball. The distance of AR2 is often determined by where the ball is (figure 8.1) and by the opponent's position near the ball. Usually, when the opposition is applying immediate pressure, AR2 must move closer to AR1 in order to provide a quick and easy pass and thereby maintain ball possession. In the attacking third of the field, AR2's distance from the ball is 5 to 10 yards (4.5 to 9 m) because of the restrictions of space and time. In this area of the field, you must offer immediate help to AR1.

Because there is more space available in the midfield, the distance of AR2 support is 10 to 15 yards (9 to 13.8 m). This area is often referred to as the building or transitional area from offense to

defense or from defense to offense. The presence of AR2 players in this area provides a series of options that can change the direction and speed of team attack play. The key to AR2 play is frequent angled movement into dangerous spaces where you can receive the ball.

In the defensive area, the threat from the opposition determines the distance of AR2 support. If there is little chance of immediate pressure, use a wide-angled support position. AR1 then has the opportunity to switch play in the opposite direction by passing the ball to AR2, who is angled in the space behind the ball and has time to change the point of attack to the opposite side of the field to create two attack advantages—open space and numbers-up. Without AR2's correct distance and angle of support, a cross-field pass in the defensive area of the field could prove costly if intercepted.

AR2 players must find a balance between being too close or too far away from the ball, referred to as spacing. If you are too close, crowded space can restrict the amount of time available to execute a skill should you receive the ball. When you are rushed to receive, control, and pass, you are likely to lose possession of the ball. If you are too far away, AR1's pass can be intercepted. The opponent might also reorganize quickly as the pass travels a greater distance away from the space alongside and behind AR1. AR2 has an im-

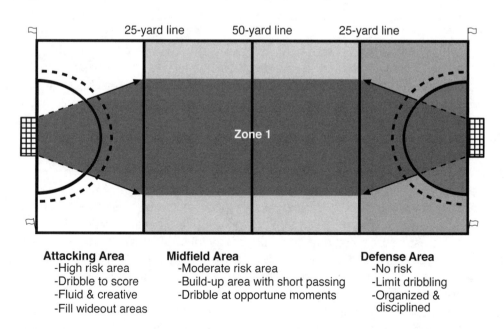

Attacking Area	Midfield Area	Defense Area
-High risk area	-Moderate risk area	-No risk
-Dribble to score	-Build-up area with short passing	-Limit dribbling
-Fluid & creative	-Dribble at opportune moments	-Organized &
-Fill wideout areas		disciplined

Figure 8.1 Three governing principles of hockey.

mediate defensive duty if AR1 loses the ball. If you are too far away from the ball when possession is lost, you must cover more ground if your role switches to DR1.

The ability to move and then receive the ball at the right moment—commonly referred to as "cutting" or "leading" to the ball—is an integral part of teamwork. Players without the ball must know where to cut, when to cut, and how to break away from a marking defender. Key elements of cutting include making eye contact with AR1 and AR2 players, pointing the stick head in a direction where you want the ball, positioning your stick near to or on the ground when the ball is in your area, and calling out verbal information. Calling out helpful information to AR1 is as important as the execution of technical skills. Communication must be brief, loud, and to the point. Verbal directives such as "With you," "Left," "Right," "Time," "Here," "I have you covered," "Through," or "Now," said quickly and loudly during play, will make AR1's confident that AR2 is ready to play the ball. Players who communicate effectively will think and attack together.

Combination Play: Two-on-One

The purpose of team attack is to create a numbers-up situations. The most fundamental AR2 attack tactic with AR1 is creating combination play—i.e., two attackers versus one defender, or a two-on-one. Combination play uses the give-and-go—the wall pass—between AR1 and AR2 to penetrate into the dangerous space behind DR1. In hockey, the give-and-go pass from AR2 to AR1 can be executed with a one-touch pass, commonly referred to as a wall pass. The point of the give-and-go (figure 8.2) is for AR1 to become a threat by forcing DR1 to step forward to tackle the ball. As soon as the defender commits, AR1 passes the ball to a nearby AR2 teammate and sprints into the space behind the defender to collect a return pass. For the give-and-go to work, both AR1 and AR2 must fulfill their responsibilities. Precise execution, correct timing of the pass and run, and an understanding of the basic tactics are essential for combination-play success.

Misstep

In preparing to set up the give-and-go, you fail to make DR1 commit before passing to AR2.

Correction

Dribble diagonally outside of the defender's lead foot. As DR1 steps forward to tackle the ball, pass to AR2.

Misstep

You pass the ball to a supporting AR2 player but she cannot execute the give-and-go.

Correction

AR2 must be 5 yards (4.5 m) away or closer, to the side of DR1. Support from a distance of more than 5 yards away will give DR1 time to adjust his position to intercept a give-and-go pass. Sprint forward after passing the ball to AR2.

To execute the give-and-go in a two-on-one situation, position yourself 5 yards (4.5 m) to the side of DR1, at a 45-degree angle from AR1. Place your stick horizontally on the ground; this is the wall. Your stick will redirect the ball along the ground. Use an open stance and face AR1 with a lead foot behind your angled stick. Redirect the pass from AR1 by executing a one-touch pass into the space behind DR1. Immediately sprint forward to support AR1 after passing the ball since another give-and-go combination could develop.

Figure 8.2 | Give-and-Go

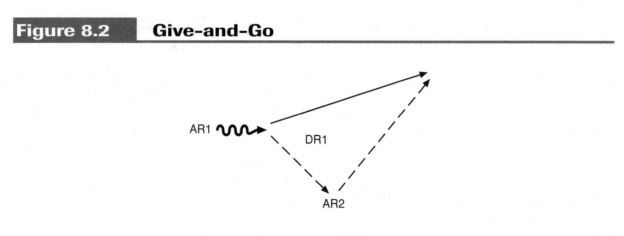

AR1

1. Face DR1 and recognize dangerous space
2. Force DR1 to commit by cut dribbling outside DR1's lead foot
3. Release the pass using the push-pass technique
4. Pass to AR2's stick
5. Sprint forward and receive a wall pass from AR2 in the space behind DR1
6. Advance toward the goal

AR2

1. Move 5 yards (4.5 m) to the side of DR1
2. Recognize dangerous space
3. Watch the ball, ready to receive it
4. Maintain an open passing lane to AR1
5. Extend a firm and angled stick to receive the ball
6. Head and right foot are behind the line of the pass
7. Strike the ball with the flat side of the stick
8. Wall pass the ball into the space behind DR1
9. Sprint forward to support on angle
10. Look for another give-and-go opportunity

Misstep

The wall pass you send to AR1 redirects off your stick behind AR1's sprinting feet.

Correction

Keep your stick firm and angle the left face so that the ball rebounds forward into dangerous space.

Misstep

An opponent blocks the passing lane between you and the ball.

Correction

Position yourself at a wide angle from the ball to create an open passing lane. Never get behind the defender or move to a narrow angle; the defender will be able to intercept the pass. Do not fill the passing lane too early.

AR2 Transitional Play

AR2's transitional play consists of interchanging the roles of attack and of counterattacking and counterdefending. Interchanging the attack roles means moving smoothly and effectively from AR2 to AR1 or AR3. Based on the awareness of the situation, quick decisions have to be made constantly in order to execute attack tactics during transition play. While AR2 scans the area to read the big-three keys of information—AR1's ball location and quality of ball possession, position of the opponent and quality of defensive pressure, and position of teammates—role interchanging can occur smoothly.

When your teammate wins possession, it is referred to as the counterattack. The attacking fast break is the ultimate tactical weapon used to counterattack and surprise the opposition, especially against pressure defenses and against a retreating defense when there is significant space behind the defense. During the attacking fast break, the AR2 player has several transitional responsibilities: to recognize that AR1 wants to immediately pass a forward penetrating ball; to immediately sprint the first 10 yards (9 m) into open space; if a penetrating pass is not available, to help switch the ball to the other side of the field by using quick support movements and two-touch passing; and to refrain from dribbling, which slows the team's chances to penetrate quickly. Taking risks is necessary for scoring success. Therefore, losing the ball is to be expected. Attack players, regardless of position, must quickly assume a defensive role in order to win the ball back, which is typically regarded as counterdefense (see step 9).

With attack transition, speed is essential—speed of skill, speed of vision, and speed of communication. Through repeated practice, you will learn to execute AR2 transition hockey and thereby improve your ability to interchange attack roles with effective counterattacks and counterdefenses.

Attack Role 2 Drill 1. *Numbers-Up Attack*

Use four cones to set up a 20-by-30-yard (18.3 by 27.5 m) area. Set goal cages, with goalkeepers at the midpoint areas behind each backline. Divide into two teams of equal numbers and decide each team's attack direction. Outside each team's defensive half of the field, on opposite sidelines, form an entry line of players to join in an attack when their team gains possession of the ball. One player from each team stands 5 yards (4.5 m) in front of the goal they are defending. Outside the midline area, a coach starts the drill by hitting a ball into play toward the center of the field. The players at the 5-yard area run to win the first touch of the ball. The team of the player who gets to the ball first becomes the attacking team and may add AR2 from their sideline entry line. The loser of the first-touch race is the lone defender with her goalkeeper. Play 2 v 1 until the ball goes out of play or until a goal is scored. DR1 can score if she wins possession of the ball. Each score earns 1 point. Play for five minutes and total your score. Play another five minutes, but increase the number of players who start on the field to two from each team. The team that wins the first touch becomes a 3 v 2 attack team. The team with the most points after two playing periods wins the game.

To Increase Difficulty

- Increase the amount of playing time.
- Add another attacker and defender inside the playing area.
- Decrease the field's width.
- Limit players to three touches or fewer.

To Decrease Difficulty

- Reduce the amount of playing time.
- Increase the width of the playing area.

Success Check

- Immediately transition from AR1 to AR2 and from attack to defense.
- AR2 executes good support movement.
- Execute the give-and-go.
- Penetrate to goal.

Score Your Success

Highest score = 5 points

Lowest score = 3 points

Your score ___

Attack Role 2 Drill 2. *Mini-Hockey*

Use four cones to set up a 25-by-30-yard (23 by 27.5 m) field area. Mark a parallel shooting line 10 yards (9 m) from the backline, across the width (25 yards, or 23 m) of the field. Set two goal cages behind each backline (total of four goals) by aligning the outside goalpost with the sideline. Divide into two teams of equal numbers and decide each team's direction of attack. Each team has three players on the field, with substitutions entering at the midline. Each team's goalkeeper defends both goals on her backline. Players may only push pass the ball or dribble; no hitting is permitted. Push shots can be taken from inside the 10-yard shooting lines. The game is officiated using normal field hockey rules, with the exception of the following:

- Free hits may be dribbled as well as pushed.
- After scores, a free push is taken from the shooting line where the goal was scored.
- A foul by the defending team in the shooting area results in a penalty play.

The attack player starts with the ball at the center of the field while all other players (both attack and defense) start in AR1's defense shooting area. When AR1 dribbles the ball, players may leave the far shooting zone to attack and defend. Play one game of two six-minute halves. The team that scores more goals wins the game.

To Increase Difficulty

- Increase the amount of playing time or number of games.
- Add another attacker and defender inside the playing area.
- Decrease the size of the field in order to limit space and time.
- Limit players to three touches or fewer.

To Decrease Difficulty

- Reduce the amount of playing time.
- Make the goals bigger.

Success Check

- Immediately transition from AR1 to AR2 and from attack to defense.
- AR2 executes good support movement.
- Execute the give-and-go.
- Force the defender to commit and then change direction to the other side of the field.

Score Your Success

Winning team = 5 points

Losing team = 3 points

Your score ____

Attack Role 2 Drill 3. *Three-Area Attack Game*

Use cones to mark three areas in the center of the field to a shooting circle. The back attack zone is 20 yards (18.3 m) wide and 15 yards (13.8 m) long. Use four cones to mark both sideline boundaries of the back attack area, starting at the 45-yard line and ending at the 30-yard line. Use the penalty corner marks to align the sidelines for all three areas. The mid-attack zone is 5 yards (4.5 m) deep, as marked from the 25-yard line to the 30-yard line or common border with the back attack area. The front attack area spans the 25-yard line to the 10-yard area inside the shooting circle. Divide into two teams of equal numbers. Team A starts as the attacking team. Place one attacker in the back area and one attacker in the front attack area. One defender starts in the mid-attack area.

The attack team designates a passer to serve balls off a board a few yards away, from behind the back attack zone. Team A's substitutes enter from the right boundary at the mid-attack zone. Team B's substitutes enter and leave from the opposite side of the same zone. All players may move within their starting zones when the passer serves the ball against the board. The passer may pass the ball to any attack player. Once the pass is made to one of the attack players on the playing field, all players may go anywhere. AR2 reads the available free space near DR1 and cuts in order to provide angled support or to combine with AR1. The game is officiated using normal field hockey rules with the exception of out-of bounds plays—the passer starts a new ball when the previous ball travels out of bounds. Team A remains on attack for five minutes before switching to defense for the second five-minute period. The attack team earns 2 points for a goal and 1 point for a penalty corner draw. A penalty stroke is taken at the conclusion of the five-minute period. A penalty corner is worth 2 points if there is a score. The team with the most points after two five-minute periods wins the game.

To Increase Difficulty

- Increase the amount of playing time.
- Add another attacker in the back zone and another defender in the mid zone.
- Decrease the width of the field.
- Limit players to two touches.
- Start game with a free hit.

To Decrease Difficulty

- Reduce the amount of playing time.
- Increase the width of the playing area.

Attack Role 2 Drill 4.
Two-on-One Buildup in Each Zone

Use four cones to set up a 30-by-30-yard (27.5 by 27.5 m) area. The 15-yard line is the half-field mark. Center a 4-yard-wide (3.5 m) goal behind each backline. Divide into two teams of equal numbers and decide each team's attack direction. Each team plays with two players on the field. Substitutions enter from behind their respective backlines, from the right of their goal cages. Team A starts as the attack team, Team B on defense. The defending team may defend with only one player in each half of the playing field. Attack players may position themselves in either half. The game starts with a pass from the first attack substitute on the backline to an AR2 player on the field. Play for six minutes. A team earns 1 point for a penalty corner draw, 2 points for a goal, or 3 points for a counterattack goal. The team with the most points wins the game.

To Increase Difficulty

- Increase the amount of playing time.
- Add another attacker and defender (3 v 3) inside a 40-by-40-yard (36.5 by 36.5 m) playing area. Defenders may have only two defenders in the defensive half of the field.

Success Check

- Prepare the ball for a pass with the first touch.
- Fast transition from AR1 to AR2 and from AR2 to AR1.
- AR2 executes good support movement at wide angles to the ball.
- Use correct pace and accurate passes.
- Communicate with AR1.

Score Your Success

Winning team = 5 points
Losing team = 3 points
Your score ___

- Increase the size of the playing field to 40 by 50 yards (36.5 by 45.5 m) and play with four players on each team.
- Limit players to two touches.
- Start each possession with a free hit.

To Decrease Difficulty

- Reduce the amount of playing time.
- Increase the width of the playing area.

Success Check

- Immediately transition from AR1 to AR2 and from attack to defense.
- AR1 prepares the ball for a pass with the first touch.
- AR2 executes support movement at wide angles to the ball and DR1.
- Adjust position in response to the ball's movement.
- Penetrate with a killer pass.

ATTACK ROLE 3 TACTICS

Attack players need to make intelligent runs in order to create confusion and to destroy the balance of the defense. Players who are not immediately around the ball are the assistant helpers, who are further from the ball. Attack role 3 (AR3) players have three primary functions: to stretch the defense by staying spread out, to create space for other teammates by making runs, and to make runs into spaces where teammates can receive the ball. Decisions of when to execute these functions depend on AR2's movement. Team attack tactics begin to take form with unlimited and creative outcomes that unbalance the defense.

The chief responsibility of all AR3 players is to create and use space that is two or more passes away from the ball (30 yards, or 27.5 m, or more). AR3 can effectively create and use space by running toward the ball, away from the ball, or through and diagonally forward of the ball. AR3 should make deceptive changes of direction with timing and speed as well as be ready to receive the ball. Make the defender worry about whether she should play the ball, play the space, or defend the player in the space. AR3's decision to create and use space is based on her knowledge of the big three—AR1's ball position and quality of ball possession, position of the opponent and quality of defensive pressure, and position of teammates. You can do the most good by simply staying wide or deep to stretch the defense, by making a run to create a space, or by running into created space with the intention of receiving the ball. By using runs to move further from the ball, AR3 can open up an area or set up space that can be used by AR1 or AR2. By using space through coordinated team play, AR3 or AR2 can receive passes that maintain ball possession from player to player. To be successful as an AR3 player, be prepared to assume and execute the technical and tactical skills of AR2 and AR1, as well as the roles of defense.

AR3 Width and Depth Support: Stretch the Defense

To maintain flowing and dangerous attack play, create space by stretching your team up and down the field and across the field. AR3 players need to provide deep and wide support in the outside spaces for AR2 players and AR1 to exploit. Width refers to the space between the ball and the attackers across the field. Proper width creates more space in which each attacker can work. It stretches opponents, which makes covering and engaging distance more difficult. It also creates gaps in the defense for through passes or AR1 runs. Depth in attack will increase the number of passing options and will help players change the point of attack without losing the ball. Depth in front of the ball often draws a defender out of the line of defense and creates dangerous space behind the defender that can be used by all attackers. Penetration happens only through the effective use of width and depth.

Organizing AR3 width and depth support in the space for AR2 and the ball depends on several factors, including the number of AR3 players, the angle of AR3 support, the distance of AR3 support, and AR3 communication with AR2 and AR1. AR3 must evaluate AR2's movement in order to time her run to use or create space and to execute one- and two-touch attack play. Generally, as the ball moves, AR3 prepares her space.

Depth in attack establishes a minimum of one or two AR3 players ahead of the ball and one or two AR3 players behind the ball. The function of the AR3 player behind the ball is to provide depth in the attack and to do what AR1 can't—pass the ball forward. The front-running AR3 players spearhead the attack, playing as deep targets who are ready to move into AR2 or AR1 positions.

Maintaining width during an attack forces the defending team to cover a larger field area, which can create gaps within its defense. To provide width, AR3 players position themselves both on the side of the field nearer the ball and, to some extent, on the opposite side of the field, which is the weak side or far side. Usually one or more AR3 players provide width on each side of the field.

AR3 players should position themselves to form angles from the nearest AR2 player, the opponent, and AR1. The angle varies, depending on the position of the opposition and teammates. The wider the angle of support, the more difficult it becomes for DR3 (see step 9) to defend the space. Narrow support angles allow DR3 to intercept long, direct passes. A position directly behind AR2 creates no advantage because the amount of space is severely reduced. AR1 has restricted vision of where you are providing deep or wide support, and you have limited vision of the field. A position directly alongside AR2 also limits attack effectiveness because of the lack of spacing between teammates and the ball. A long-distance pass made from AR1 to you has a greater chance of being intercepted by a covering opponent. A rule for all attack players is to never stand where you want the ball! Providing correct angles of width and depth will help you recover into a defensive role if your team loses possession of the ball.

When moving into a support angle in front of the ball, always try to win the ball-side position in the passing lane so that AR1 can easily see that you are ready to receive the ball. When providing angles of support behind the ball, position yourself on the goal side of AR1 and on a 45-degree angle to AR2 teammates in case AR1 loses the ball. This positioning is especially important when you are close to your own defensive goal for several reasons: because a safety pass will change the point of attack, defense can be used quickly if required, more passing possibilities are available, and AR3's vision of the field is improved because there is more time and space.

Misstep

AR1 cannot see you, which restricts the use of space and which limits her passing options.

Correction

Avoid positioning yourself directly behind or directly alongside AR2, because your position will reduce the number and size of the passing lanes available for AR1. Form wide, 45-degree angles from AR2 players to increase the depth and width of the space.

As a general rule, there should be no more than 50 to 60 yards (45.5 to 55 m) between the last player behind the ball and the deepest AR3 player in front of the ball. Because the hockey field is 60 yards wide, AR3 players providing width should have 35 to 50 yards (32 to 45.5 m) between each other. Generally, AR3 helpers are two passes away from the ball, or approximately 30 yards (27.5 m) away. Depending on the opposition's positioning, AR3 attempts to secure positions 7 to 10 yards (6.4 to 9 m) away from the nearest defender (DR3), behind or to the side of DR3.

AR3 has an immediate defensive duty if AR1 loses the ball. It is crucial to drop back into dangerous space behind the ball line to a ball-side position or to a position to deny the pass to the other side of the field. Often AR3 players find themselves far away from the area where possession was lost. For successful team defense, AR3 must sprint to recover into a defensive role.

Although talking is an important part of effective AR2 support, AR3's communication is less important because she is further from the ball. Nevertheless, communication between two attackers who understand each other's plans and who respond together remains an important part of attack tactics. You are working in spaces that are far from the ball, so calling for the ball would not be effective because defenders would have time to organize. AR3 players must communicate by calling whenever AR1 has her head down or whenever AR2 and other AR3 players are not aware of their presence. Nonverbal body language makes up 70 percent of human communication. AR3 communicates her intentions not just by words but by gestures, head position, eye contact, ball position, stick position, posture, and even by the direction she faces. These same elements can be used to deceive opponents.

Effective AR3 communication with AR2 and AR1 will help you penetrate with the ball. Penetration happens only by using width and depth during an attack. AR3's responsibility is to arrive in a space at the same moment as the ball. If you arrive before the ball, you will quickly be marked by the defense. If the ball arrives before you do, it will likely be picked up by a cover defender or be allowed to roll over the backline, which will result in a 16-yard defense hit. A team can penetrate successfully by using short, sharp cuts before cutting or leading to receive the long through pass. Fake or dummy lateral movements by AR3 tend to drag defenders out of position, which allows the ball to be passed through into space.

AR3 Runs: Create and Use Space

Various types of runs can create space for AR3 to use. If AR3 moves and the opponent moves with her, space is created for another AR3 as well as for AR2. If AR3 moves and the opponent does not move with her, space can be used for an immediate pass to AR3. Space can be created through the combined movements of two or more attack players.

The diagonal run (figure 8.3) is a tremendously effective way for role 3 attackers to penetrate through the opponent's defense in the attacking third of the field. Begin your run from the outside of the field and travel toward the center of the defense, running diagonally through the defense; or begin from the central area and move toward the outside of the field. In either scenario, diagonal runs penetrate the dangerous space and force the opposition to mark you, possibly drawing defenders into bad defensive positions. A diagonal run may also clear the area of defenders, allowing AR2 or AR1 to move forward into open space. Should you receive the ball while moving diagonally through the defense, from the

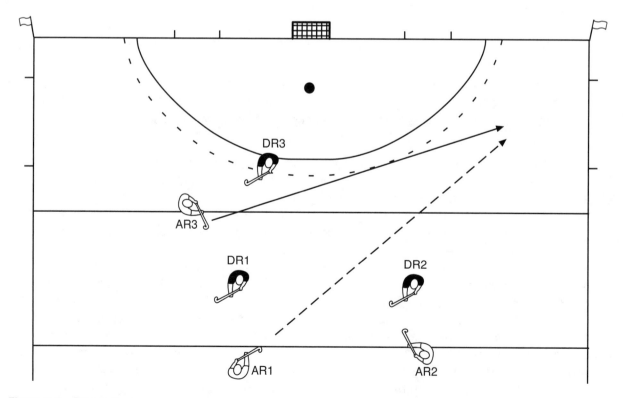

Figure 8.3 Diagonal run.

outside to the center, you will be in an excellent position to penetrate and shoot. A diagonal run from midfield (two-dimensional cutting) out to the side is used to create space. A long diagonal run will help an attacker occupy many areas in a short amount of time, causing confusion in both zone defenses and man-to-man defenses.

Space in the middle of the field can be created with a split diagonal run (figure 8.4). A split diagonal run involves two AR3 players moving in opposite directions from the middle of the field to the outsides so that space is created between the central defenders. This space is then used by AR2 attackers or by AR1 moving forward from deep positions.

A run that is made behind a defender is referred to as a "blind-side run" or a "backdoor cut." The opponent cannot defend the run of AR3 if he cannot see him. A blind-side run (figure 8.5) can create space by forcing the covering defender across the field, when opens up the area behind DR1. The blind-side run from the middle of the field to the outside wing areas often stretches the width of the opponent's defense.

A run from behind AR1 to the outside of the ball is referred to as an overlap run (figure 8.6).

Effective to either create or use space, the overlap run is most effective to the outsides of the field to increase attack width. Decide at what moment to make the overlap run by determining the defensive position ahead of the ball. Accelerate to move ahead of the ball and communicate with AR1 when to hold the ball to take on the DR1 player and when to pass the ball forward to force a two-on-one.

Checking runs (figure 8.7) are short, sudden bursts of speed that are designed to make the defender think that you are moving into the space behind her. Bluff a run forward, past the defender, then suddenly check back toward the ball or to the space away from the nearest defender. Use the checking run to create distance between you and the opponent marking you, which often develops in the attacking area of the field. Because defenders attempt to maintain a goal-side position when marking or covering, the distance between you and the defender increases when you suddenly stop and check back toward the ball. The checking run lets you take advantage of the separation space to receive the ball.

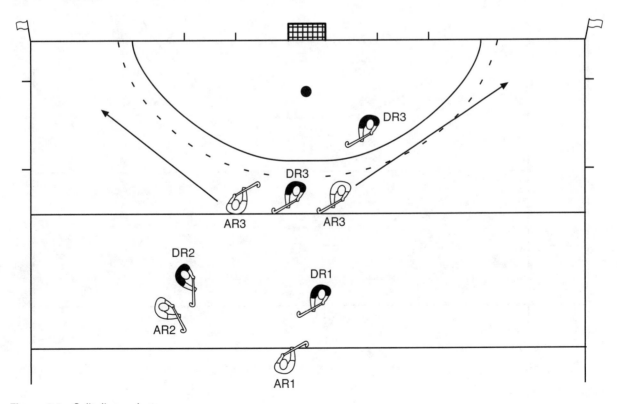

Figure 8.4 Split diagonal run.

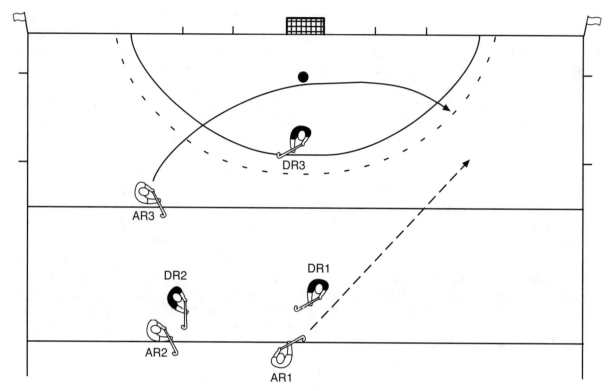

Figure 8.5 Blind-side run.

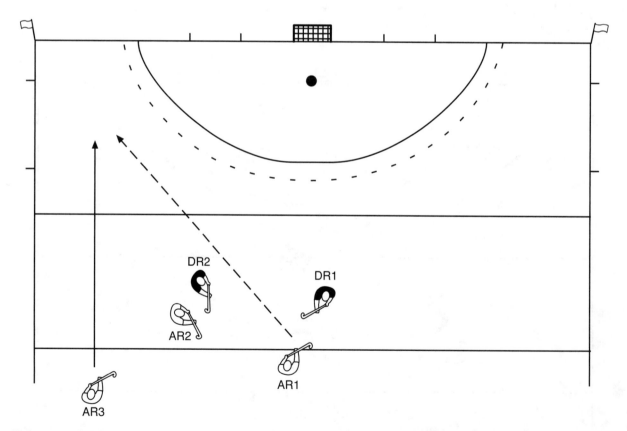

Figure 8.6 Overlap run.

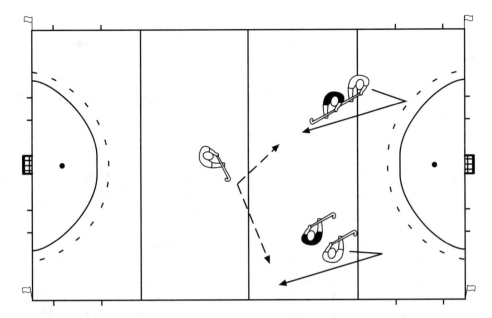

Figure 8.7 Checking run.

Misstep

Through passes are always intercepted by the opponent.

Correction

You have arrived too early. Time your run or checking run to receive the through ball at the same moment that the ball arrives.

Because of limited space and because of the pressure of the opponent in the attacking area, two-dimensional cuts and combination movements with other attack players can break down a defense. AR3 must decide whether to use space by moving to the ball or whether to create space by taking defenders away. While watching her AR2 teammates, AR3 must concentrate on their next move and react quickly to it. Sharp, accurate movement and combination play, which include one- and two-touch passing, will produce scoring opportunities. Keep the ball in your view while you attempt to lure defenders into bad defensive positions. When using space in the attack areas, you must move at the right moment, whether unmarked or marked. Keep as wide a view of the field as possible.

AR3 players must be ready to score. AR3 prepares to receive the ball from cross passes directed to the wideouts and to the middle of the shooting circle. With cross passes, it is important to concern yourself with the angle and timing of the run and with the shot on goal. When receiving a crossed ball, move into the line of the ball rather than attempt to move across it. If the angle is correct, it will be easier to time your run. Because of the precise timing needed to strike the ball, it is difficult to make contact while running across the path of the ball. Timing your run correctly is crucial. The run should be made late but fast. Defenders will be able to quickly reorganize their marking assignments if you move too early and then have to wait for the ball to arrive. Scoring in the circle involves redirecting the ball to goal. Keep your stick still and at the correct angle while timing your run to the pass.

Misstep

You have difficulty getting the ball when it is crossed into the attack area.

Correction

Concentrate on the line you move along to receive the ball. Time your move toward the line of the passed ball. Keep your stick still and correctly angled in order to redirect the pass to your target.

When the ball is in the midfield, all attackers must coordinate their efforts to control this area. A patient but quick attack creates penetration opportunities. For the AR3 player, constructive runs ahead of the ball are useful for creating space. Diagonal runs in front of the opponent disrupt and stretch man-to-man and zone defenses. Blind-side runs are similar to diagonal runs in the midfield, except that the blind-side run has less depth. Overlapping runs can be used to attack from the midfield into the attacking area.

When the ball is in the defensive area of the field, maintaining possession is important. Playing the ball safely to the outside of the field helps a team keep possession of the ball. AR3 players must attack the opposition with combined runs in order to create and use space. Usually your combined runs are made behind the opposition's defenders.

AR3 Transitional Play

Even the best attacking situations can break down. When you have a numbers-up attack situation that breaks down, the counterattack by the opponent can be devastating. When your team loses possession, immediately determine which defensive role you should assume. You must be able to adjust in order to regain possession or to break down the opponent's counterattack. The AR3 player who can effectively move from attack to defense to anticipate the opponent's most obvious attacking alternatives will often create the all-important goal-scoring opportunity.

When her team wins possession of the ball, AR3's responsibility is to immediately provide forward depth or lateral width for the counterattack, such as for the fast break. A crucial part of AR3's transition game is the readiness to move smoothly into AR2 support or to receive the ball and become the new AR1. The ability to interchange attack roles as the ball travels is crucial for successful team attack. Ball movement from player to player will result in longer periods of ball possession, penetration into dangerous space, and scoring opportunities—the ultimate goal of team attack play.

Misstep

The role 3 attack player fails to adjust her position in response to the movement of the ball.

Correction

An attack player who is 30 yards (27.5 m) or more from the ball finds herself in a state of constant transition. As the ball is played from one area of the field to another, evaluate AR2's movement and adjust your position to provide passing options in the area away from the ball.

Attack Role 3 Drill 1. *Four-Goal Game*

Use four cones to set up a 60-by-60-yard (55 by 55 m) area. Center a goal cage behind each side of the square to create a total of four goal lines. Divide into two teams of six players, with a goalkeeper at each goal. Place extra game balls behind each goal cage to keep the game moving. Team A starts the game with a free hit. The objective is to create open space with AR3 runs so that AR1 and AR2 can use free space to go numbers-up while maintaining possession. The team that scores takes a free hit 5 yards (4.5 m) in front of the goal cage. You may not score consecutive goals in the same goal cage until the ball has been moved to another goal area. The game is officiated using free hits for fouls and for when the ball rolls out-of-bounds. Play a 12-minute game. The team with the most goals wins the game.

To Increase Difficulty

- Increase the amount of playing time.
- Add another attacker and defender.
- Reduce the size of the playing field to 50 by 50 yards (45.5 by 45.5 m).
- Limit players to two touches.
- Start each possession with a free hit.

To Decrease Difficulty

- Reduce the amount of playing time.
- Play without goalkeepers.
- Attack team has extra player.

Success Check

- Immediately transition from AR3 to AR2, or AR1, and to defense roles.
- Open space by using diagonal runs, split diagonal runs, and overlap runs.
- AR2 moves at wide angles from the ball and DR1.
- Adjust your position in response to the movement of the ball and AR2.

Score Your Success

Win game = 5 points

Lose game = 3 points

Your score ___

Attack Role 3 Drill 2. *Possession Game*

Use the portion of the field between the 25-yard lines, a 60-by-50-yard (55 by 45.5 m) rectangle. Free hits are awarded for fouls or for balls that roll out of bounds. The objective of the game is to have AR3 players stretch the width and depth of play so that ball possession can be maintained during any number situation—numbers-up, even numbers, and numbers-down. Divide into two teams of eight players or more. Team A, the attack team, starts the game with seven players and with a free hit. Team B, the defense team, starts with four defenders. When Team A completes three consecutive passes, team B adds a defender to make it 7 v 5. Team B adds a defender every time team A completes three consecutive passes. Team A's objective is to maintain possession in order to earn the ultimate challenge (numbers-down) of competing against eight defenders. If team B wins possession of the ball, they try to pass the ball to the outside space and to keep possession as long as possible. Play a seven-minute period. Play another seven-minute period in which team B plays possession attack roles 1, 2, and 3. The attack team that reaches 7 v 7 or 7 v 8 the most times is the winner. Maintaining possession with three consecutive passes earns the following points:

Against four defenders = 1 point

Against five defenders = 2 points

Against six defenders = 3 points

Against seven defenders = 4 points

Against eight defenders = 5 points

To Increase Difficulty

- Increase the amount of playing time.
- Start the game using five defenders instead of four.

- Reduce the size of the playing field to 50 by 40 yards (45.5 by 36.5 m).
- Limit players to two touches.

To Decrease Difficulty

- Reduce the amount of playing time.
- Increase the size of the playing area.
- Attack team has eight players.

Success Check

- Make immediate, smooth transitions to all attack roles.

- AR3 creates and uses space by executing blind-side, diagonal, split-diagonal, and overlap runs.
- Maintain clear passing lanes to the ball.
- Adjust your position in response to the movement of the ball and AR2.

Score Your Success

12 points or more in 7 minutes = 5 points

9 to 11 points in 7 minutes = 3 points

6 to 8 points in 7 minutes = 1 point

Your score ___

Attack Role 3 Drill 3. *Directional Game*

Use the game field from the backline to the 50-yard centerline. The shooting circle has a goal cage and a goalkeeper. Set a 4-yard-wide (3.5 m) target parallel to the backline, near the long hit mark on both sides of the field. Set another 4-yard-wide target (3.5 m) parallel to the centerline, on the 45-yard area near both sidelines. Free hits are awarded for fouls and for balls that roll out-of-bounds. The objective of the game is to have AR3 players stretch the width and depth of play so that ball possession can be maintained while penetration occurs during any number situation—numbers-up, even numbers, and numbers-down. Divide into two teams of eight players or more. Team A, the attack team, starts the game with seven players and with a 16-yard free hit. Team A attempts to maintain possession and to score on the target goals at the 50-yard line. Team B, defense, starts with four defenders. When team A advances the ball with a pass or a dribble through the target goals, which are set at the right and left sides of the centerline, team B adds another defender and team A restarts with a 16-yard free hit. Use the following scoring for team A:

Against four defenders = 1 point for pass through target goals, 2 points for dribble

Against five defenders = 2 points for pass through target goals, 4 points for dribble

Against six defenders = 3 points for pass through target goals, 6 points for dribble

Against seven defenders = 4 points for pass, 8 points for dribble

Against eight defenders = 5 points for pass, 10 points for dribble

A dribble through is worth double the points. If team B wins possession of the ball, they attempt to earn points by accomplishing the following:

Score a goal = 5 points

Draw a penalty corner = 3 points

Hit through the target goals set near the long hit marks = 3 points

Dribble through the target goals at long hit marks = 6 points

Play a 10-minute period and total your score. Team A and team B then switch roles and direction and play another period. The team with the most points wins.

To Increase Difficulty

- Increase the amount of playing time.
- Start the game using five defenders instead of four.
- Reduce the width of the playing area.
- Limit players to two touches.
- Use for outlet practice (16-yard defense hits), with backs, midfield, and forward positions.

To Decrease Difficulty

- Reduce the amount of playing time.
- Increase the size of the targets.

Success Check

- Make immediate, smooth transitions to all attack roles.
- AR3 creates and uses space by executing blind-side, diagonal, split-diagonal, and overlap runs.
- Maintain spacing from teammates and clear passing lanes to the ball.
- Adjust position in response to the movement of the ball and AR2.

Score Your Success

Winning team with 13 points or more = 5 points

Winning team with 10 to 12 points = 3 points

Winning team with 8 or 9 points = 2 points

Winning team with 7 points or fewer = 1 point

Your score ____

Attack Role 3 Drill 4.
Flow Through for Transferring the Ball

Use the full field, with goalkeepers at both goals. This drill is organization rehearsal. While in other field areas, a team must maintain possession using forward and back, or side-to-side movements, or both, with AR2 and AR3. The four backs for team A start with a 16-yard (14.5-m) hit by the outside left back. The five defenders of team B (three forwards and two midfielders) defend the side of the field where the ball is positioned. Team A positions two midfielders on the right inside area to ready the space for passing the ball. Three forwards on team A start above the 50-yard line in the attack half of the field against team B's four backs. If the ball moves across the field, team B's five defenders slide to keep the ball in front of them and they try to prevent the transfer ball from passing through to team A's midfielders or forwards (AR3). If team B wins possession, they run toward the goal and attempt to score. A restart ball is taken when team B loses the ball out of bounds or when team B fails to take a free hit quickly from the spot of a foul. A total of 10 restart balls are played by team A—five restart balls on the left-side back position and five on the right-side back position. Team A scores 1 point for each ball that is transferred through the midfield area and is received by AR3. Team A receives 2 points if they take a shot on goal or draw a penalty corner. Team A receives 3 points for a goal. Team B receives 3 points for a winning possession that results in a shot and 5 points for a goal. Free hits are awarded for fouls or for balls that roll out-of-bounds. Total your team score and play a second time with team B completing 10 restart balls.

To Increase Difficulty

- Increase the number of restart balls at each position.
- Limit players to two touches.
- Use for other team movement strategies such as outletting (16-yard defense hits).

To Decrease Difficulty

- Reduce the number of restart balls.

Success Check

- Immediate, smooth transition into all attack roles.
- Maintain spacing from teammates and clear passing lanes to the ball.
- Adjust your position in response to the movement of the ball and AR2.
- Penetrate with the ball after a transfer.

Score Your Success

10 points or more = 5 points

8 or 9 points = 4 points

5 to 7 points = 3 points

2 to 4 points = 2 points

Fewer than 2 points = 0 points

Your score ____

SUCCESS SUMMARY OF SUPPORTING THE LEAD ATTACKER

Playing off the ball requires teamwork, correct decision making, and skill execution. Attack teamwork includes everything a player can do to help others on the team when she does not have the ball. This includes supporting, creating options, creating space, making runs to space, confusing the defense, distracting the defense, stretching the defense, and communicating. Remember, the purpose of any offensive scheme is to create sufficient time and space in the opposition's area, which should result in a scoring opportunity. When your team is attacking and you are without the ball, execute the responsibilities of either attack role 2 or attack role 3.

The most important lesson is that the attack tactics used by you and your teammates should reflect the quality of skills within your team. The greater your skill level, the more effective and varied the attack tactics available to your team. Using attack team tactics is very satisfying when you and your teammates think and play together.

Each of the drills described in step 8 has been assigned a point value based on player performance. Record your scores and total the points to get an assessment of your ability level.

Attack Role 2 Drills

1. Numbers-Up Attack   ___ out of 5

2. Mini-Hockey   ___ out of 5

3. Three-Area Attack Game   ___ out of 5

4. Two-on-One Buildup in Each Zone   ___ out of 5

Attack Role 3 Drills

1. Four-Goal Game   ___ out of 5

2. Possession Game   ___ out of 5

3. Directional Game   ___ out of 5

4. Flow Through for Transferring the Ball   ___ out of 5

Total   ___ *out of 40*

A combined score of 32 points or more indicates that you have sufficiently mastered the tactical responsibilities of attack role 2 and attack role 3. You are now prepared to move on to step 9. A score in the range of 26 to 31 is considered adequate. Review and practice AR2 and AR3 tactical movements again before moving on to step 9. If you scored fewer than 26 points, you have work to do before moving on to the next step. Review all the material again and perform all the drills at least one more time to improve your team's scores. The additional practice will boost your confidence and performance, preparing you for steps 9 and 10.

Supporting the Lead Defender

While each player must be able to execute the defense role 1 techniques and tactics discussed in step 7, the team will not be successful unless all players think and work together to achieve the same defensive objective. To effectively play team defense, players must work together to deny opponents the space and time necessary for scoring goals. Every player, including the goalkeeper, needs to understand each defensive role in order to successfully execute the tactics and skills of team defense. A thorough understanding, and subsequent execution, of off-ball defensive responsibilities—defense role 2 and defense role 3—helps a field hockey team think and defend together.

Players must be able to evaluate and organize transitional flow from one defensive role to another. "Drop, evaluate, communicate, and anticipate" (DECA) is the defensive motto to remember when supporting the lead defender. Effective role-to-role transition, crucial for potent team defense, requires immediate calculated pressure. A player must know when to drop back to cover the immediate dangerous space, as well as the opponents in that space, and to provide balance to protect the dangerous field space 30 yards (27.5 m) or more from the ball. Because defense role 2 (DR2) players, or helpers, are nearest DR1, their prime responsibility is to help DR1 by marking the nearest opponent or by controlling space near the ball. The assistant helpers of the defense are the defense role 3 (DR3) players. DR3 is responsible for covering and controlling dangerous spaces of greater width and depth from the ball than what DR2 covers. DR3 marks and covers AR2 near the ball and marks and covers AR3 two passes or more—30 yards (27.5 m) or more—from the ball. When DR1 has support from DR2 and DR3, he can use defensive tactics to block penetration, prevent goals, and win back the ball.

In field hockey, play is always changing, which presents numerous decision-making situations. Defenders not only must be physically fit and determined, but they also must make good decisions about when to challenge for the ball and where to get in position for best coverage and defensive balance. The defenders away from the ball are responsible for executing good decisions for the organization of their team's defense. Improve your decision making by learning to organize and evaluate what is most important to defend—the ball, the opponent, or the space. To be a successful problem solver within team defense, stay aware of the big three—ball, opponent, and teammates—discussed in step 8. Using the correct defensive skill at the right moment is critical for organized and aggressive team play that will win back the ball. Defending away from the ball requires discipline, intelligence, and anticipation. Every player should understand each defensive role. Doing so will lead to good decisions during team defense.

Defense roles 2 and 3 facilitate cooperation among players. A team that is able to blend all three defensive roles will be able to influence how the opponent plays, reduce the opposition's scoring opportunities, and increase its chances to win the ball back. By learning defense roles 2 and 3, you will learn to intercept passes, interrupt opponents when they change positions, prevent give-and-go attacks by covering space, and shift

positions in the direction of the ball in order to provide balance. Defensive balance protects the open space on the side of the field opposite the ball. As with attack play, understanding the relationship of time and space on the field is crucial for good team defense. The less space you make available to attackers, the less time they will have to receive, control, pass, or shoot. A great deal of organization is necessary to get into position and to effectively communicate with teammates so that you can mark the opponent, restrict space, and cover the dangerous space. Defense roles 2 and 3 provide the tactical organization to win back the ball.

DEFENSE ROLE 2 TACTICS

It is fundamental to deny the opponent passing options against both possession-style offenses and, especially, in fast-break attack play. The moment your team loses possession of the ball, rapidly counter into space behind DR1 as you transition into team defense—DECA (drop, evaluate, communicate, and anticipate). DR2 players are helpers who support DR1 by controlling or restricting space and by marking the opponent near the ball. It is DR2's responsibility to see the pressure on the player with the ball, to communicate, to mark AR2, and to control the spaces immediately around the ball in order to limit passing options and to create narrow passing lanes. To help DR1, DR2 must control or block passing lanes that are one pass away from AR1. The basic passing lanes run behind the ball, alongside the ball, and in front of the ball. DR2's primary responsibility is to protect the space around DR1.

To successfully defend passing lanes that support DR1's immediate pressure, DR2 must be able to mark. Marking is defending an opponent who is near the ball. Effective marking includes changing direction and speed as well as being ready to challenge for the ball if it is passed to the AR2 player being marked. In addition to DR1 skills, DR2 players need vision, anticipation, and communication skills in order to mark and control space. Proper defensive positioning enables the team to consistently control space and to mark the opponent in the vicinity of the ball. A lack of help leaves DR1 isolated and increases the

chances that she will be beaten. Organizing capable support for DR1 depends on several factors, including the number of DR2 helpers, the angle of DR2 help, the distance of defensive help, and communication.

The number of DR2 helpers near the ball is critical. Having several DR2 players near DR1 may limit AR1's choices near the ball, but having too many can be a disadvantage because congestion creates chaos. When space around the ball becomes congested, players must organize marking and passing-lane coverage. As a guideline, AR2 players must be marked if they are moving to create forward and penetrating passing options such as diagonal and through-passing lanes.

DR2 players need a clear view of the ball and of the AR2 player being marked. DR2 players should position themselves away from DR1, the opponent, and other DR2 teammates in order to form angles that will allow pass interceptions and quick adjustments to the opponent's movement. DR2's angle varies according to DR1's position and AR2's movement. A position directly behind DR1 creates no defensive advantage because the opponent's passing options are improved. Positioning yourself directly alongside DR1 limits the depth between you and the ball. Without depth, a penetrating pass behind you, from AR1 to AR2, has a good chance of being completed. Too much depth by DR2 is also a problem in transition because too much ground has to be covered to effectively move from defense role 2 to dangerous attack roles.

When defending passing lanes in front of the ball, read the pressure on the ball. If effective pressure is present within 5 yards (4.5 m) of AR1, try to win the ball-side position in the passing lane against AR2. If DR1 is more than 5 yards from the ball, choose a marking angle on AR2's side or on the side of the goal. Read the quality of pressure and play the space to AR2.

Generally DR2 helpers are one pass away from the ball. The distance of DR2 from DR1 is often determined by where the ball is on the field (figure 9.1), by the quality of DR1 pressure on the ball, and by the opponent's position near the ball. Usually when DR1 is applying effective, immediate pressure, DR2 must move closer to AR2 in order to control the space and size of passing lanes near the ball. In the defensive area of the field, DR2's distance from the ball is 2 to 3 yards (1.8 to 2.3 m) because of space and time restrictions. In this area, you must immediately help DR1 in tight-defense situations. Opponents must be denied time and space in the shooting circle, especially in the vital scoring zones in the front and center.

The midfield area is often referred to as the "transition area" from defense to offense and from offense to defense. The correct positioning of DR2 players in this area provides immediate organization and control around the ball and can change the direction and speed of team defensive play.

In the attack area, the threat from the opponent determines the distance of DR2 help. If there is little chance of immediate pressure, use a wide-angled position. Without DR2's correct distance and angle of support, an unsuccessful tackle by DR1 could prove costly. A long outlet pass by the opponent could result in a dangerous numbers-up fast break.

The ability of players to position themselves correctly and to intercept the ball at the right moment is integral to defensive teamwork. DR2 players who are one pass away from the ball must keep their stick heads near or on the ground and give verbal information about defensive decisions. Call out helpful information to assist DR1 if DR1 gets beaten. DR2's communication must be brief, loud, and to the point. Verbal directives such as "Drop," "Left," "Right," "Go," "Stay," "Hold," "Step up," "Switch," delivered quickly and loudly during play, will build DR1's confidence and DR2's readiness to play the ball. "Step up" means that DR2 should move closer to the ball to deny a pass to AR2 or that DR2 should assume the DR1 role. "Stay" means to mark, while "Hold" means to hold the space. Occasionally DR2 players must communicate to other DR2 players when switching while marking AR2 around the ball. DR2 players who communicate effectively will help their teammates transition from role to role.

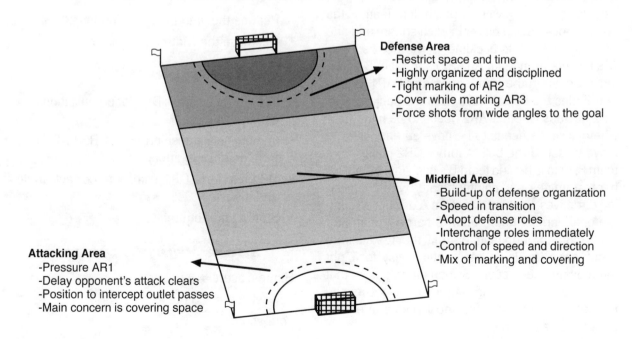

Defense Area
-Restrict space and time
-Highly organized and disciplined
-Tight marking of AR2
-Cover while marking AR3
-Force shots from wide angles to the goal

Midfield Area
-Build-up of defense organization
-Speed in transition
-Adopt defense roles
-Interchange roles immediately
-Control of speed and direction
-Mix of marking and covering

Attacking Area
-Pressure AR1
-Delay opponent's attack clears
-Position to intercept outlet passes
-Main concern is covering space

Figure 9.1 Principles of defensive play.

Misstep

AR1 beats DR1 with the dribble, and the DR2 player fails to get in proper position to cover.

Correction

Tell DR1 to delay her tackle and to force AR1's dribble in another direction so that you have time to get in position at a 45-degree angle from DR1 in order to stop AR1 from moving into the immediate dangerous space.

Misstep

DR2 near the point of attack does not have enough time to recover to a position on the goal side of the ball.

Correction

Tell DR1 to drop and delay until DR2 can recover to help.

Defense Role 2 Drill 1.
Simple Organization and Communication

Use cones to mark two 20-by-20-yard (18.3 by 18.3 m) squares (40 yards, or 37 m, total length). Set goals 7 yards (6.4 m) behind each backline of the back square and front square. Divide into two teams of equal numbers and decide each team's attack direction. Team A, the attacking team, places one player in each square and one player behind team A's backline. Team A places a passer outside each sideline, 3 yards (2.8 m) outside the back square. The player behind the backline organizes her teammates, and communicates with them, when team A loses possession, using the directives go, drop, step up, stay, hold, switch, right, or left. Team B, the defense, places one player in each square and one defender behind its backline, in the front square. The players from team A (AR2) and team B (DR2) must remain in the front square until AR1 passes or dribbles the ball forward from the back square. DR2 decides whether AR2 needs to be marked or whether space needs to be covered and when to move closer to the ball. Another DR2 player from team B, who is behind team B's backline, organizes her teammates, and communicates with them, using directives. Each attack-team A dribble through the goal earns 1 point. Team B earns 2 points for each score through team A's goal that results from a defensive tackle or interception. Play for eight minutes and keep score. Switch directions so that team B uses passers, and play another eight-minute period. The team with the most points after two periods wins the game.

To Increase Difficulty

- Increase the amount of playing time.
- Allow passers to pass the ball forward into the front square.
- Increase the size of both squares.
- Add one attacker and one defender in the back square or in both squares.
- Place playing squares outside the shooting circles and run toward the goal.

To Decrease Difficulty

- Reduce the amount of playing time.
- Decrease the width of the playing area.

Success Check

- DR2 correctly reads DR1 for organization and communication.
- Immediately transition from DR2 to DR1 or from defense to attack.
- DR2 supports DR1 using the correct angle and distance.
- Start a counterattack.

Score Your Success

Highest score = 5 points

Lowest score = 3 points

Your score ____

Control Immediate Space

Everyone defends. When a team does not have the ball, all defenders assume a defensive role to stop penetration, deny space, and regain the ball. To control space near the ball, drop back into the space closer to your goal and slide toward the ball to help DR1.

When DR1 applies pressure, defenders away from the ball drop back or recover to a position closer to the ball and goal. To recover is to move to a defensive position between the ball and the goal, in the dangerous space being defended. Dropping or falling back on defense buys time to recover and organize your team's defensive strategy for winning back the ball. Always move quickly along the shortest possible route to protect the area in front of the goal. Evaluate the situa-

tion by keeping track of the opponent, the ball, and your teammates. From a goal-side position (figure 9.2), you will be able to keep the ball and the opponent you are marking in view while you provide cover and balance for your teammates. Be aware of your goal, and keep the ball and opponent in front of you. Determine the space and time you need—i.e., how far to drop and at what angle to slide. DR2 players move to a position on the ball side of the opponent (figure 9.3) to reduce the space available to AR2 players near the ball. Defenders away from the ball should slide toward the center of the field as they recover. Coordinating the recovery to the ball side of the goal is a team discipline that is necessary for controlling space.

Help DR1 by reading pressure and by covering to control space. To play team defense well, DR2

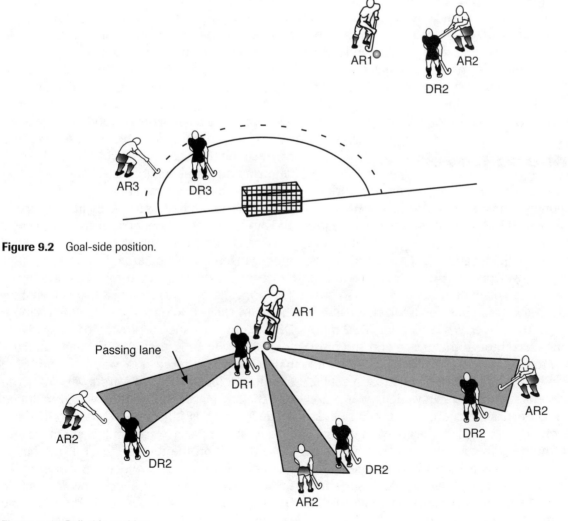

Figure 9.2 Goal-side position.

Figure 9.3 Ball-side position.

players help DR1 by controlling the space around the ball. While DR1 pressures, DR2 players fall back and organize to defend the opponent who is one pass away from the ball. Effective, immediate pressure may force AR1 to slow down and to play into the defense, where passes are limited. Drop back so that immediate cover defense can be set up before DR1 tackles the ball or forces it in a direction the attacker does not want. Covering is defending space behind and beside a teammate. If DR1 cannot cleanly tackle to gain possession, she should delay or force the attacker to pass backward in order to give DR2 players time to drop back and slide toward the ball so that they can provide help near the ball. DR2 players help control space by blocking the forward space available to AR2 players. When controlling space, DR2 must pay close attention to other teammates, the ball, and the opponent. Be aware of risks and priorities that affect team depth, control of space, and position balance. Keep the ball and opponent in front of you so that you can intercept an opponent's pass into the space behind DR1. The farther you are from the ball, the deeper your position must be in order to see the opponent and the ball, which will enable your team to control and block the space behind you.

Mark and Cover

Defense role 2 players are responsible for marking the opponent who is near or one pass away from the ball. All DR2 players have either a marking assignment or a covering-space obligation in every area of the field (figure 9.1, page 177), unless there is no cover player. A cover player defends the space behind marking teammates. To successfully mark, get in position to block a passing lane to the AR2 player. While marking, DR2 must prevent a pass through that space and she must be ready to challenge AR1 if AR1 beats DR1 with the dribble. DR2 must be prepared to use a double team defense with DR1. How tight you mark depends on AR2's direction, speed, and skill, as well as on her proximity to the goal and the ball, and on the need to cover for nearby defenders. Marking is generally tighter when the defender is near the ball or the goal, when AR2 is slow and unskilled, and when AR1 is turned while DR1 is putting excellent pressure on the ball. When the

ball is near the sidelines, mark in a ball-side position. Defenders must mark in front of the attackers when the ball is near the center of the field.

Marking the opponent while controlling space is essential for preventing goals. Most goals are scored from the open center space or from zone 1 (figure 6.3, page 120) in front of the goal. Role 2 defenders mark and control space in the most dangerous shooting areas. While defending the space behind the defense, you must limit the number of receiving choices available to AR2. If you tightly mark AR2, you force AR1 to attempt a longer pass, which forces errors and opportunities to intercept the ball. If you position yourself on the ball side of the passing lanes, in order to control diagonal-forward and through passes, you force AR1 to lift an aerial ball or to pass the ball square or back to a supporting AR2 teammate. As discussed in step 2, aerial passes are time-consuming and easier to defend. Also, flat cross-field passes and back passes toward the opponent's goal allow your defense more time to mark players and to control space.

Force the opponent away from center. Since a small, congested area is easier to defend than a large space, force the ball wide in order to limit the opponent's passing options and to delay direct penetration to the goal. Work hard to keep the ball near the side of the field, which will minimize defensive adjustments. By restricting space, you prevent the opponent from making fast cross-field passes that stretch the defense. By limiting space and by forcing the opponent away from the center area, a defense can eventually gain control of the most dangerous scoring area.

Cover to provide depth to your team's defense. The principle of cover-defense play is based on the team skill of defensive depth. One or more DR2 teammates should provide cover or depth for DR1, who pressures the attacker with the ball. Defensive depth is a way of countering attack overloads. DR2 players away from the ball should stagger their positions and maintain 45-degree angles from one another so that sufficient time and space are available to move and play the ball on the forehand side if the ball is passed forward. Defensive depth provides cover for your teammates and reduces the open space between teammates. Too much depth will allow the opponent to play closer to your goal.

Misstep

DR2 moves into position directly behind DR1 and fails to prevent AR1's pass through the space beside DR1.

Correction

Move into position on an angle from the ball, in the space behind and to the side of DR1.

Transition

The ability to change roles and to play effectively completes the organization (DECA) of team defense. DR2 transition play consists of interchanging defensive roles as well as counterdefending and counterattacking (discussed in step 8). Interchanging the defensive roles refers to moving smoothly from DR2 to DR1 or DR3. Constant decisions have to be made when interchanging defensive roles. Decisions are based on the situation—i.e., the location of the ball, the location of the opponent, the quality of AR1's ball possession, and the positions of your teammates—with special attention paid to the quality of defensive pressure by DR1.

Team defense begins at the moment just before the opponent gains possession of the ball. When defending a counterattack, all players, regardless of position, must quickly assume a role on defense in order to prepare for an opponent who is approaching fast. The moment your team loses possession, you should transition into your counterdefense. The choice of tactical weapon that your team uses against the opposition's fast break is crucial to counterdefense. To avoid being beaten by a team who outnumbers your team in transitional play, regain possession immediately, if possible; slow down the attack and keep the play in front of you; retreat and delay your defense; force play to the outside or keep the ball in the same area of the field so that you need less defensive organization; protect the center of the field and prevent movement and passing through the center; and, finally, approach the ball when there is a strong scoring threat or when you are positioned at an angle to prevent centering passes.

Win the Ball

Finishing the defensive motto of DECA—drop, evaluate, communicate, and anticipate—will help you win the ball. Patiently watch for when DR1 forces the ball to your area of coverage. Intercept the ball, thereby gaining possession of it. Finish your interception by controlling the ball and then making a strong, accurate attack pass.

Misstep

DR2 is too far from DR1 to provide help.

Correction

When determining the proper distance from which to help, consider the ability of DR1, the area of the field, and the location of the AR2 player you need to mark.

Defense Role 2 Drill 2. *2 v 2 Marking*

Use cones to set up a square (20 by 20 yards, or 18.3 by 18.3 m, or less). Two attackers and two defenders start in the square. DR2 players mark the attack players and then move into position to control the ball-side passing lanes. The defender's backline is the dangerous space they should protect while marking AR2 in order to block passes. Attack passers, one outside each sideline, pass the ball to each other and attempt to complete passes to their teammate inside the square. If the ball goes out of play or if a foul occurs, the nearest passer serves the ball into play. DR2 receives 2 points for each intercepted pass and 1 point for breaking up an attack play without a foul. The attack team is awarded 1 point for receiving a pass and 2 points for dribbling over DR2's backline. The defensive team is awarded 3 points—2 points for the interception and 1 point for the score—when they successfully score after an interception. Play for two minutes before substituting new players for the attackers and defenders in the square. After eight minutes, the defensive team becomes the attack team. Play another eight minutes. The team with the most points after two periods wins the game.

To Increase Difficulty

- Increase the amount of playing time.
- Add another defender, who must keep a foot on the goal line.
- Increase the size of the playing square.

To Decrease Difficulty

- Reduce the amount of playing time.
- Decrease the width of the playing area.

Success Check

- Maintain a defensive stance while sliding to win ball-side space.
- Organize and communicate with the other DR2 player.
- Move into position to intercept forward passes.
- While marking, provide angle and distance cover for your teammate.
- Immediately transition from DR2 to DR1 or from defense to attack.
- Win the ball early in the defined space.
- Start a counterattack.

Score Your Success

Highest score = 5 points

Lowest score = 3 points

Your score ____

Defense Role 2 Drill 3.
Numbers-Down Organization and Communication

Use cones to set two 20-by-20-yard (18.3 by 18.3 m) squares (40 yards, or 37 m, total length). Set one goal 7 yards (6.4 m) behind each backline of the back square and the front square. Divide into two teams of equal numbers and decide each team's attack direction. Team A, the attacking team, places one player in each square and one player behind team A's backline. This player can join the game when the ball is served into the playing area. Team A places a passer outside each sideline, 3 yards (2.8 m) outside the back square, to serve the ball. Team B, the defensive team, places one player in each square and one defender behind its backline of the front square. The players from team A (AR2) and team B (DR2) must remain in the front square until AR1 passes or dribbles the ball forward from the back square. DR2 determines whether AR2 needs to be marked, or whether space needs to be covered, and when to step closer to the ball. Another DR2 player behind team B's backline organizes and communicates and then joins in when the backline attack player joins in. Each dribble through the goal

earns 1 point for team A. Team B earns 2 points for each score that results from a successful tackle or interception. Play for six minutes and keep score. Switch directions so that team B uses passers, and then play another six minutes. The team with the most points after two periods wins the game.

To Increase Difficulty

- Increase the amount of playing time.
- Add a goalkeeper, who defends a 10-yard-wide (9 m) goal.
- Increase the size of both squares.
- Add one attacker and one defender in the back square or in both squares.
- Place playing squares outside the shooting circle and run toward the goal. Add a goalkeeper.

To Decrease Difficulty

- Reduce the amount of playing time.
- Decrease the width of the playing area.

Success Check

- DR2 successfully reads a numbers-down situation.
- DR2 organizes the defense and communicates to DR1.
- The DR2 player who joins in organizes the defense and communicates to initial DR2.
- Immediately transition from DR2 to DR1 or from defense to attack.

- Win the ball early in the front square.
- Start a counterattack.

Score Your Success

Highest score = 5 points

Lowest score = 3 points

Your score ___

Defense Role 2 Drill 4.
Weak-Side Defender Organization

Use cones to set up two 20-by-20-yard (18.3 by 18.3 m) squares (40 yards, or 37 m, total length). Set a goal 7 yards (6.4 m) behind each backline of the back square and the front square. Divide into two teams of equal numbers. Team A, the attacking team, places one player in each square and two attack passers (one on each sideline) 3 yards (2.8 m) outside the back square. One of the attack passers may join the game with or without the ball. Team B, the defense team, places one player in each square and one defender 3 yards (2.8 m) outside both sidelines of the front square. The players from team A (AR2) and team B (DR2) must remain in the front square until AR1 passes or dribbles the ball forward from the back square. DR2 determines whether AR2 needs to be marked, or whether space needs to be covered, and when to step closer to the ball. The weak-side defender on the opposite side from the joining passer may join the front square in order to organize DR2's transition. If team B gains possession of the ball, they have just 30 seconds to pass or dribble through the goal. The ball is restarted by the attack passers after a score. Each team-A dribble through the goal earns 1 point. Each team-B (defensive team) pass or dribble through the goal earns 2 points. Play for six minutes and keep score. Switch directions so that team B uses passers, and play another six minutes. The team with the most points after two periods wins the game.

To Increase Difficulty

- Increase the amount of playing time.
- Add a goalkeeper, who defends a 10-yard-wide goal.
- Increase the size of both squares.
- Add one attacker and one defender in the back square or in both squares.
- Place playing squares outside the shooting circle of the field and run toward the goal. Add a goalkeeper.

To Decrease Difficulty

- Reduce the amount of playing time.
- Decrease the width of the playing area.

Success Check

- Weak-side DR2 organizes and communicates to DR2 teammate.
- DR2 organizes and communicates to DR1.
- Immediately transition from DR2 to DR1 or from defense to attack.
- Win the ball early in the front square.
- Start a counterattack.

Score Your Success

Highest score = 5 points

Lowest score = 3 points

Your score ___

Defense Role 2 Drill 5.
Ball-Side and Weak-Side Marking

Use cones to mark a 30-by-30-yard (27.5 by 27.5 m) square with a 7-yard (6.4 m) alley that runs north to south in the middle of the square. Divide your team in half, with forwards and midfielders on the attack team and backs and midfielders on the defense team. Only defenders are permitted in the alley. Position one attacker and one defender in each square, on the left and right sides of the alley. Place an attack passer 3 yards (2.8 m) outside each sideline. The weak-side passer may enter the square when the ball is passed in to AR2. The attack team attempts to move the ball over the defense's endline, and the defense attempts to win possession and move the ball over the attack team's endline. The weak-side defender must cover the passing lanes of two AR2 players on the weak side of the playing area. DR2 learns to drop toward the ball-side space and to read plays in order to intercept attack passes headed for AR2 on the weak side. Earn 1 point for an attack team score and 2 points for a defense interception that results in a score. Play for five minutes and keep score. Attack teams and defensive teams switch roles and play another five-minute period. The team with the most points after two periods wins the game.

To Increase Difficulty

- Increase the amount of playing time.
- Add a 4-yard-wide (3.5 m) goal 7 (6.4 m) yards behind the endlines.

To Decrease Difficulty

- Reduce the amount of playing time.
- Decrease the width of the playing area.

Success Check

- Weak-side DR2 organizes and communicates to DR1 teammate.
- DR2 drops into the alley on the ball's side in order to defend the passing lanes of the two AR2 players.
- Immediately transition from DR2 to DR1 or from defense to attack.
- Position yourself to intercept advantage and penetration passes.
- Start a counterattack.

Score Your Success

Highest score = 5 points

Lowest score = 3 points

Your score ___

Defense Role 2 Drill 6. Recovery Drill

Play on one half of a field hockey field, with a regulation-size goal and shooting circle. Use cones to set two targets 3 yards (2.8 m) wide, parallel to the backline at the 40-yard area opposite both penalty corner marks. Divide your team in half with forwards and midfielders on the attack team and backs and midfielders on the defense team. Start with three defenders and three attackers on the 30-yard line. One of the three attackers starts on the 25-yard line closer to goal. Place a passer and a stack of balls at the long hit mark—the replay area—on both sides of the field. Position an attacker in each of the target areas set on the 40-yard area. The attack player in one of the target areas starts the drill by passing a ball to AR2, who is at the 25-yard line. As soon as

AR2 touches the ball, all players on the 30-yard line start playing. The defense recovers and organizes to win back the ball. If the ball goes out of play, a replay ball from the right side is passed into play. The defense attempts to score by passing or dribbling the ball between the cone targets. If the attacker at the cone target receives the ball before it travels through, she joins the attack, creating a numbers-up attack. The defensive team earns 1 point for each score. The attack team receives 1 point for a goal. Free hits are awarded on foul calls. After each score, repeat the drill until a total of four balls are used from the start area. Play a set of four balls using the replay ball from the right side and four balls using the left-side replay balls.

To Increase Difficulty

- Add more reset balls.
- Add more players.
- Recover from a greater distance.

To Decrease Difficulty

- Use fewer reset balls.
- Decrease the recovery distance.

Success Check

- Defenders sprint to recover along the shortest line to goal.
- Position yourself to organize defensive roles.

- Slow or stop penetration to the central area of the attack third of the field, or zone 1 (see figure 6.3, page 120).
- Listen to the goalkeeper's directions.
- Immediately transition from DR2 to DR1 or from defense to attack.
- Start a counterattack.

Score Your Success

Highest score = 5 points

Lowest score = 3 points

Your score ___

DEFENSE ROLE 3 TACTICS

One objective of attacking play is to get behind the opponent to create scoring chances. Because attacks on artificial turf surfaces are fast and controlled, defensive players need to recover quickly and organize a defense that will keep the attack play in front of them in order to deny penetration into the dangerous space. If you are not in the group of defenders near the ball, be aware of the dangerous space that the attackers seek to enter. You are in defense role 3 (DR3), an assistant helper who aims to prevent any forward penetration either by the ball or by a running AR3. It is with this role that your team-defense tactics become organized and balanced.

To maintain organized defensive play, DR3 must learn to cover and control the dangerous space that is farthest from the ball. Get in position to keep the ball and the opponent in your view and to deny a penetration pass in order to shut off the opponent's direct route to the goal. To execute effectively, you must determine your distance from the ball, which is a prerequisite for covering and

controlling dangerous space. Organizing capable support for DR2 depends on several factors, including the number of DR3 helpers, angle of DR3 help, distance of DR3 players, and communication of DR3. DR3 must always concentrate on the next move, adjust quickly to cover AR3 players, and control the dangerous space.

Depth in defense requires one or two DR3 players ahead of the ball and one or two DR3 players behind the ball. The function of DR3 behind the ball is to provide depth in the defense and to do what DR2 is not able to do because of a lack of time and space—intercept or tackle the forward ball. Controlling the width available to the attack forces the opponent to perform attack skills in a narrow area. When role 3 defenders are two passes away, or 30 yards (27.5 m) or more from the ball, they drop to deeper ball-side and goal-side positions toward the center of the field in order to restrict space and provide balance. Usually one or more DR3 players provide balance in coverage on each side of the field.

Misstep

DR3 is too close to DR2, and as a result, the team is vulnerable to a long cross-field pass into the dangerous space.

Correction

Stay compact, with teammates on AR3's ball side, in order to reduce the number and size of the passing lanes. When the ball is played 30 yards (27.5 m) or more into open space, you will have sufficient time to recover while the ball is rolling, provided that you are not too close to DR2, and you can therefore sprint into your recovery.

The number of DR3 helpers away from the ball is significant. As a guideline, the passing lanes to AR3 must be covered when AR3 players are moving to create dangerous passing options for diagonal and through passes. Because your goalkeeper is the last line of defense, a limited number of DR3 players are needed to provide depth and width coverage away from the ball.

Read the pressure on the ball. Step up to block passing lanes if pressure is being applied and if DR2 has met his responsibilities. DR3 players should position themselves to form narrow angles from the DR2 players and the ball, which will allow them to intercept long, direct passes. Angles vary according to the positions of the opposition and teammates. The narrower the angle of support, the easier it is for the DR3 player to defend the space. Taking a position directly behind DR2 creates a disadvantage because it increases the amount of dangerous space and because the DR3 has limited vision of the field. A position directly

alongside DR2 lacks depth between teammates and the ball. Without depth, AR1 has a greater chance of completing a penetrating pass to AR3. Too much depth by DR3 players allows the opposition to move into the space near the goal.

When defending passing lanes in front of the ball, win the ball-side position in AR3's passing lane. When you are defending passing lanes behind the ball, get in position on the goal side of AR3 in case DR2 gets beaten. This positioning is especially important close to your defensive goal because interchanging defensive roles can be done quickly, if required, because a limited range of passing possibilities is available to the opponent, and because AR3's vision of the field is decreased with less time and space. Positioning on correct angles in relation to the ball, the opponent, and your teammates provides a greater chance to intercept the pass. Maintaining correct angles of width and depth will also enhance your transition into an attack role if you gain possession of the ball.

Misstep

The DR3 player fails to adjust his position in response to the ball's movement.

Correction

When playing away from the ball on defense, positioning must constantly change. As the ball is played from one area of the field to another, adjust your position to control passing-lane options to AR3 in the area away from the ball.

As a general rule, there should be 50 to 60 yards (46 to 55 m) between the last field player behind the ball and the deepest DR3 player in front of the ball. Because the hockey field is 60 yards (55 m) wide, DR3 players defending width should be 35 to 50 yards (32 to 46 m) from the ball and in line with the near goal post. Because DR3 helpers are two passes or more away from the ball, the actual distance of DR3 is often determined by where the ball is (figure 9.4) in relation to the goal, by the quality of DR1 pressure, by the cover and control of DR2 near the ball, and by AR3's position away from the ball. Generally when DR2 is effectively marking an attacker, DR3 can get closer to AR3 and thereby cover and control the dangerous space. In the defending area of the field, DR3's distance from the ball and from AR3 is based on the restrictions of space and time. In this area, you must offer immediate help to DR2

in tight defensive situations. Opponents must be denied time and space in the shooting circle, especially in the vital scoring zones in the front and center of the goal.

The midfield area has more space to defend. This area of the field is often referred to as the "transitional area." Use it to organize your defensive roles. The correct positioning of DR3 players to protect dangerous space in this area will determine organized team-defense play.

In the attack area, DR3's distance can be greater because DR3's main concern is covering space. When the ball is in this area, DR3 must cover the passing lanes that would allow a long outlet pass behind teammates, which would result in a dangerous numbers-up fast break.

It is vital to communicate with teammates in front of you and to follow directions from your goalkeeper or from other DR3 teammates. In ad-

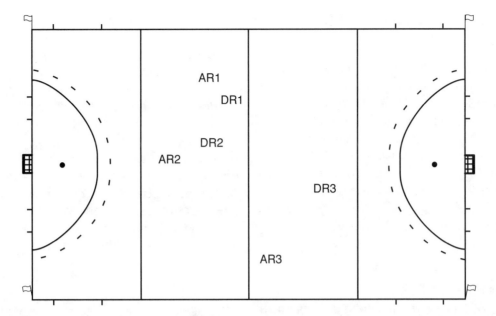

Figure 9.4 Position of DR3 cover.

dition to DR2's directives, a DR3 in cover position says, "Go," when she wants DR2 to take the space because cover or marking is being provided by DR3. Use effective communication to deny width and depth. DR3 can coordinate team play to block areas and discourage the opponent's ball movement. Successful team defense depends on DR3's ability to perform the following responsibilities:

Protect Dangerous Space

The chief responsibility of all DR3 players is to protect the dangerous space, which in turn helps DR2. It is your assignment to assess the situation while DR1 and DR2 are closing down the point of attack and to protect the depth and width space that is 30 yards (27.5 m) or more from the ball.

To be successful, DR3 must drop to the ball-side and goal-side positions in order to cover passing lanes to AR3 in the dangerous space. Cover defenders such as DR3 are concerned with keeping their defensive team compact (i.e., blocking the dangerous central space) and avoiding being lured to outside or weak-side space. From here you will be able to read the situation and provide cover for your teammates while reducing space available to AR3 players away from the ball. Recovering to protect dangerous space provides balance in handling the possible threat against DR2 and DR1. DR3's decision to cover dangerous space is based on knowing the position of the ball and the goal, the quality of DR1 pressure on the ball, where DR2 teammates are providing help, and where the opponent is positioned.

Misstep

AR3 receives through passes to the dangerous space.

Correction

Protect the dangerous space. Get in position diagonally behind DR2, along a line of balance extending toward the far goalpost. From here, you will be able to keep the opponent and the ball in view and to also intercept a penetrating ball. Remember that the line of balance changes with the movement of the ball.

Mark and Cover AR3 Runs

Because AR3 is farthest from the ball, she does not pose an immediate threat. DR3 can support DR2 and DR1 as they attempt to win the ball. But it remains crucial that you see and cover AR3 runs while you protect the dangerous space. Ball watching is a frequent mistake that DR3 players make, which can prove costly in the defensive area (figure 9.1, page 177) of the field. AR3 players make runs for only two reasons—to create space and to use space. DR3 players have to determine quickly what type of run is being made and for what purpose. The most dangerous runs use space, such as a run from the wings to the middle of the field. While keeping AR3 and the ball in view, DR3 must remain on either AR3's goal side or ball side while remaining aware of the goal's position. The least dangerous AR3 runs create space from the middle out to the wing areas. Should AR3 receive a pass, you would have sufficient time to adjust and engage because of the greater distance that the ball has to travel. If AR3 plays the ball directly from AR1, attempt to intercept the pass, prevent AR3 from turning and changing the point of attack, delay penetration to the center of the field, or tackle.

Misstep

AR3 beats you to a long diagonal ball.

Correction

Read the pressure from DR1 and DR2 and concentrate on your angle as you cover the passing lane to AR3. Get on AR3's ball side so that you are nearer to the ball than AR3 and can therefore intercept it. Time your move to the line of the passed ball. Keep your stick and body in a ready position.

Provide Balance

DR3 provides balance to establish cover or defensive depth for DR2. DR3 players away from the ball must be staggered but compact, in support in the dangerous space across the field. Also, DR3 must be at a 45-degree angle from her teammates so that sufficient time and space are available to move and play the ball on the forehand side if the ball is passed forward. A DR3 player who is on the side of the field opposite the ball gets in position along an imaginary diagonal line that starts at the ball and travels toward the far goalpost. By sliding toward the middle and by keeping the ball and the opponent in view, you can intercept a pass into the space behind DR2. The farther you are from the ball, the deeper you must be to see the opponent and the ball, which will enable your team to control and protect the dangerous space. From a position along the line of balance, DR3 can protect the space behind DR2 as well as keep the ball and the AR3 player she is marking in view (figure 9.4, page 187).

Only cover attack players for a certain distance. Balance your running coverage between moving away too far and not moving at all so that you have the opportunity to intercept a pass to the outside, to move close to the attacker, and to protect the central area of the field. A DR3 player who is lured all the way to the outside of the field opens up the central area. AR1 and AR2 will use this area to execute dangerous attacks to goal. The goalkeeper must be prepared to help protect the open space behind DR3 and to communicate the need for defensive balance.

Transition

When a team loses possession of the ball, its immediate goal is to protect dangerous space against the fast break. A crucial part of DR3's transition game is the readiness to transition smoothly into the DR2 marking role or into DR1's leadership role. The ability to interchange defensive roles as the ball travels is crucial for successful defense-team tactics. Organized team defense (figure 9.5), accompanied by determination, patience, and anticipation will help your team deny penetration into dangerous space and eventually win back the ball. The DR3 player who can move from defense to attack by anticipating the opponent's obvious attacking alternatives will often create a numbers-up opportunity.

Figure 9.5 | Team Defense

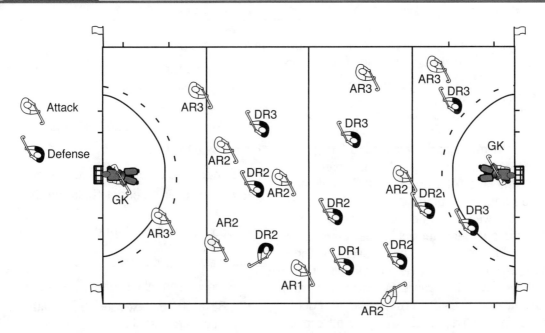

DR1

1. Position yourself goal side, close to AR1
2. Call out, "Ball"
3. Establish a defensive posture with your lead foot
4. Right shoulder is aligned with the ball
5. Maintain balance and stick control
6. Focus on the ball
7. Slow down and direct AR1's dribble or pass
8. Challenge for the ball with help from DR2
9. Win the ball
10. Start a counterattack

DR2

1. Protect space near DR1
2. Read the pressure, and position yourself at the proper angle and distance to DR1
3. Mark AR2 near the ball
4. Keep the ball and opponent in view, with your feet facing the attack backline
5. Intercept any ball passed into the space behind DR1
6. Assume the DR1 role if the ball is passed to the AR2 that you are marking
7. Drop back and evaluate when DR1 is beaten on a dribble
8. Win the ball using communication from DR2 and DR3
9. Start a counterattack

DR3

1. Protect the space diagonally behind DR2
2. Position yourself along a line of balance that extends toward the far goalpost
3. Keep the ball and opponents in view
4. Move along the line of balance in response to the ball's movement and AR3's runs
5. Intercept any passes sent into the space behind DR2
6. Win the ball
7. Start a counterattack

Defense Role 3 Drill 1.
Recovery Against Numbers-Up Attack

Play on one half of a hockey field, with a regulation-size goal centered on the backline and a stationary passer stationed on each long hit mark. Use markers to designate two 5-yard (4.5 m) mini-goals 50 yards (46 m) apart on the 50-yard line. Position a goalkeeper in the regulation goal; do not use goalkeepers in the mini-goals. Designate a four-player attack team and a four-player defense team. Position two attackers (AR2 or AR3) off the ball, near the circle's edge, both of whom are marked by two DR2 or DR3 players. From the remaining players, one attacker and one defender get in position near the mini-goals. Play starts with the recovery defender at the right-side mini-goal. He passes ball 1 to the attack player, who is 5 yards (4.5 m) ahead, and immediately runs to catch up or recover in order to provide defensive help. Attack players attempt to penetrate and then score before the defense can organize a 3 v 3 counterdefense. If the defensive team wins possession, it attempts to pass the ball through one of the mini-goals for 1 point. Award 1 point to the attack team for a goal. Regulation field hockey rules apply, and play continues until a point is scored or until the ball goes out of bounds over the endline of the attack team. Continue the sequence: a long hit with ball 2 is crossed into play; after this ball, the recovery defender on the left side plays in ball 3; ball 4 is played from the left long hit mark. Play for 15 minutes and keep track of points.

To Increase Difficulty

- Increase the amount of playing time.
- Add a neutral player, who always plays with the attacking team.
- Add one AR3 and one DR3 opposite the ball.

To Decrease Difficulty

- Reduce the amount of playing time.
- Add a cover defender (DR3) on the 25-yard line.
- Decrease the width of the playing area.

Success Check

- Recover along the shortest line to the far post.
- DR2 and DR3 execute DECA with marking and covering skills.
- Slow or stop penetration into dangerous space by forcing the ball to the outside of the field.
- Prevent shots from the central area of the attack-third of the field or from zone 1 (see figure 6.3, page 120).
- Start a counterattack.

Score Your Success

Highest score = 5 points

Lowest score = 3 points

Your score ___

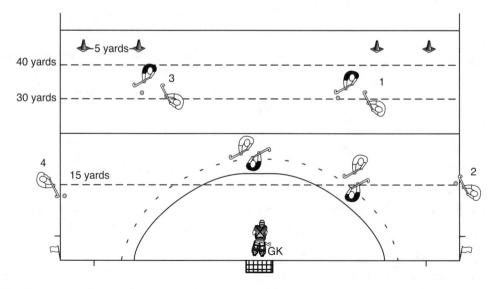

Figure 9.6 Recovery against numbers-up attack.

Defense Role 3 Drill 2.   *DR3 Cover and Balance*

Play on one half of a hockey field, with a regulation-size goal centered behind the backline in the shooting circle. Attack passers on each sideline may stand on the field, 5 yards (4.5 m) from the sideline. Use markers to define a 15-yard-wide (13.8 m) alley that runs north to south in the middle of the field—in zone 1. Divide your team in half, with forwards and midfielders on the attack team and backs and midfielders on the defensive team. Only defenders are permitted in the alley—in zone 1—outside the shooting circle. Anyone is permitted inside the shooting circle and in zone 1 inside the shooting circle. Position two attackers and two defenders in each side area to the left and right of the zone 1 alley. The attack passer starts the drill by passing the ball into the playing field to a teammate. The attack team attempts to move the ball to goal in order to score and the defense team attempts to win possession of the ball and then clear it over the 50-yard line. One DR3 defender slides to the middle of the field (zone 1 alley) to provide cover for her DR1 and DR2 teammates while the other DR3 player slides ball side to provide defensive balance by defending the passing lanes to two AR3 players on the weak side of the field. DR3 drops toward the ball-side space and reads the play in order to intercept attack passes that are headed for AR3 on the weak side. The defense receives 1 point for each successful interception or possession win that results in clearing the ball over the 50-yard line. Award the attack team 2 points for a goal. Play for 10 minutes and keep score. The attack and defense switch roles for a second 10-minute period. The team with the most points after two periods wins the game.

To Increase Difficulty

- Increase the amount of playing time.
- Allow the passer on the ball side of the field to join the attack.
- Place a 4-yard (3.5 m) target at the 50-yard line. To score, the defensive team has to place the ball in the target area.

To Decrease Difficulty

- Reduce the amount of playing time.
- Decrease the width of the playing area.
- Restrict the attack team to three touches or fewer.

Success Check

- Weak-side DR3 organizes DECA to provide cover and balance.
- Cover and prevent penetration via a pass or dribble to zone 1.
- Immediately transition from DR3 to defense and attack roles.
- Balance on the side of the field opposite the ball.
- Start a counterattack.

Score Your Success

Winning team = 5 points

Losing team = 2 points

Your score ____

Defense Role 3 Drill 3.   *Balance: 5 v 4*

Play on one half of a hockey field, with a regulation-size goal centered on the endline. Place a 5-by-5-yard (4.5 by 4.5 m) distribution square in the center of the field, 45 yards (41 m) from the backline. Organize one team of five attack players (two forwards and three midfielders) and one team of four defense players and a goalkeeper. Designate an additional attack player as the distributor; she gets in position inside a 5-by-5-yard (4.5 by 4.5 m) distribution square, marked 45 yards (41 m) from

the goal line. The distributor receives a pass on the 50-yard line from a stationary hitter, and she must pass the ball to either the left- or right-side attackers. The distributor's pass may not roll forward. The defensive team must quickly drop and slide to the ball side in order to adjust to the lateral pass, which will keep the ball in front of the defenders and on that side of the field. When the defense wins possession, they clear the ball to the outside of the field above the 25-yard line. Award the defense 2 points for each interception and clear that result from correct cover and balance play and 1 point for each successful tackle and clear of the ball. The attack team scores 1 point for each goal and for a successful point-of-attack change through zone 1 inside the 25-yard line. Play for 10 minutes and keep track of points.

To Increase Difficulty

- Increase the amount of playing time.
- Allow the distributor to join the attack.
- Place a 3-yard target on the 50-yard line on the right side of the field. To score, the defensive team must put the ball into the target.

To Decrease Difficulty

- Reduce the amount of playing time.
- Decrease the width of the playing area.

- Limit the attack team to three touches or fewer.

Success Check

- Apply pressure at the point of attack.
- Cover and prevent penetration via the pass or dribble to zone 1 inside the 25-yard line.
- Immediately transition from DR3 to defense and attack roles.
- Balance on the side of the field opposite the ball.
- Start a counterattack.

Score Your Success

Winning team = 5 points

Losing team = 2 points

Your score ____

Defense Role 3 Drill 4.
Flow-Through for Defense Organization

Play on the full hockey field, with regulation goals centered at each end. Decide which defense your team wants to play: man-to-man, zone, or match-up zone. On one half of the field, four back defenders from team A take positions at 16 yards (14.5 m) against two forwards and three midfielders from team B. On the other half of the field, four back defenders from team B get in position at 16 yards against two forwards and three midfielders from team A. The coach starts the drill by hitting the ball to the backs on team A. They attempt to play the ball forward. If team B's midfielders win the ball, team B goes to goal. Team A's midfielders may not drop back to defend. Team A is awarded 1 point for each play through to their midfielders in the other half of the field. The flow-through team earns 2 points when they take a shot on goal or draw a penalty corner. If the ball goes out of play over the sideline of the defending team, another ball is passed to the backs at the 16-yard line. Team A gets 10 balls to play before it is team B's turn to start 10 balls at the other end. The team that earns the most flow-through points wins.

To Increase Difficulty

- Increase the number of repetitions.
- Play three forwards and two midfielders.
- Add one recovery defender from midfield.

To Decrease Difficulty

- Reduce the number of repetitions.

Success Check

- Apply pressure at the point of attack.
- Cover and prevent penetration via the pass or dribble to zone 1 (figure 6.3, page 120) inside the 25-yard line.
- Immediately transition into all defense roles.
- Organize cover and balance on the side of the field opposite the ball.
- Start a counterattack.

Score Your Success

Winning team = 5 points

Losing team = 2 points

Your score ____

SUCCESS SUMMARY OF SUPPORTING THE LEAD DEFENDER

Successful defensive pressure, marking, and covering require coordinated help by DR1, DR2, and DR3 players as well as outnumbering the opponent between the ball and the goal. Each defender must read the situation correctly, anticipate the actions of his teammates, and react accordingly. Poor communication, lack of help, incorrect positioning of DR2 and DR3, failure of DR1 to effectively pressure the ball, or poor recovery efforts can all negatively affect a team's defense. Although DR1 skills are the foundation of good defense, the defenders covering players in the space away from the ball also must not be beaten. Based on the assessment of the opponent's attack threat, the organization of a team's defense is improved by the tactical and technical efforts of DR1 discussed in step 7.

Your defensive strategy will influence the organization of all three defense roles. As DR1 pressures the ball, DR2 players support DR1 and cover the nearest AR2 players. DR3 players cover less-threatening AR3 players and then try to protect the space behind the defense in order to provide balance. By denying space, your defense can prevent goals and regain possession of the ball. Record your scores in the following chart and then total the points to get an estimate of your level of competence.

Defense Role 2 Drills

1. Simple Organization and Communication	___ out of 5
2. 2 v 2 Marking	___ out of 5
3. Numbers-Down Organization and Communication	___ out of 5
4. Weak-Side Defender Organization	___ out of 5
5. Ball-Side and Weak-Side Marking	___ out of 5
6. Recovery Drill	___ out of 5

Defense Role 3 Drills

1. Recovery Against Numbers-Up Attack	___ out of 5
2. DR3 Cover and Balance	___ out of 5
3. Balance: 5 v 4	___ out of 5
4. Flow-Through for Defense Organization	___ out of 5
Total	___ *out of 50*

A combined score of 38 points or more indicates that you have sufficiently mastered the tactical responsibilities of defense roles 2 and 3 as described in step 9. You are now prepared to move on to step 10, Organizing the Team's System of Play. A score in the range of 30 to 37 is considered adequate. Review and practice DR2 and DR3 tactical movements again before moving on to step 10. If you had fewer than 30 points, you have work to do before moving on to the next step. Review all the material again and perform all the drills at least one more time to improve your team's defensive performance scores. The additional practice will boost your confidence and performance, preparing you for step 10.

Organizing the Team's System of Play

The final phase of field hockey tactics is the unified organization of all 11 players on the field. Commonly referred to as a system of play, team organization is based on the style of play that your team is capable of performing. The tactics of the attack and defense roles that you have learned thus far are universal to all systems, differing only in individual and team abilities and in the tactical objective of the opponent. The system of play is only a frame that offers your team an unlimited variety of tactics.

Several distinct systems of play have been used at all levels and within various entities of field hockey competition. Many teams play with two or three forwards; others play with four forwards. Occasionally, one forward spearheads the attack. On defense most teams engage a full-time cover defender, commonly called a sweeper. But some teams play without a true sweeper in a three- or four-back alignment. Some teams play a man-to-man defense; others play a zone defense, while others play a combination of both, referred to as a match-up zone. None of these systems are better than the others, and all are effective if played correctly, i.e., with an understanding of attack and defense roles and of incorporating position responsibilities based on player abilities. Teams use different systems partly because of their field hockey philosophy, the style of

play they are capable of playing during certain playing conditions, and the opponent's players and style, but the choice of the system depends primarily on the unique talents and abilities of a team's players.

The shape of a system reveals how a team wants to attack and defend. For example, the formation of the forward positions may resemble a backward or forward arrowhead. A forward arrowhead may indicate a center forward who wants to provide attack depth as soon as her team wins possession. A backward arrowhead may show a center forward who has breakaway speed and counterattack passing skills that allow her to start and join attacks from behind. A diamond shape in the midfield creates natural angles of support to the forwards and the back positions.

The system of play defines each player's positional responsibility within the team. For example, four players may be aligned as backs but have significantly separate expectations. One might be strictly a defensive back whose sole task is to mark the opponent's dangerous and speedy wing forward, whereas another might be an attacking back who creates scoring chances for teammates. For good teamwork, each player must understand his positional responsibility. An expectation that is a constant in all systems of play is the ability to transition into all attack and defense roles.

A system of play is a plan that gives your team an advantage. Advantages allow your team to exploit an opposing team's weaknesses, capitalize on your own strength, counter the opponent's strength, or cover a weakness in your team. Before adopting a system of play, you should understand your team's style of play and your positional responsibilities. Remember, all that the team formation or system of play can do is give a general direction for your team based on your team's ability to execute various attack and defense roles.

STYLE OF PLAY

Two teams competing against each other may use essentially identical systems of play. Yet there may be major differences in the styles they use. Tactics performed from team to team and in different stages of the game can be translated through different manners or styles. Teams develop different styles of play based on the mental and physical abilities of the players, the tradition of the team, the coach's philosophy, and the environments in which some games are played. For example, the Canadians have played a hit-and-rush style; the Germans have played a structured and methodical man-to-man style; the British have played a highly aggressive style with one-on-one toughness and speed; the Americans work hard for physical dominance; the Australians and Koreans have played a fast, wide-open attacking style using direct passes across wide spaces; and the Dutch have played an aggressive but controlled game full of varied tempo, rhythm changes, and cleverly designed tactics. Many South American teams, notably those from Argentina, are characterized by their ability to counterattack, short passes, and dazzling stick handling. As with India and Pakistan, their style is rich in techniques and full of magical ball-handling abilities. Common factors that influence style of play are listed here.

Mental and physical abilities. Your mental and physical abilities will shape your style of hockey, and they are vital to the team's style and system of play. The importance of a team's attitude toward the game and its surroundings is well represented by the fact that a team can use the same players and the same system during home and away games, yet achieve vastly different results. Mental abilities consist of courage, will power, confidence, perseverance, and discipline—essentially those emotions that drive or motivate performance. Strong and determined mental tools are necessary for acquiring and using competitive hockey skills.

To have success, your level of physical ability must meet the demands of the game. Physical gifts that you and your teammates possess will influence your team's style of play. Players who are fast, skilled, and fit will obviously use a style that is different from what players who are slow but skilled will use. Since inadequate physical preparation is a limiting factor in acquiring hockey skills, it also will be a factor in how your team is organized.

Tradition. The duplication of certain hockey skills from player to player or from last year's team to this year's team often leads to the handing down of a tradition of play. Because tradition helps expose specific traits and because it provides constant inspiration and wisdom, you and your teammates can work toward common goals. Teams that exhibit strong traditions demonstrate a strong interest and commitment to field hockey, a desire to succeed, and a willingness to put in great amounts of time and effort to win. Tradition is built on the expectation of success. Often expectation of success determines the effort that you and your team give to preparing your mental and physical skills. If you expect to be skillful and dangerous on attack, then you most likely will be. If you expect not to recover when your teammate loses possession of the ball, then you most likely won't. Your team's tradition of play is another factor that influences the style and subsequently the system of play.

Coach's philosophy. Two teams can be arranged in the same way in the back positions, midfield positions, and forward positions and yet play different game styles. A reason for this difference, apart from the players' abilities, can be the instruction given by the coach. Based on a philosophy, the coach's instructions to her players are designed to get a reaction or a performance. Instructions that produce desired responses are based on *how* the coach gives instructions, not so much on what he or she says. To use philosophy with athletes is to reveal your beliefs and how you stand for these beliefs. The philosophy of a coach provides guidance and direction and helps to interpret the events that surround the team; it also helps to formulate training rules, discipline and conduct, a competitive outlook, and team goals and objectives. The style that you and your teammates play will reflect the coach's philosophy and system of play.

Environment. All team formations should be flexible so that teams can adjust to weather and field conditions, opponents, and the type of competition. On a cold, hard, icy surface, small players can keep their footing better than taller players because they have a lower center of gravity; players who are not physically fit can struggle on a humid afternoon; and on muddy grass fields, strength is required. On watered artificial surfaces, technical skill and speed are essential. While good coaches prepare to use specific tactics to counter the strengths and weaknesses of the opposition, knowing the type of competition is also an important factor. A tie may be good enough in a scrimmage but not in a tournament semifinal in which only the winner advances.

POSITION CHARACTERISTICS AND RESPONSIBILITIES

When field hockey players learn to retreat in order to defend and to advance in order to attack, they are ready to execute overlapping attack and defense roles. Team systems or formations are developed from the players' characteristics and from requirements of game positions. General descriptions of player positions can provide the player with an understanding of the responsibilities of the attack and defense roles. Regardless of their positions, all players assume attack roles when their team has the ball and they perform defense roles when the opponent has the ball. Use the following list of positional characteristics and responsibilities to help you understand a chosen system of play.

Goalkeeper

The goalkeeper (see step 6, page 117) prevents goals from being scored, clears the ball out of the circle to a safe space or to a teammate, directs team defense in the circle, covers and clears balls that penetrate behind her teammates, tackles breakaway forwards, uses directions to coordinate the positioning and play of the backs and sweeper, defends penalty strokes, and organizes the defense of all defensive penalty corners. Goalkeepers must have good concentration and an ability to quickly determine the angle of the shot. Courage, confidence, quick reflexes, mental toughness, excellent vision, excellent eye–hand and eye–foot coordination, gymnastic ability, strength and agility, an ability to read the game, and a willingness to lead are all characteristics of a good goalkeeper.

Backs

The backs mark opposing forwards or midfielders in their area of the field, set up attack play by distributing balls to midfielders and forwards, coordinate with nearby teammates to defend against the opponent's attack, provide depth support to change the point of attack, assist with or take free hits in the defensive area of the field, use tackling and positioning for marking and covering, communicate attack and defense directions, and assist in set pieces of the attack and defense penalty corners.

The *sweeper*, or *fullback*, must read the game as well as anyone else on the field because it is essential for the sweeper to spot the danger in an opponent's attack. Sweepers need to be skilled in winning the ball in one-on-one situations, in marking or covering in all defensive situations, in coordinating all defense roles, in taking 16-yard (15-meter) defense hits, in demonstrating agile footwork with composure, and in being a good leader. All sweepers must be able to pass the ball hard and accurately over long distances.

The *right side back* provides balance and cover when the ball is on the opposite side of the field, takes most sideline hits on the right side, assists or takes deep defensive hits, and prevents shots on goal. This player needs good speed and mobility to mark the opposing, left, outside forward and needs to be in position to support the midfielders and forwards during a counterattack. The right back must have composure and be skilled at intercepting and passing, particularly at making the through pass that runs parallel to the right sideline and at making the long centering pass from the right side of the field to the left.

The *center back's* main responsibilities are to tightly mark the opposing center forward and to demonstrate good tackling skills. To stay close to a particular opponent throughout a 70-minute match, a center back must be very fit. Center backs need to be physically strong and mentally tough in order to concentrate on marking tightly. Other skills needed to effectively play center back include the abilities to pass and to intercept the opponent's passes, to assist in free hits out of the defensive area, and to take or assist free hits in the midfield and attack areas.

The *left back* provides balance and cover when the ball is on the opposite side of the field, takes most left-sideline hits, assists or takes deep defensive hits, and communicates attack and defense roles with the left midfielder, center back, left wing, and sweeper. It is important that the left back have good foot speed because her main assignment is to mark the opposing right outside forward, who is usually a fast sprinter. The left back must be able to mark tightly and to tackle the ball with strength in order to prevent right-side attacks. When the left back wins the ball, she must be able to pass the ball and especially to hit passes accurately from the left side of the field to the center and right side of the field.

Midfielders

Midfielders provide a link between backs and forwards; mark opposing midfielders in attack, midfield, and defensive regions of the field; get in position to control space in the midfield in order to limit the opponent's passing options; help teammates with marking assignments; take midfield free hits and assist on free hits outside of the defensive zone; tackle, mark, and cover; attack and finish the attack; communicate attack and defense roles with nearby teammates; and assist in set pieces of the attack and in defense penalty corners. To effectively play any midfield position, players must be able to execute transitional play in all the attack and defense roles.

The *outside midfielders* must have quickness and speed, along with endurance, because they cover and control the most space (the space between the 25-yard lines). They must have excellent vision and they must be very skilled at controlling the ball when building the attack play. In addition to being good combination-style passers with the ability to think quickly and to locate the best pass to give, outside midfielders must have an instinct to score. They usually set up successful attacks by threading intelligent passes through the opponent's defense. Equally important is their ability to fulfill the responsibilities of all three defense roles, particularly of marking.

The *center midfielder* marks the opposing center midfielder in the attack and midfield region of the field, assists in marking the inside forwards in the defensive region, provides an AR2 link between backs and forwards, assists the center back in controlling the midfield, supports forwards and provides depth to the attack in order to allow the point of attack to change quickly or to allow dangerous penetration, and provides a passing option out of the defense. The center midfielder is a total field hockey player who possesses creative and imaginative attack play and determined defense skills that keep the opponent's attacks to one side of the field. This player needs to see all options and must be able to choose the best option while under pressure, and she must do so with composure. These players must be tactically sound with great leadership abilities and have the same abilities as the outside midfielders. A good center midfielder has an exceptional ability to receive and control passes that come at her from all sides and to pass accurately to teammates in AR2 and AR3 roles. It is the busiest position in terms of processing visual information.

Forwards

Forwards create and finish goal-scoring opportunities, combine with nearby teammates to build attacks, create depth and width for ball penetration and for stretching the opponent's defense, use space created by others, get in front of midfielders, play defense roles in all three regions of the field, and assist in set pieces of attack and defense penalty corners.

The *center forward* needs physical and mental strength—and she must be a risk taker—to play in a tight or crowded space so that she can get to the ball first. It is vital that the center forward be able to score goals with a quick release and be able to anticipate centering passes. Swiftness, good close-ball control, and one-on-one skills with and without the ball are requirements that enable center forwards to move into space near the goal. On defense, the center forward should cover the attack moves of the opponent's center back.

The left and right outside forwards, the *wing forwards*, must use speed and quickness with the one-on-one dribble in order to spot and play the space behind the opponent. Also, wing forwards need to be able to hit hard, accurate centering passes and to be a threat to score goals. In addition to executing all attack roles, they must execute all three defense roles while covering and marking the opponent's corresponding side backs.

TEAM ATTACK AND DEFENSIVE TACTICS

When selecting a system of play, a coach must consider which kind of team attack and team defense his team is capable of performing. Again, this decision is based on the team's style of play. Environmental factors such as field conditions and climate may also influence game performance, but it is still important to learn how to play effectively in various environments, regardless of the game conditions.

Tactics for Team Defense

Team defense tactics such as man-to-man marking, zone defense, and a combination of both—the match-up zone—may influence the choice of which system to play.

In *man-to-man marking*, one defender takes on the specific responsibility of marking one opponent. Although the opponent may have difficulty escaping and using space, man-to-man marking requires strict discipline from every player on the team. If one player fails to perform her defensive assignment soon enough, there is an immediate chance that the team defense will become weak and disorganized.

With *zone defense*, each defender takes responsibility for any opponent that enters her zone of defense. The zone concentrates on the region of greatest danger but also ensures that cover is provided around the zone should the point of attack shift to another area of the field. The ability to maintain discipline and organization is critical to zone defense. Zone tactics have many benefits: the ball can be kept in an area of the field by using intelligent positioning, DR2 and DR3 interceptions can lead to counterattacks,

defenders learn to play against an extra attacker, and the zone defense is less physically demanding. The weakness of a zone occurs when a zone is overloaded, which allows the opponent to execute two-on-one attacks.

The combination of both zone and man-to-man marking—the *match-up zone*—is the most effective team-defense tactic. The match-up zone defends areas of the field and marks man-to-man when opponents enter the areas of greatest danger. Actually, the defense roles and the combination defense tactic are the same. Both provide efficient marking of the attack players around the ball and cover for balance in spaces away from the ball. Good match-up zone defenses will force the opponent to play the ball square or back because they have denied the opponent the opportunity to penetrate.

A team must thoroughly understand the principles of both zone and man-to-man defenses before executing an efficient match-up zone. Along with understanding all three defense roles, effective communication is necessary in the transition from each defense role that a match-up zone requires. The inability to move quickly and purposefully into each defensive assignment may cause much confusion against an attack team that uses short, well-paced passes and deft dribbling skills.

Tactics for Team Attack

Team attack tactics include the fast break and the possession attack.

Although field hockey is a highly technical game with various unpredictable situations, it also has certain recurrent patterns. For example, one team may play possession hockey, controlling the ball for long periods, while the opponent occasionally initiates quick counterattacks, or *fast breaks*. Despite the possession team's apparent dominance, the score may be close or the fastbreaking team may win. Fast breaks into the dangerous space behind the opponent usually start from a turnover at midfield or from a poorly placed clear to the center of the field by the goalkeeper. The space behind the defense is used by making through passes into it or by fast dribbling into it if there is no opponent between the ball and the goal. Speed of execution is the key to fast break success against retreating defenses or pressure defenses.

Possession attack uses frequent square and back passes to build up the team attack. To play this style within a system, your team must have excellent support help, movement, communication, and one- and two-touch passing skills. An effective means of attack, the possession style can be used to protect a scoring lead or to draw out a team that retreats and sets up its defense near the defensive 25-yard (23-meter) area.

COMMON SYSTEM ALIGNMENTS

Hockey coaches gravitate toward two fundamental alignments based on either a defensive scheme or an attacking scheme. If based on defense, the choice is to play with a designated cover player or sweeper or to play an alignment without a designated cover. Playing without a designated cover requires players in the back positions to assume cover responsibilities, along with marking, when the situation warrants. If the system of play is based on an attacking scheme, the choice is how many forwards and midfielders to use during the attack so that the attack and defense roles can be successfully interchanged and executed. Team personnel and abilities allow the coach to determine which system or alignment will best use the strengths of the team.

In describing a system of hockey play, the first number refers to the forwards, the second to the midfielders, the third to the backs, and if necessary, the last to the sweeper. The goalkeeper is not included in player numbering. The following hockey systems are just two of the most common alignments used in modern field hockey.

3-3-3-1 System

One of the most widely used alignments in field hockey is the 3-3-3-1 system (figure 10.1). Derived from European hockey (primarily from the Dutch), the 3-3-3-1 system employs a sweeper back who is generally designated as the free cover defender. Strong and fast AR1 skills are especially

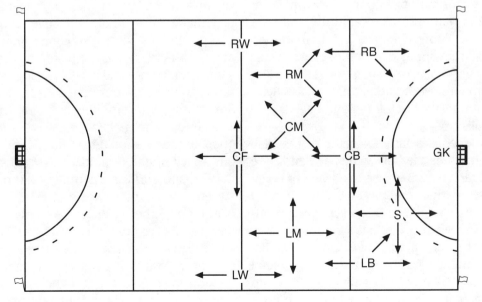

Figure 10.1 3-3-3-1 system.

needed by the forwards in the 3-3-3-1 system. The three forwards are organized with two outside players, or wings, and the inside center forward. The forwards are free to run anywhere to create width and depth in order to produce disorder in defenses that play zone, man-to-man, or match-up zone.

In a three-player forward line, the diagonal run is the most effective attack run. Many one-on-one breakaways can occur when an opponent fails to effectively interchange defense roles, resulting in drawing penalty corners and goals. On defense, the three forwards look to mark or cover the passing lanes to the opposing backs and sweeper and to back tackle for double-teaming defense.

The three midfielders must be very fit and must be able to execute tactical and technical skills. Close man-to-man marking is generally employed by the two outside midfielders, making it extremely difficult for the opposition's corresponding forwards and midfielders to receive the ball and to break away into open space. The side midfielders support the forwards on attack and provide a line of defense in front of the backs. The center midfielder has the freedom to move laterally or even to overlap on attack, which can create more space for an attack. The defensive marking scheme is generally a zone or a match-up zone. It is crucial for all midfielders to transition well both when attacking and defending.

The backs usually mark opponents closely in the midfield and defensive regions of the field in order to prevent the opposition's forwards from receiving the ball and penetrating to goal. The center back is more effective in a man-to-man marking of the opposition's most dangerous inside forward but can also be effective using a match-up zone in the attack half of the field. Backs must be very disciplined and have strong tackling skills.

The sweeper is a fast evaluator of the play and often receives the ball with space and time to set up attack play. Because the sweeper is not assigned to mark a specific opponent, a good sweeper can make the 3-3-3-1 system very effective if she can provide leadership and cover for the other three backs. The sweeper is a vital position for any system that employs a designated cover player. The ability to field loose balls, to make a final one-on-one tackle before an attacker penetrates the circle, to join the attack when coverage is assumed by a teammate, and to be a willing participant in all special situations makes the sweeper highly important in the 3-3-3-1 system. The 3-3-3-1 system, or any system using a sweeper, such as a 4-2-3-1 or 5-3-2, requires an agile, explosive goalkeeper who can support the sweeper and read the play. It is essential that the goalkeeper be an excellent defender against the penalty corner.

3-3-4 System

In the 3-3-4 system (figure 10.2), players are spread out over the field to provide balance between attack and defense. This system is usually suited for teams with young, inexperienced tactical players or for a team that does not have a bona fide sweeper. The forwards, midfielders, and backs are in place to play the ball to the outside of the field. Although this system of balance may initially lose some of its flexibility in order to vary game tactics, it can become a more adaptable formation as the team improves its tactical understanding and technical skill.

The three forwards occupy the front of the attack and have responsibilities similar to those of 3-3-3-1 forwards. Speed is an asset for the wing forwards, and finishing skills are a must for the inside center forward.

The center midfielder is an important player in the 3-3-4 system and must be a total player. He must be able to read the game so that creative play making is swift and effective. Good passing and dribbling skills are required, along with an ability to penetrate and finish. On defense, the center midfielder must be a strong ball tackler because the outside midfielders cover and position off the center midfielder's movement.

The four backs align themselves to mark the opposing team's forwards and the most dangerous attack-oriented midfielder. The inside backs have responsibilities similar to those of the sweeper and center back in the 3-3-3-1 system, working together so that one marks the center forward and the other provides cover. The outside backs usually match up against the opponent's outside forwards or side midfielders and they provide cover and balance. The 3-3-4 system requires that the backs and midfielders contribute

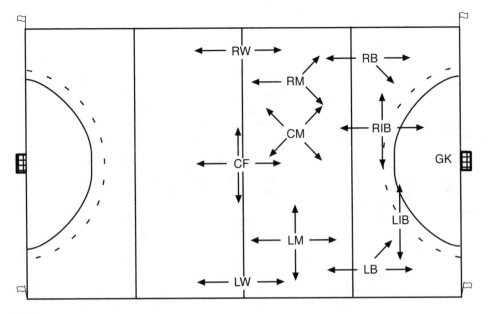

Figure 10.2   3-3-4 system.

to their team's attack by using overlapping runs from behind.

Alignments such as 2-4-4 (figure 10.3) or 2-5-3 (figure 10.4) are created from the 3-3-4 in order to provide a greater emphasis on player mobility and on the interchanging of positions. The trend in field hockey is to load the midfield area in order to cover space and press better. Backs start attack play and join attack play with the midfielders in order to use attack space better. At the highest level of competition, alignments favor four backs because of the tactical flexibility available within the system. It is common to see teams switch formation during the game—for example, by having one of their backs play in front of the other backs instead of behind the backs that are in man-to-man or match-up zone defenses. Or the four backs play zone defense flat across the field and move into a match-up zone below the 30-yard area.

The use of four or five midfielders in the midfield also provides greater tactical assignments. On defense, double teaming with DR1 and pressing coverage are possible in both zone and man-to-man defenses. Often the outside midfielders

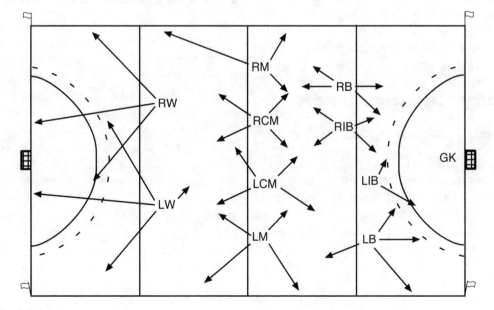

Figure 10.3   2-4-4 system.

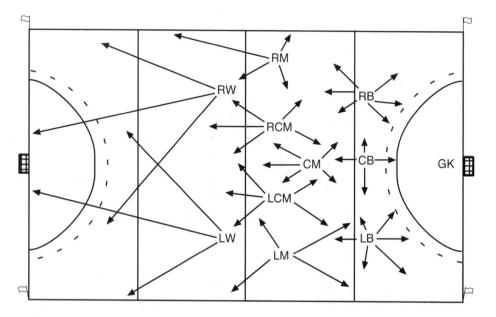

Figure 10.4 2-5-3 system.

become forwards in the attack third of the field. The inside midfielders can change the shape of their positioning from flat to triangle or diamond, giving emphasis to attack or defense counters.

No matter what formation your team uses, the roles of attack and defense, discussed in steps 7, 8, and 9, are critical to understanding and executing hockey.

ORGANIZING THE PENALTY CORNER

An integral part of organized team play is the penalty corner. The penalty corner is an important situation in which the attacking team will seek to maximize its goal-scoring opportunities while the opponent organizes a defense to deny a scoring chance. How a team chooses to organize itself for a penalty corner, on both attack and defense, is based on players' abilities.

Penalty Corner Attack

In principle, with only five defenders to beat, every penalty corner should produce a quality shot at goal. Because the rules place no restrictions on how many attackers may take part in the penalty corner, it is important to exploit those areas of the shooting circle (figure 10.5) that the defenders find difficult to protect. Numerous organized attack plays may be devised for the attack penalty corner. But the most organized team attack will only be as successful as your team's ability to execute with speed and accuracy three

fundamental attack techniques—push passing, receiving, and hitting.

Penalty Corner Defense

The penalty corner defense consists of five players, each of whom has critical and disciplined assignments. As the leader of the penalty corner defense, the goalkeeper has important responsibilities. Positional play is fundamental to goalkeeping. The goalkeeper is expected to organize her defense and to concentrate on the ball the moment the penalty corner is awarded. Always alert for a quick push out from the opponent, the goalkeeper moves quickly from the goal line to block the path of the shot. The goalkeeper should avoid being screened or blocked from the sight of the ball by focusing on the ball as it is passed from the backline, during a trap or stick stop, and when it is shot. Because most penalty corner shots at goal are taken from 13 to 14 yards (12 to 13 meters) away, the goalkeeper must develop

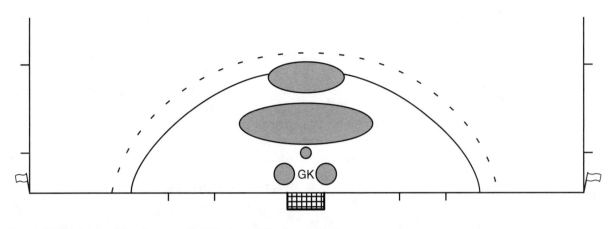

Figure 10.5 Areas of the shooting circle that are difficult to defend.

and master a style of defense as well as have an organized penalty corner defense system that can be practiced.

Three styles of goalkeeping are used in defense of the penalty corner: the upright style, the lying position, and the running slide.

Upright Style

The upright style is the most effective position. It reinforces goalkeeping techniques previously learned and should be practiced before other styles. Goalkeeping while standing in ready position requires the ultimate in skill and reaction, and this style is used as basic training on all playing surfaces and with players of varying abilities.

To execute the upright position, quickly advance 3 to 5 yards (about 3 to 5 meters) from the goal line. The distance will vary for each goalkeeper because of her size and reaction time. Coordinate your reaction time with your position away from the goal line. Use breakdown footwork

to move into the ball's line before the ball is shot at goal. Concentrate and stand in a balanced, ready position at the time of the shot. Your eyes are focused on the ball so that you can quickly respond to the speed and direction of the shot.

A team's decision to use one or two post players will depend on the goalkeeper's abilities. If two post players can defend the shot near the goalpost, then the goalkeeper can defend the shot between the post players. If only one post player is used (figure 10.6), then the goalkeeper is responsible for the rest, or three-fourths, of the goal.

The remaining defenders include a flyer, who is the first runner off the goal line. The flyer lines up to the goalkeeper's left side when the shot is taken from the right side of the circle. The flyer's assignment is to pressure the initial shot. The right cover player takes a position outside the left post and runs from the goal line, even with the goalpost, to cover the flyer. The right cover's assignment is to cover the flyer's right side and

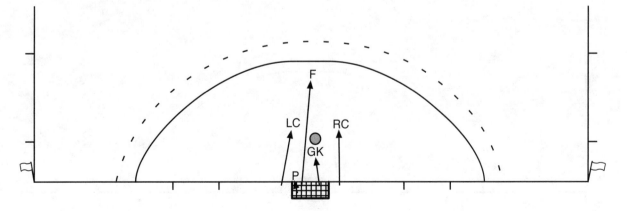

Figure 10.6 Defending the goal during a penalty corner, with one post player and the goalkeeper in upright position.

203

to pick up any rebounds or lay-off passes to the right. When one post player is used, a left cover player covers the flyer's left side and breaks up play behind the flyer.

Lying Position

The lying position is sometimes referred to as "logging" and can be a dangerous style if the goalkeeper is not fully protected. The lying style is effective if the goalkeeper has poor reaction time and skill when defending the initial shot from an upright position. The objective is to block horizontal space along the ground because the initial shot, if struck with a backswing, can score only if the ball is hit 18 inches (45.72 cm) or lower over the goal line.

To execute the lying position, move 2 or 3 yards (about 2 or 3 meters) from the goal line. Rest your body weight on the right foot and on the inside of the left foot. Lean to your right. Drop to the ground on your right side as the ball is struck in order to create a wide barrier with your body. Bend at the waist, and support your weight on your right hand and stick or on your stick and elbow, and raise your left glove hand. Keep your head in line with the ball. Shots to your right are saved using both the glove and stick together. Shots to your legs are saved with the feet, but your glove and head move to the ball. In the lying position, you will have more difficulty stopping shots above your waist, legs, and extended stick.

Except for the flyer, the penalty corner assignments of the other defenders change when the goalkeeper uses the lying position (figure 10.7). The left post player comes out level with or slightly behind the goalkeeper's feet in order to clear balls that bounce off the goalkeeper's pads or hand. She must also cover the space in front and to the left of the goal in the shooting circle. The right post player comes out and covers the area to the goalkeeper's right side. She clears saved shots away to her extreme right and defends attackers who run into the penalty-spot area. A fifth defender, a runner, covers the flyer's left or right side.

Running Slide

The running slide (figure 10.8) is used occasionally at the most advanced levels of play as a variation of the lying position. It is meant to surprise the attackers. It is the least used method of goalkeeping because it leaves the right and left sides vulnerable to passes.

To execute the running slide, run as fast as possible from the goal line toward the ball and then slide down and smother the ball as it is hit. Use the double-leg slide (stack) to create a large barrier with your body between the goal line and the ball. It is crucial to keep your eyes focused on the ball in order to time your slide correctly, because the slide tackle requires perfect timing.

Defensive assignments for the remaining defenders are similar in principle to the lying goalkeeper's assignment. Because the goalkeeper becomes the flyer, a right cover player defends space to the goalkeeper's right side and a left cover player positions herself to cover the goalkeeper's left side. Usually two post players remain near the goal line to protect the space in front of the goal.

When a goalkeeper masters an effective style for defending the penalty corner, your team will enjoy challenge of protecting your goal.

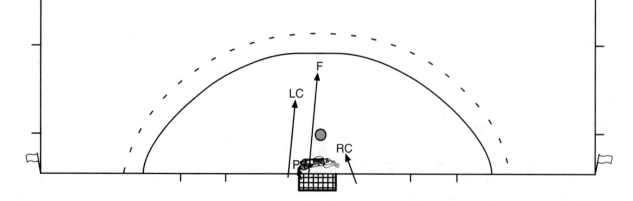

Figure 10.7 Defending the goal during a penalty corner, goalkeeper in lying position.

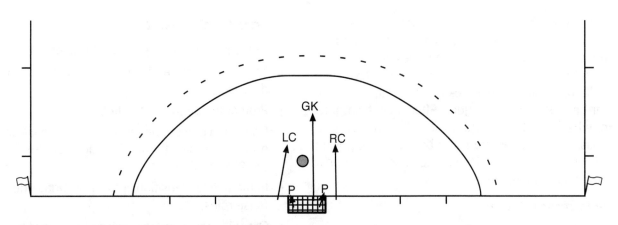

Figure 10.8 Defending the goal during a penalty corner, goalkeeper using the running slide.

Team Organization Drill 1.
Skeleton Drill for Team Attack

Play on a regulation-size field with goals. Select the system to be used and move into position on one half of the field. The goalkeeper gets in goal with a supply of balls. A back begins the drill by taking a 16-yard defensive hit. From that point, you and your teammates collectively two- or three-touch pass the ball down the field and shoot it into the opposing goal. Do not use any opponents other than a goalkeeper in this exercise. Every attack player should focus on moving correctly in relation to the ball as you pass the ball downfield toward the goal. After each score, return to your original positions. Repeat the exercise 10 times at half speed and 15 times at game speed against an opposing goalkeeper. Award 1 point for each accurate shot on goal and 2 points for a score that is finished with two shots or fewer.

To Increase Difficulty

- Limit players to one or two touches when passing, receiving, or shooting the ball.
- Add six opponents who try to prevent your team from advancing the ball down the field.

To Decrease Difficulty

- Reduce the number of repetitions.
- Slow the speed of the drill.

Success Check

- Provide width and depth in attack.
- Provide support for AR1.
- Immediately transition into all attack roles.
- Adjust your position in relation to the movement of the ball.

Score Your Success

20 points or more = 5 points

17 to 19 points = 3 points

15 or 16 points = 2 points

12 to 14 points = 1 point

11 points or fewer = 0 points

Your score ___

Team Organization Drill 2.
Skeleton Drill for Team Defense

Use the same setup as the previous drill and add an opposing team. Get in position to defend a goal while the opponents get in position in the opposite half of the field. The opponent's back has the ball and begins the drill with a 16-yard defensive hit. The opponent attempts to move the ball down the field in order to shoot at your goal. You and your teammates work together, using all three defense roles, to prevent shots, gain possession of the ball, or both. Award your team 1 point each time you win ball possession. The attacking team earns 1 point for each shot on your goal. After a shot on goal, or when your team tackles the ball or intercepts a pass, immediately return the ball to the opposing sweeper or back for a 16-yard defensive hit. Repeat 20 times at game speed.

To Increase Difficulty

- Increase the number of repetitions.
- Require the defending team to play with only eight field players.

To Decrease Difficulty

- Reduce the number of repetitions.
- Limit attacking team to three touches or fewer when passing, receiving, or shooting the ball.

Success Check

- Apply pressure at the point of the attack.
- Pressure, mark, and cover, and balance on defense.
- Protect the center of the field.
- Cover and prevent penetration via the pass or dribble to zone 1 (figure 6.3, page 120) inside the 25-yard line.
- Immediately transition into appropriate defense roles.
- Organize cover and balance on the side of the field opposite the ball.
- Start a counterattack.

Score Your Success

Yield 5 points or fewer = 5 points
Yield 6 to 8 points = 2 points
Yield 9 points or more = 0 points
Your score ___

Team Organization Drill 3.   *11 v 11 Board Game*

You will need a drawing of a hockey field, graphed on a piece of paper (figure 10.9), as well as pencils and two dice. You may also use a cloth field that is a minimum of 36 inches long by 26 inches (91.44 cm by 66.04 cm) wide. You'll need dime-size magnets in two contrasting colors, as well as a magnet of a different size and color to represent the ball. The field (either paper or cloth) must be marked to scale with graphed squares, each representing 5-by-5-yard (4.5 by 4.5 m) squares. The hockey field is 60

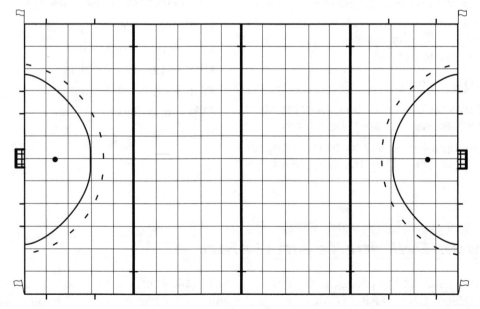

Figure 10.9 11 v 11 board game.

yards (55 m) wide; therefore, the field is 12 squares wide. The length of the hockey field (100 yards long, or 91.5 m) is represented by 20 squares.

Two or more players can play. Divide the players into two teams and place 11 game pieces on the field as you would to start a real game. If you use a paper game field, write each player's position in a square on the paper. For example, LB, CB, and RB stand for left back, center back, and right back in a three-back system. On a cloth field, use magnets to mark player positions.

The basic game rules are as follows:

1. Only one player or piece may occupy a square.

2. You may not move the ball or players through a square space that is occupied by an opponent.

3. You may move players diagonally, square, forward, and back.

4. A player from each team rolls the dice to determine which team will start the game with the ball. The team who rolls the higher number begins the game with a roll of the dice.

5. The team with the ball continues rolling until they lose the ball or until a score occurs. If a score occurs, the team that is scored on restarts the game at the 50-yard line.

AR1 rolls the dice. The outcome of AR1's turn is determined by the following chart:

2 = Ball over your attacking backline; 16-yard hit for the defense

3 = Defense intercepts; executes two passes

4 = AR1 sets up a give-and-go plus one pass

5 = Lose ball; opponent wins possession at this spot on the field

6 = AR1 dribbles laterally one square and forward two squares

7 = Opponent intercepts and makes one pass

8 = AR1 dribbles two squares and passes

9 = AR1 passes plus one more pass

10 = AR1 passes

11 = AR1 passes and dribbles two squares

12 = AR1 beats DR1 with a pass and then another pass

Next, roll the dice to determine the number of spaces AR2 or AR3 can move. The outcome of this roll is determined by the following chart:

2 to 4 = may move six squares or less

5 to 7 = may move four squares or less

8 to 10 = may move three squares or less

11 or 12 = may move five squares or less

After the attack team makes a move, the defense rolls and moves its players according to the following chart:

2 to 4 = may move six squares or less

5 to 7 = may move four squares or less

8 to 10 = may move three squares or less

11 or 12 = may move five squares or less

On a turnover (initial roll of 3, 5, or 7), the defending team rolls the dice to determine how many defenders may recover:

2 or 3 = one recovers

4 to 6 = two recover

7 to 9 = three recover

10 to 12 = four recover

The defense keeps throwing the dice until all defenders recover.

If the ball enters the circle, the goalkeeper rolls one die:

1, 3, or 6 = score

4 = goalkeeper saves; roll the dice again

2 or 5 = 16-yard hit by defending team

Play for 15 minutes. The team with the most goals wins.

To Increase Difficulty

- Increase the length of the game.
- After each roll of the dice, a decision must be made in three seconds or less.

To Decrease Difficulty

- Reduce the length of the game.
- Permit five seconds for a decision to be made.

Success Check

- Organize the defense around the ball.
- Protect the center of the field in all defense roles.
- AR2 provides support for the lead attacker, allowing the lead attacker to move the ball.
- AR3 provides an angle of support from AR2.
- Provide width and depth in attack.

SUCCESS SUMMARY OF ORGANIZING THE TEAM'S SYSTEM OF PLAY

Each system of play has strengths and weaknesses, both in team style and in positional responsibilities. It is the coach's responsibility to evaluate her players and to select a system that best fits the team's capabilities. No system can overcome inaccurate passing or shooting, improve ball control, help players who will not help each other, or hide players who cannot or will not run. A team can play as many forwards as it wishes, but if it cannot win and maintain possession of the ball, then the system employed will not produce goals.

Furthermore, a team can place as many defenders as it wishes in front the ball and the goal, but if they cannot interchange defense roles effectively, then the system will not prevent goals.

Each player has a responsibility to become familiar with the system of play, to understand his or her positional responsibilities within the system, and to execute the attack and defense roles. Doing so will allow you to achieve technical, tactical, physical, and psychological success in the exciting game of field hockey.

Team Organization Drills

1. Skeleton Drill for Team Attack — ___ out of 5
2. Skeleton Drill for Team Defense — ___ out of 5
3. 11 v 11 Board Game — ___ out of 5

Total — ___ *out of 15*

Your total score will depend on how many formations your team rehearses in the drills. The team should average at least 3 points per drill and per formation of play. Scoring less than 3 points indicates that more practice is needed. Decide how your team wants to play tactically and then rehearse the formation until the movements become natural. Develop into a team that thinks and executes together.

Functional Training

The demands of fitness vary from sport to sport. Preparing the body to meet the demands of field hockey should be a shared responsibility between the athlete and the coach. Exercise, nutrition (including water), and rest must be monitored and maintained in order to achieve a fitness level that is sufficient for successful performance. This step focuses on a dynamic field hockey warm-up and fitness program that is designed to prepare and train the player for the physical demands of hockey.

A field player may be required to run more than 5 miles in a typical 70-minute game. Hockey running includes changing direction sharply, sprinting, jogging, walking, running backward as well as forward, and power-step footwork that is similar to the shuffle and acceleration patterns used in tennis at various distances and speeds. These movements require endurance and explosiveness and, therefore, both the aerobic and anaerobic energy systems need to be stressed during practices. Field hockey players who use functional training for their warm-ups and fitness training will increase strength, speed, power, and endurance.

Sport-specific activities for field hockey involve coordinated, multijoint movements and torso training that are designed to improve speed, strength, and power. Agility, which is the ability to change the position of the body or any of its parts rapidly while remaining in control, is critical for successful field hockey performance. Controlling the speed of power movements (the product of force and velocity) and being flexible (the ability to move normally through the full range of mo-

tion of each joint without restriction) enable players, including goalkeepers, to maintain balance, which is crucial for executing technical skills. A prerequisite for proper hockey technique is correct and constant foot-to-ball distance combined with coordinated stick handling, good hand-eye coordination, and agile foot movement. No matter what the player's position on the field, a field hockey player must squat with a low center of gravity and then move and control that low center of gravity, as with lunging and power footwork. To effectively perform hockey movements, the player must maintain balance (the ability to assume or maintain any body position with control and stability), making interrelated groups of muscles and joints work in unison. Each player must learn to control his or her own body weight and center of gravity in the various activities that field hockey requires.

Good physical conditioning for hockey emphasizes core-strength of the key joints and stabilizing muscles in the hips, legs, and knees; torso (abdominals and lower back); and scapula of the posterior shoulder. The aim is to use exercises that train the muscles in the same way that they are used in the sport of field hockey. Ultimately, training for speed and power, and improving the endurance of both, will lead to improved field hockey performance.

Field hockey is a speed and power sport in which the best players are the ones who can move the most proficiently and explosively for more than 70 minutes. To play at your potential is the mark of a successful field hockey player and, eventually, a successful hockey team. Players who develop quick and strong execution of fundamental hockey skills exemplify the splendor of team play.

Although field hockey is a team game, individual execution of the fundamental hockey skills is critical to a team's success. Regardless of a player's skill level, balance is the foundation for the performance of hockey techniques. Superior balance is the most fundamental trait of the best hockey players who have developed speed, coordination, and power. Balance is achieved through a purposeful warm-up and through functional fitness training that builds strength in the core stabilizing muscles and that develops speed, power, and endurance through anaerobic and aerobic exercises.

DYNAMIC WARM-UP

Effective field hockey performance requires players to warm up in preparation for the physical demands of field hockey. Before every practice or game, perform a series of sport-specific warm-up activities. Exercise that is designed to warm up the body by using movements that will be used during the game is referred to as a *dynamic warm-up*.

Dynamic warm-up exercises are designed to stimulate the nervous system by increasing heart rate and blood flow, which in turn elevates muscle temperature and helps prevent muscle and joint injuries during the practice or game. A warm muscle contracts more forcefully and relaxes more quickly. Warm-up exercises also improve muscular contraction, response time, and flexibility.

The joint's active range of motion (ROM) during movement is known as *functional flexibility*. Training functional flexibility benefits the field hockey player because body control is reinforced throughout the ROM. Stabilizing and balancing the body while moving at the required speed is crucial for executing technical hockey skills. With any functional movement, the body will only allow ROM that it can control. In contrast, *static flexibility* is the passive ROM of a joint without movement. Experts have learned that static stretching that is performed before a game can reduce a player's explosive power, which field hockey demands. In other words, static stretching may inhibit explosive performance, and therefore it is most effective *after* a game, during the cooldown or after the workout.

The length of the dynamic warm-up varies for each individual, but 15 to 20 minutes is generally enough time to elevate muscle temperature. A good indication that the muscle temperature is elevated is sweat. It is important to elevate your heart rate from the resting rate, increasing blood flow to muscles, before performing dynamic stretching exercises.

The two components of the dynamic warm-up are the five-minute, sport-specific warm-up and the ballistic and functional-flexibility exercises. The five-minute, sport-specific warm-up of hockey techniques includes cadence-style running and basic movements. Ballistic and functional-flexibility exercises progress from a slow to a fast tempo. Generally this component lasts 10 to 15 minutes.

Remember, your goal is to warm up your muscles using the same movements that you will use during the practice or game. This step provides a few dynamic warm-up routines that you can use or modify to build and maintain the physical demands of field hockey movements.

Five-Minute Sport-Specific Warm-up

Choose one or more hockey skills, such as dribbling with a ball or passing and receiving with a teammate while jogging, to increase blood flow to the muscles and to raise the overall body temperature. Here are some examples of passing and receiving warm-up routines. Use one of these five-minute sport-specific routines as the first component of the dynamic warm-up or create one of your own.

Routine 1. Partners start 7 yards (6.4 m) apart and push and receive the ball. Emphasize proper push passing and receiving techniques. Compete with other pairs of teammates to see which pair can complete 15 (or any chosen number) push and receiving passes first. The pair who stops the 15th pass on their stick first wins the contest. Pairs of players then compete with pushing, reverse pushing, and quick hits at distances of 15 yards (13.8 m). Next, at a distance of 25 yards (23 m), pairs of hockey players hit and receive passes.

Routine 2. Divide team into shuttle groups of five players per group. Two players stand in a line 25 yards away, facing the remaining three players in the other line. Each group has one hockey ball. For five minutes, players execute skills, with the specific technique changing every 30 seconds. For example:

1. Player 1 starts with the ball. She pushes the ball 2 to 5 yards (1.8 to 4.5 m) out and accelerates to regain the ball on her stick, then push passes to player 2 in the opposite line. Player 1 runs to the rear of player 2's line as player 2 receives the ball and repeats. As they wait their turn, players 3, 4, and 5 stay in constant motion by jogging, skipping, or hopping in place.

2. For the next 30 seconds, players move from accelerated push passes to small lifts of the ball off the ground while running forward, followed by a push pass to the teammate waiting in the opposite line.

3. For the third 30 seconds, players sharply change direction with the ball, moving to the left and to the right, followed by a push pass to a teammate who is waiting in the opposite line.

4. For the next 30 seconds, players sharply change direction with the ball, moving to the right and to the left, followed by a push pass to a teammate who is waiting in the opposite line.

5. For the next 30 seconds, players push the ball out and away from the body while turning the lead shoulder and hitting the ball to the shuttle teammate.

6. For the next 30 seconds, players execute fakes and hits.

7. For the next 30 seconds, players run right and then left with the ball on the stick and then make a hit pass.

8. For the next 30 seconds, players run left and then right with the ball on the stick and then make a hit pass.

Continue creating your own patterns. Play for five minutes. Try to receive every ball without a rebound off the stick by focusing on receiving the ball with your head and shoulders over the ball. Keep your stick in a vertical position out in front of your right foot, and maintain relaxed, soft hands. With your eyes focused on the ball, follow the ball's path in order to keep the ball close to your stick.

Ballistic Exercises and Functional Flexibility

Ballistic activity and functional-flexibility exercises that progress from a slow speed to a fast speed make up the second part of the dynamic warm-up. Ballistic exercises consist of dynamic, quick movements of the lower body. The following are two examples of ballistic exercises:

1. Straight leg swings across the front of your body, 10 repetitions with each leg. Face a wall, fence, or goal cage and place your hands on the object to help you balance. Swing your leg in front and across your body while balancing on the opposite leg.

2. Leg swings forward and back, 10 repetitions with each leg. Turn one side of your body toward a wall or fence. Place the hand of the arm nearer the wall on the wall for balance. Maintain balance and control of your torso without bending at the waist or moving your head. Swing the leg nearer the wall forward and back while balancing on your support leg.

Ballistic exercises improve explosive movements and the speed of hockey skills. Because field hockey demands intense explosive and reactive movements for passing and receiving, ball control and dribbling, and tackling, it is important to do ballistic exercises.

Here is a sample routine of functional-flexibility exercises that can be used to complete the dynamic warm-up.

Perform slow-tempo functional-flexibility exercises while standing or while walking forward and back over a distance of 10 yards (9 m). Follow this sequence:

1. Golfer pick up. Walk forward. Bend from the waist and reach down with one arm to pick up something or to touch the ground. Alternate the reach arm and support leg.

2. Knee up. Pull one knee to your chest and then the other.

3. Foot back. Grab the instep of your foot and pull the leg back under your hip. Point your knee downward. Switch to other foot.

4. Leg cradle. Walk forward. Lift your foot off the ground. Grab the foot in front of your body and pull it up to your stomach, keeping your bent knee in a hurdle-seat position.

5. Sumos, down and up. Assume a wide crouch-like stance, like a sumo wrestler, with buttocks at knee level. Place your hands on your right ankle, then move them to your left ankle in a right-center-left motion.

6. Stand up. Walk forward and backward, reaching both arms toward the right ankle, left ankle, out in front of the feet, then down close in front of the feet.

7. Inchworm. While standing, reach down and place hands on the ground in front of your feet. Walk your hands out until you are in an extended push-up position. Then keep your hands in place and walk your feet to your hands.

8. Spiderman. Place your hands on the ground in front of your feet. Walk your opposite leg and arm forward like a spider.

9. Dog in the bush. Place your hands on the ground and walk forward on your feet and hands like a dog. Alternate lifting your legs like a dog using a bush or fire hydrant.

10. Curtsey. Bow or bob over front knee and twist.

11. Back reach over leg. Right hand reaches back to grab left foot. Pull left leg toward lower back. Switch to right-leg reach.

Perform quick-tempo functional-flexibility exercises by briskly skipping or jogging a distance of 15 to 20 yards (13.8 to 18.2 m), then back, for each exercise. Follow this sequence:

1. Straight-leg march (like a Russian soldier) with opposite hand to foot forward. Jog backward.

2. Open-hip skip forward and backward. Pull knee up and outside of hip.

3. March forward and backward with your knee up and with open hip flexors. Rotate the bent knee up and out.

4. Power skips forward and backward. Skip as high and far as possible.

5. Backward run. Stretch heels up in rear.

6. Quick carioca forward and backward.

7. Accent carioca forward and backward. Lift knees to waist height.

8. High knees. Run in place for three seconds with high knees, and push forward into a quick sprint start. Do two sprint starts while running forward and then return.

9. Power slide steps. Turn the side of your body to the finish line. Assume a defensive position and slide laterally. Do not allow your feet to come together.

10. Quick start and turn to each side. Turn your back to the finish line. Run in place with high knees, then turn to your right 180 degrees and sprint. Turn left on return.

The warm-up is complete and your body is now prepared for the practice or game. At the end of each practice session or after a game, do a warm-down. A warm-down consists of exercises that allow your bodily functions and heart rate to return to resting levels. Jog or walk, and then perform static stretching exercises for each major muscle group. Pay attention to the lower-back muscles when doing static stretches. Use a stretch strap to help maintain correct form and range of motion. Static stretching after a game or after a strenuous practice session will help prevent muscle soreness. Stretch each major muscle group for 30 seconds and repeat if necessary. Focus on the glutes, hamstrings, quadriceps, groin, calves, and Achilles tendons. Here are some examples of static stretches:

1. Hurdle seats (quadriceps). Sit with a one leg straight forward. Bring the foot of the other leg into the middle of your body as far as is comfortable. Turn or twist your shoulders to the side of the bent leg and reach your hands behind your hip. Stretch the quadriceps, keeping the outside of the hurdle leg against the ground.

2. Seated hamstring (hamstrings, lower back, calves). Sit on the ground and spread your

legs as far as is comfortable. With your arms outstretched, reach toward your left foot, toward your right foot, and then forward, keeping your head and shoulders up.

3. Butterfly (groin). In a seated position, bring both feet to the middle of your body as far as comfortable. Hold both feet with both hands, and pull your chest to your feet.

4. Lateral groin stretch (groin, hamstrings). Squat over your right leg. You may keep the right heel flat or balance on your toes. Facing forward, extend your left leg laterally, resting your foot on your heel. Lean your upper body forward or to the left and point your left foot upward.

5. Lying lower back (lower back). Lie on your back, with your arms outstretched at 90 degrees to the sides of your body. Raise your left leg (which may be straight or bent)

to a position perpendicular to the turf, and then lower it to your right hand.

6. IT band stretch (iliotibial band, glutes). From the butterfly position, maintain the position of your right leg but place your left leg behind your body. Try placing your chest on top of your right knee. Repeat to your left knee.

7. Three-point lunge (hamstrings, hip flexors, glutes). Kneel with your left knee on the turf, lower left leg behind your body. Place your right leg in front of your body, with your foot flat on the turf and your knee at 90 degrees. For position 1, keep your upper body in an upright position while pushing forward. For position 2, turn to the left and lower your right elbow toward the turf, to the inside of your right leg. For position 3, grab your left foot with your right hand. Pull it to your buttocks and lean forward.

FUNCTIONAL TRAINING FOR OVERALL FITNESS

After the completion of the dynamic warm-up, implement a functional training routine. Functional training should take five to eight minutes after the dynamic warm-up. Functional training is a method of practicing and of building and maintaining muscles that you use in field hockey. Choose a different routine each day, or create your own routine. If you elect to incorporate a functional training routine into your practice preparation, choose from the following functional-training routines. Perform functional training after the end of the dynamic warm-up.

Mini-Band Routine

Secure an elastic mini-band or surgical tubing around your ankles. Make certain that the band remains taut, stretched to about shoulder width. Do not bring your feet together. Grip your field hockey stick and complete the following exercises, forward and back two times each, in eight minutes or less:

1. Lateral slide 10 yards (9 m) forward and back. Assume a balanced, defensive stance,

and move laterally while maintaining your defensive posture.

2. Lateral slide 2 yards (1.8 m), and take three power steps forward, 10 yards and back.

3. Monster walk 10 yards and back. Stay in a slightly crouched position and walk with your legs wider than shoulder-width apart, like a monster.

4. Speed skater (with quick feet), 10 yards and back. Glide along the turf.

5. Ice skater, 10 yards and back.

Finish with the standing hip-flexor exercise. Perform 10 repetitions with each leg. Place the mini-band around both ankles. Start by lifting the left knee. Rotate the knee to the left side at hip height. Balance on the right power point and repeat with the right knee.

Medicine Ball Routine

During the eight-minute routine, maintain an athletic stance and grasp the medicine ball with your hands on either side of the ball. (You can substitute a field hockey stick for the medicine ball.) Perform 8 to 10 repetitions of each exercise, or do each exercise for 10 seconds. Comfortably hold the ball out away from the body between your hip and chest height to begin each of the following movements:

1. Twist from side to side while watching the medicine ball.

2. Dynamic twisting.

3. Balance on your right foot and twist from side to side. Repeat while balancing on your left foot.

4. Bring the ball down toward your left ankle and then up over your right shoulder. Reverse, bringing the ball down toward your right ankle and then up over your left shoulder.

5. Lower the ball to between your feet and then raise it over your head.

6. Move the ball making a hitting motion. Take the ball back to the outside of the right hip and pull with the left side of the body (left shoulder and left hip) to bring the ball through on a downswing.

7. Balance on your left foot and lower a hand to touch the ball on the ground. Repeat on your right foot.

8. In a down-and-up motion, pull the ball behind your right thigh and then over your left shoulder. Keep your feet shoulder-width apart while balancing on your power points. Repeat to the other side, pulling the ball behind your left thigh and over your right shoulder.

9. Move the ball from hip to hip.

10. Repeat the hitting motion as in 6.

11. Balance on your left foot and touch the ground with the ball. Do three repetitions. Repeat on the right foot.

12. Perform a wood-chopping motion with the ball to three levels: both sides at waist level, knee level, then ground level.

13. Move the ball in a big figure-8 motion.

14. Touch the ball on the ground, and then bring the ball off the ground using a vertical jump.

15. Balance on your left foot. Hold the ball and twist. Repeat on your right foot.

16. Balance on one foot. Touch the ball to the ground in front of your body and to the ground on both sides of your body.

17. Balance on one foot and squat. Extend the ball straight out.

Hip Flexors and Claws Routine

The hip-flexor exercises in this section will develop and stretch the torso muscles that help with stabilization, lateral flexion, and rotation as you perform hockey skills. The routine takes six minutes.

1. While standing, walking, or jogging, drive or pull your knee to your chest and drive the bent knee down to the ground. Flex your foot in a claw-like position, lightly touching the ground before bringing the opposite knee up and down to repeat. Do 25 repetitions with each leg.

2. Hip lift. Lie on your back with your feet and shoulders on the ground and bend your knees to 90 degrees (up a bridge position). Lift your hips up and down on one leg at a time. Do 10 hip lifts on each leg from a bridge position.

3. The Cook stretch (named after physical therapist Gray Cook) will teach you to distinguish between hip extension and back extension so that you properly use the gluteus and hamstrings as hip extensors. Most field hockey players need to improve their range of motion in their hip joints so that they can maximize their performance during explosive hockey skills. The hip extensors are used not only in many field hockey techniques, such as in hitting and tackling, but also in change-of-direction running. Tight hip flexors will limit hip extension and contribute to lower back pain when you handle the ball with the stick. To perform the stretch, lie on your back with your feet flat on the ground. Place a tennis ball on your ribs and pull one knee to your chest and hold the ball in place. From this position, push down through the foot that is still on the ground and extend the

hip while keeping the ball tight against the ribs with the other leg. Do eight repetitions with each leg.

4. Without the tennis ball, do eight repetitions of the straight-leg Cook stretch with each leg. Keep the raised leg straight and the other foot flat on the ground.

Roped Medicine Ball Routine

Some medicine balls come with a sturdy rope attached. The roped medicine ball is used for dynamic training exercises of varying degrees of difficulty. Roped medicine ball routines are meant for collegiate and more experienced players. The attached rope allows the field hockey player to train for explosive rotational movements, which are used to strike the ball. The roped medicine ball must be used properly to prevent injury. Follow these guidelines when using a medicine ball:

- Use only against hard, smooth surfaces.

- Never add air to the roped medicine ball; the manufacturer determines the ball's weight and volume.

- Young people should use medicine balls only with adult supervision.

Progress through the routine of core exercises at your own pace. Stand with your feet shoulder-width apart, and hold the rope of the medicine ball in both hands, right hand below the left. Do two sets of 10 repetitions for each exercise.

1. Circle the ball above your head like a helicopter blade. Use the central stabilizing muscles of the shoulders, abdominals, and lower back and the surface back muscles, commonly called the "lats" (latissimus dorsi), a large muscle of the back that draws the arm down and back and that rotates the arm. Be sure to keep your feet on the ground to generate rotational force with the body and not with the hands. Complete the helicopter exercise by rotating the roped medicine ball clockwise and then counterclockwise.

2. Grip the rope portion of the roped medicine ball, hands out in front and away from your body. Maintain a shoulder-width stance and circle the ball clockwise in front of your body for two sets of 10 repetitions. Use your central stabilizing muscles to maintain balance and control of your body and the weighted ball. Repeat, circling the ball counterclockwise.

3. Stand with feet shoulder-width apart and grip the rope of the medicine ball, holding it in front of your body. Keep your arms relatively straight and begin moving your arms in a figure-8 motion.

4. Sit on the ground with your legs straight out. Grip the roped medicine ball as in the previous exercises. Swing the roped medicine ball so that the ball strikes the ground on either side of your hips. Keep your hands and arms away from your body.

5. Sit on the ground with your legs straight out and securely grip the rope of the medicine ball, with your right hand below your left. Strike the ball on the ground toward the outside of the right foot. Immediately swing the ball diagonally up and behind your left shoulder to hit the ball on the ground. Repeat in the opposite direction (outside the left foot and behind the right shoulder).

6. Stand with your back 12 inches (30.5 cm) in front of a solid wall. Hold the ball with a secure rope grip. Maintain a slight bend in your knees and keep your hips against the wall. Use your shoulder-width stance and a steady head to maintain balance on the power points of your feet. Start by forcefully extending your arms to the left and then to the right as if you were swinging a baseball bat. Keep the rope under tension and accelerate the roped medicine ball away from your body and toward the wall. Target your core stabilizing muscles by keeping your shoulders and hips close to the wall at all times. When the ball rebounds, swing your arms and rotate at the hips in the opposite direction in order to accelerate the ball across the front of your body so that it strikes the wall on the opposite side.

7. Set up as in the previous exercise. While twisting through your body's midsection, bring the ball down toward the opposite leg. Reach down until the ball touches the

ground on the outside of your foot. Reverse the diagonal movement and bring the ball back to the starting position. Switch the roped medicine ball to the other side of your body and repeat.

8. This exercise is similar to the previous exercise except that you stand in a low squat with your buttocks a few inches above the bend in your knees. From this squatting position, maintain balance on your power points and keep a shoulder-width stance during the exercise. The roped medicine ball should hit the wall at knee height or lower.

9. Set up in the same position as in the previous exercise, but move the roped medicine ball diagonally from outside the foot on the wall to over the opposite shoulder on the wall. Maintain a steady head and balance. Repeat to the other side of your body.

10. Stand 6 to 12 inches (15 to 30 cm) in front of a solid wall. Keep your torso erect and knees slightly bent, standing in a balanced shoulder-width stance on the power points of your feet. Secure your hold on the roped medicine ball by inserting your left wrist through the rope handle and then grasping the rope with the left hand. Use the right hand to grasp the rope below the left hand using a hockey stick grip. Swing the roped medicine ball so that the ball strikes the wall directly over your head. As the ball rebounds, forcefully swing your arms down so that the ball goes between your feet. For safety purposes, keep the rope under tension during the exercise.

11. Grip the roped medicine ball with your left hand at the end of the rope and your right hand below the left, touching your left hand. Balance with your feet shoulder-width apart and your knees bent. Turn the left side of your body to your target as you start the hitting motion. Keep your left arm straight as you make your backswing in the direction of the right hip. Generate force with the left hip and shoulder as you start the downswing, bringing your arms down and through in the direction of the left hip. Keep your arms and hands away from your

body. Keep your head steady and your torso upright. Repeat on the backhand side, with your right side facing the target.

Plyometric Routine

Whether you are dribbling the hockey ball, changing direction or speed while dribbling, passing the ball while moving, or challenging for the ball by tackling, you will need a great deal of body coordination. All field hockey skills require good hand-eye and foot coordination and balance for correct technical performance.

Jump rope activities improve agility, and plyometric exercises—exercises that enable a muscle to reach maximum strength in as short a time as possible—can increase much-needed power. Plyometric training consists of jumps, hops, leaps, bounds, and skips performed with great speed and intensity over a planned progression. Be sure to protect your legs by jumping on a soft surface.

Jump rope activities will improve agility and aerobic capacity. The proper technical use of a jump rope will allow you to train efficiently while developing coordination and balance. A variety of skips, jumps, hops, and runs should be performed on the power points of the feet. Grip the jump rope handles as you would when you shake hands with someone. Keep your hands slightly forward at hip level and turn the rope with your wrists. Depending on your level of conditioning, you can increase or decrease your pace for the following rope-jumping exercises:

1. Two-foot hop: Jump over the rope with both feet for a total of 50 hops.

2. Right-foot hop: Jump over the rope with the right foot only for 25 hops.

3. Left-foot hop: Jump over the rope with the left foot only for 25 hops.

4. Jog step: Jog for 50 rope turns under the feet.

5. Skier's hop: Jump side to side using two-foot bunny hops for 50 hops.

6. One-leg skiers: Jump side to side using a one-foot hop for 25 hops on each foot.

7. Boxers: Jump with both feet, crossing your feet front and back, for 50 jumps. For example, land with your left foot in front of

the right, and then reverse it on the next jump and landing.

8. Double jumps (pepper): Pull your knees up high in front, keeping your feet under your hips on each jump. Whip the rope around twice (rapid fire) under your feet before you land on your power points and jump again. Do three consecutive double jumps.

To perform plyometric exercises, use a boundary line on the field or place a cone on the ground to mark an area or obstacle to jump, hop, skip, or bound up and over. As you become more experienced with plyometric exercises, the natural progression is to intensify your workout by increasing the size of the obstacle or cone and to perform the exercise under the pressure of time. Use the following plyometric exercises as a basic routine:

1. Two-foot vertical jump: Jump straight up as high as you can six times. Be sure to land in balance on the power points of your feet, with your knees slightly bent and feet shoulder-width apart.

2. One-foot vertical jump: On one foot, jump up as high as you can five times. Switch to the other foot and repeat.

3. Two-foot forward and back jump: Using both feet, jump forward and back across a line 10 times.

4. Two-foot lateral jump: Turn one side of your body toward a line. Stand 12 inches on the side of the line. Jump laterally across the line and back for 10 repetitions.

5. Two-foot diagonal lateral jump: Stand beside a line with feet shoulder-width apart. Jump diagonally forward across the line and immediately back to your starting spot. Repeat the pattern 10 times. Switch to the other side of the line and jump 10 times diagonally forward and back.

6. One-foot forward and back jump: Stand on one foot behind a line. Jump 12 inches across the line and back. Repeat the forward and back jumps on one foot for 10 repetitions. Switch to the other foot for 10 jumps.

7. One-foot lateral jump: Stand on one foot, 12 inches away from a line. Jump laterally over the line and back for 10 repetitions. Repeat on the other foot.

8. One-foot jump turn: Stand on one foot. Jump forward 12 inches over a line and turn halfway around to face the starting area when you land. Immediately jump back over the line and turn. Repeat for 10 repetitions. Switch to your other foot and repeat.

9. Tuck jump: Stand with your feet shoulder-width apart and your body vertical. Do not bend at the hips as you jump and bring your knees to your chest. Grasp your knees with your hands before your feet return to the ground. Land in a vertical position without bending forward. Immediately repeat the jump for six repetitions.

10. One-leg tuck jump: Do another tuck jump, but raise only one knee to your chest. Do four one-leg tuck jumps with your left leg and four repetitions with your right leg.

SUCCESS SUMMARY OF FUNCTIONAL TRAINING

Because field hockey requires good endurance and strength, a player must warm up the body; properly condition the body by doing the appropriate amounts of sport-specific exercise, by eating well, and by resting; and perform a suitable warm-down. Remember, a poorly conditioned athlete will perform skills poorly, lack confidence, and make bad decisions. Successful performance depends on physical preparation and technical perfection. Whenever possible, include a ball and stick in warm-up exercises to incorporate skill training. Inadequate warm-ups and warm-downs will limit performance. Take care of your body and enjoy creating routines for success.

⊡ Glossary

advantage pass—A forward pass in which a player maintains possession of the ball.

advantage space—The forward space between the ball and the opponent in which the defense can block the offense's movement toward the goal.

angle, narrowing the—When the goalkeeper moves nearer to the ball in order to reduce passing or shooting space near the goal.

assistant helper—Another term for role 3 players.

backhand—Maneuvering the stick in order to execute skills on the left side of the body.

balance in defense—Defensive position that provides depth and support; defenders nearest the ball mark opponents while teammates on the side of the field opposite the ball cover dangerous space behind the defense.

ball check—A ball-control technique used to momentarily stop or control the ball so that a change of direction and speed may occur.

ball control—Keeping the ball within good-contact distance and preventing it from rolling beyond a balanced reach. See *control box*.

ball-side positioning—Refers to a defender who is positioned on the side of the opponent that is closest to the ball.

blind-side run—A method of off-ball running that is made outside of the opponent's vision and behind a defender in order to use or create space.

blocking space—Defender gets in position to intercept the ball or to take away the opponent's chance for a forward pass or dribble.

block tackle (open-stick tackle)—A defensive skill used to steal the ball from AR1 by extending both arms out in front of the body and placing the stick horizontally on the ground in the path of the ball.

breakdown steps—Short, intense, running footwork intended to bring the body into a balanced position after the player takes longer sprint strides.

centering—The act of passing a cross ball from the wing into the middle of the field of play.

channeling—A defensive act (railroad running or forcing) used to force AR1 in the direction that the defensive team wants her to go so that a tackle attempt can be made by a defensive teammate.

checking run—Movement used by attackers to put more distance between the defender and the ball. Attack player runs toward the goal-side defender, then suddenly stops and cuts back toward the ball.

chip shot—A powerful aerial shot, often used to shoot the ball into the upper part of the goal. The wrists are slightly open on the downswing and at impact.

chop shot (squeeze shot)—A raised shot executed from behind the back foot by using the stick to contact the upper back of the ball, which presses the ball into the ground.

clip hit—The act of quickly hitting the ball while power dribbling by allowing the left hand to slide down the stick to join the right hand (choke-up grip).

close down—When a player reduces the space between herself and an opponent who has (or does not have) the ball.

controlling space—Positioning by defenders that restricts space and thereby forces opponents to slow their attack to a predetermined area.

control box—Area in front of a player that is defined by that player's hand reach from a squat position and shoulder-width distance, where ball control and other AR1 skills can best be executed.

counterattack—A transitional attack (fast-break) tactic that creates a numbers-up situation.

counterdefense—A transitional defense tactic that is used to defend against a numbers-up counterattack.

cover—Defensive support; as a defender challenges an opponent, she should be supported by a teammate who is located behind her in the event that the challenging defender is beaten.

cut the ball—Running diagonally forward while dribbling the ball.

dangerous space—The space between the ball and the goal you are defending.

DECA—Acronym for the defense organization of Drop, Evaluate, Communicate, and Anticipate.

defender, committing the—While with or without the ball, attracting the attention of a defender by moving him or her from occupied space.

defense stance—A balanced, ready position assumed by a defender in which the stick head is close to the ground and a lead foot is established so that a skill or a change of direction is possible.

dive shot (sliding shot)—Deflection shot taken while sliding along the ground.

double-leg stack—An advanced goalkeeping technique used when close to the ball in order to slide and smother a shot on goal. See also *stack slide*.

drag flick—A powerful flick shot taken from the back foot in which the ball starts on the stick shaft and the player coordinates foot speed with the whip action of the stick.

dropkick clear—A half-volley kicking technique used by the goalkeeper after successfully blocking an aerial shot with the glove hand.

drop step (attack and defense)—An individual ball-control technique for AR1 that creates space away from DR1 from a forward to back direction. A defensive player uses a drop step when he or she is beaten on the lead-foot side.

dynamic warm-up—Exercises that employ movements that are similar to movements used in a game.

engaging distance—The approach distance needed to set up for DR1 pressuring skills.

flick—A push stroke that raises the ball off the ground to various heights at various speeds.

forehand—The maneuvering of stick skills on the right side of the body.

functional flexibility—A joint's active range of motion.

goal-side position—Nearer to the goal; position between the goal being defended and the opposing player being marked.

instep kick—A goalkeeping technique in which the midline side of the foot, from the big toe to the ankle, is used to kick the ball.

jab tackle—A defense technique that provides a greater reach with the left hand and an easier shift into other tackles; utilizes a panhandle grip with the left hand. Execution resembles a push or poke action with the stick, which is driven by the legs from a balanced-stride position.

killer pass—A pass that penetrates through and behind an opponent.

lead foot—In a staggered stance, the foot that is slightly forward of the back foot. Establishing a lead foot enables easier backward movement while maintaining balance and agility.

lifted dribble—A small lift of the ball over a defender's stick that is low on the ground.

line of recovery—The path the defender takes when running toward his or her goal in order to establish a position on the goal side of the ball.

man-to-man defense—Defensive system in which each player is responsible for marking a particular opponent.

marking—Tight defensive coverage of an opponent that blocks the direct passing lanes to the AR2 players.

match-up zone defense—Defensive scheme of playing man-to-man defense when an opponent enters a player's zone of defensive responsibility.

open field dribble—The act of tapping the ball ahead when in possession of the ball in the open field and of moving or breaking away over a short distance so that the player can scan the field.

point of attack—The center of attack where the ball is located.

possession pass—A low-risk pass that maintains control of the ball.

possession space—Space where ball control is maintained in order to make dangerous space more vulnerable (via a lateral or back pass).

power dribble—Dribbling technique used to maintain possession of the ball in tight, crowded space. The ball is kept close to the stick at all times.

power points—The balls of the feet.

quick hit—A striking technique using a short grip and small take-back swing.

rebound clear—A goalkeeping technique in which a shot is saved and cleared with one touch of the foot.

receiving box—A visualized area or space where an attack player traps the ball using proper breakdown footwork to achieve body balance and ball control.

scanning—Observing one's immediate area, while in possession of the ball, so that decisions of when to pass, move, or change direction can be made. Types of scanning include distance, peripheral, and photo.

shaft—The area of the hockey stick between the handle and the stick head.

shake-hands grip—The basic hockey grip from which all other grips originate. The forefinger and thumb of both hands form a V so that a straight line from the tip of the V runs down and bisects the middle line of the handle and toe; sometimes called the "split grip" or "receiving grip."

skeleton play—A method of coaching that allows players to execute skills and movements without opposition.

slide (shuffle)—Defensive footwork used to maintain a balanced defensive stance while moving sideways.

split angles—Term used to describe goalkeeper positioning; goalkeeper is positioned in the center of the space between the ball and the goal.

square pass—A lateral pass across the field.

stack slide—A one-on-one goalkeeping technique executed from pressure distance. The double-leg stack is used in order to slide on the ground into the ball to block a shot on goal by AR1.

static flexibility—A joint's passive range of motion without movement.

step up—A defensive communication that is used to encourage a teammate to move closer to the ball and the opponent while positioning herself in the passing lane.

sweep hit—A passing technique of striking the ball with the stick shaft instead of the curved stick head.

tactics—A strategy or plan.

transition—Players moving from role to role in both attacking and defensive play.

trapping—The action of controlling, stopping, or receiving the ball.

triple threat—AR1 ball position in which the ball is on the stick and to the right side of the body, near the right foot, ready for a shot, pass, or dribble.

two-touch passing—Type of passing in which the receiving player (AR1) controls the ball with her first touch and passes to a teammate on her second touch.

wall pass—Combination passing (give-and-go) with a teammate in which one player's stick serves as a wall to block and redirect the path of the ball. A player usually runs forward to receive a return wall pass around an opponent.

width in attack—Tactic of using the width of the field in order to attempt to draw defending players away from central positions. The objective is to create space for scoring opportunities in the most dangerous space (attacking zones).

zone 1—Center area in the defensive circle from the goal out to the 25-yard line.

zone 2—Diagonal areas on both the right and left of zone 1.

zone 3—Area 5 meters (about 5 1/2 yards) from the backline on both sides of the goal cage.

zone defense—System of play in which each player is responsible for defending a certain area of the field when the ball or the opponent, or both, enter that area.

■ About the Authors

Elizabeth R. Anders is a dominant figure in field hockey. Her accomplishments include being the winningest coach in college field hockey, leading her teams to nine NCAA National Championships, and serving as head coach of the U.S. national field hockey team for three periods: 1985, 1990-93, and 2003-04. During her 35 years as a field hockey player, Anders twice earned a spot on the U.S. women's Olympic field hockey team and is the current Olympic Games record holder in scoring, winning a bronze medal in 1984. She was inducted into the United States Field Hockey Association Hall of Fame in 1989.

Anders has coached and taught field hockey for over 30 years. She is currently the head field hockey coach at Old Dominion University in Norfolk, Virginia. Ten of her former players have earned spots on the U.S., Dutch, and Argentine Olympic teams, and five are currently on the national team. A frequent writer on the sport, Anders is the author of *Lessons in Field Hockey, Fitness Training for Field Hockey, Summer Training for Field Hockey,* and *On the Rebound: The Hit.* She resides in Virginia Beach, Virginia.

Sue Myers has 35 years of experience coaching and teaching field hockey internationally and nationally. She is currently an assistant field hockey coach at Old Dominion University. Sue was on the U.S. national team from 1972 to 1979 and played on the very first U.S. World Cup team in 1975. Myers was a player on and cofounder of the Red Rose Field Hockey Club based in southeastern Pennsylvania from 1975 to 1985. With the club, she won five national team championships coaching alongside Anders.

In her free time, Myers enjoys gardening, reading, and playing golf. She resides in Virginia Beach, Virginia.